Aesthetic Thinking

Historical Materialism
Book Series

Editorial Board

Loren Balhorn (*Berlin*)
David Broder (*Rome*)
Sebastian Budgen (*Paris*)
Steve Edwards (*London*)
Juan Grigera (*London*)
Marcel van der Linden (*Amsterdam*)
Peter Thomas (*London*)

VOLUME 247

The titles published in this series are listed at *brill.com/hm*

Aesthetic Thinking

Essays on Intention, Painting, Action, and Ideology

By

Fred Orton

BRILL

LEIDEN | BOSTON

The Library of Congress Cataloging-in-Publication Data is available online at https://catalog.loc.gov
LC record available at https://lccn.loc.gov/2021052520

Typeface for the Latin, Greek, and Cyrillic scripts: "Brill". See and download: brill.com/brill-typeface.

ISSN 1570-1522
ISBN 978-90-04-50329-8 (hardback)
ISBN 978-90-04-50333-5 (e-book)

Copyright 2022 by Koninklijke Brill NV, Leiden, The Netherlands, except where stated otherwise.
Koninklijke Brill NV incorporates the imprints Brill, Brill Nijhoff, Brill Hotei, Brill Schöningh, Brill Fink, Brill mentis, Vandenhoeck & Ruprecht, Böhlau Verlag and V&R Unipress.
All rights reserved. No part of this publication may be reproduced, translated, stored in a retrieval system, or transmitted in any form or by any means, electronic, mechanical, photocopying, recording or otherwise, without prior written permission from the publisher. Requests for re-use and/or translations must be addressed to Koninklijke Brill NV via brill.com or copyright.com.

This book is printed on acid-free paper and produced in a sustainable manner.

Contents

Acknowledgements VII
'Present, the Scene of ... Selves, the Occasion of ... Ruses': Fred Orton's
    Art History VIII
        Steve Edwards
Publications by Fred Orton XXIV

1 Beginning ... with Intention 1

2 Painting Out of Time 22

3 Action, Revolution and Painting (Resumed) 42

4 Ideology: Reading Paul de Man Reading Marx and Engels 81

Bibliography 177
Index 188

Acknowledgements

Among those who helped write the essays collected here, who gave advice, criticism and encouragement, I thank Joanne Crawford, J.R.R. Christie, T.J. Clark, Neil Cox, Gail Day, Steve Edwards, Andrew Hemingway, Jon Kear, Martin McQuillan, Alex Potts, Nick Ridout, Richard Shiff, Tom Steele, Nick Till and Lindsay Waters. Among those no longer with us who also helped in one way or another, I remember with thanks David Craven, Charles Harrison, Michael Podro, Hugh J. Silverman and Richard Wollheim.

'Present, the Scene of ... Selves, the Occasion of ... Ruses': Fred Orton's Art History

Steve Edwards

This book consists of four interlinked essays by the art historian Fred Orton.[1] One essay is published here for the first time and the others have been rewritten for this volume. All are concerned, in various ways, with painting and ideology, particularly with acts of beginning and intention.[2] Orton wrote: 'Setting beginnings and endings is a tricky business. They are always underway before they are recognised as such. Beginnings are always endings. And endings are always new beginnings'.[3] In this respect these studies represent a searching critique of what Orton calls 'the dominant theory of modern art'. That is to say, an account of painting that finds explanations for artworks in biography, intention and expression. The first essay addresses Jasper Johns's beguiling painting of the flag of the United States, made in 1954–55. Here Orton returns to a central question in modern criticism: what is the relation between an artist's intention and the work that actually gets made? The second text is focused on Paul Cézanne's landscape painting. In this piece Orton looks at the contradictions between the account of Cézanne's work in the dominant theory of modern art (including the artist's own statements) and what he actually did at his easel. The third section considers the critic, and one-time Trotskyist, Harold Rosenberg's account of Abstract Expressionism and the idea of painting as an arena of revolution. The final long study examines the distinct, but related, critiques of ideology in the work of the young Karl Marx and the literary criticism of Paul de Man. The four sections add up to an inquiry into aesthetic ideology.

Fred Orton has been a presence in Marxist art history since the late 1970s, writing acclaimed studies and teaching on the highly influential M.A. in the

---

1 Chapters 1, 2 and 4 all have connections to a seminar Orton ran, as visiting Professor at Wimbledon School of Art at the turn of the century. Participants included his ex-student Gail Day, Nick Ridout, Nick Till, Dominic Rahtz and John Mitchell. Orton has always emphasised the importance of this experience.
2 A central impetus for this work is Edward Said, *Beginnings: Intention and Method*, Columbia University Press, 1985. That book alerts us to a certain continuity in Orton's work between 'theory' and more traditional literary-critical concerns.
3 Fred Orton and Griselda Pollock, 'Memories Still to Come ... An Introduction', *Avant-Gardes and Partisans Reviewed*, Manchester University Press, 1996: vii.

Social History of Art at the University of Leeds.[4] Unlike many former allies, he has not wavered from this intellectual-political commitment. As with a number of other British art historians, Orton began his education in art school. In his case, this was Coventry College of Art. Terry Atkinson, who taught there part time during his final year, and Michael Baldwin, a fellow student, went on to found the highly significant Conceptual Art collective Art & Language.[5] The group subsequently developed as an international network, before an acrimonious reformation that saw the creation of the British incarnation of Art & Language, consisting of the artists Mel Ramsden and Baldwin along with the late critic Charles Harrison.[6] Orton subsequently maintained a close interest in Art & Language and during the first part of the 1980s that interest tipped over into conversation and collaboration. He became a member of the group, both writing and painting under their aegis.[7] But with this we are jumping ahead: after graduating in 1967, Orton left art practice to study for an M.A. in Art History at the Courtauld Institute of Art.

The Courtauld Institute was at the time a bastion of the establishment (despite having as its Director the Communist spy Sir Anthony Blunt), but new approaches to art history were beginning to circulate. On leaving the Cour-

---

4 The M.A. was initiated by T.J. Clark in 1979, but it would have been 1983 or 1984 before Orton took a central role.

5 Strictly, Art & Language emerged from the famous, or infamous, art theory course devised by Atkinson and Baldwin between 1969 and 1971, when it was closed by the authorities, who decreed that artworks had to be physical things. Mark Dennis, *Strategic Anomalies: Art & Language in the Art School 1969–1979*, unpublished Coventry University PhD. 2016. Charles Harrison, *Essays on Art & Language*, Blackwell, 1991, p. 70.

6 Charles Harrison, *Essays on Art & Language*, Blackwell, 1991. Charles Harrison and Fred Orton, *A Provisional History of Art and Language*, Paris: Editions Fabre, 1982. It should be said, these are partisan histories, much disputed by other participants in the expanded circle of Art & Language.

7 Orton met Baldwin in 1964, but they renewed contact when Art & Language presented a seminar in Leeds in 1978. As curator of the Leeds University Gallery, Orton gave Art & Language an exhibition in 1980, where they showed the first versions of *V.I. Lenin in the Style of Jackson Pollock*. In 1983, he helped mount their exhibition of the 'Studio' pictures in Icon Gallery Birmingham (Orton appears in all of these works). He was also in Vienna that year as part of the Art & Language residency associated with an exhibition at Galerie Grita Insam. They visited the Kunsthistorisches Museum together and Orton alighted on Lucas van Valckenbroch's *Winter Landscape* (1586), which was to be the point of departure for their 'snowing' paintings. All these works are discussed in Harrison, *Essays on Art & Language*. Important publications emerged from the discussion: Charles Harrison and Fred Orton, *A Provisional History of Art and Language*, Paris: Editions Fabre, 1982; Charles Harrison and Fred Orton eds., *Modernism, Criticism, Realism: Alternative Contexts for Art*, London: Harper & Row, 1984; and Charles Harrison and Fred Orton, 'Jasper Johns: Meaning What You See', *Art History*, Vol. 6, No. 1, March 1984: pp. 78–101.

tauld, Orton taught for a while at Leicester Polytechnic, and in the following year T.J. Clark, who was appointed Professor of Art History at the University of Leeds in 1976, recruited him, along with art historian Griselda Pollock and Terry Atkinson, to teach fine art (with Orton having some responsibility for work in the studios). Orton and Pollock met at the Courtauld as post-graduate students in 1972, and after joining Leeds, they regularly collaborated on a series of iconoclastic critiques of their discipline. This was the period of the emergence of, what we would now call, second-wave Marxist history of art, and the group at Leeds constituted one central nucleus for the British formation.[8] Their last joint publication appeared in 1996.[9] As with many others of the generation who pioneered the Marxist critique of art history, sometimes called the Social History of Art, Orton began working on nineteenth-century French art, in his case the Post-Impressionism of van Gogh and others. The essay in this volume on Cézanne is a late echo of that early interest, though the intellectual mode is very different. Sometimes alone, but often writing in collaboration with Pollock, Orton produced a series of groundbreaking studies that helped demystify the cult of Impressionism, insisting on the presence of class and capital in the making and reception of this art. Orton and Pollock were particularly committed to debunking the myth of van Gogh as 'primitive' or mad genius and the investment of art history in such ideologically loaded categories, which occlude the work of making paintings.[10]

Important interventions followed, particularly the essay co-written with Pollock on Gauguin in Brittany and the fantasy of an escape from modern social

---

8   Others were based at Middlesex University producing the important journal *Block* and at the Open University. There were other outposts, such as Portsmouth Polytechnic. There was an uneven interchange between these groups: Clark, Pollock, Orton and Atkinson all published in *Block* and contributed radio and TV programmes to Open University modern art courses, but, for various reasons, there was little interchange between the Middlesex crew and the O.U.

9   Fred Orton and Griselda Pollock, *Avant-Gardes & Partisans Reviewed*, Manchester: Manchester University Press, 1996.

10 See: Fred Orton and Griselda Pollock, *Vincent van Gogh: Artist of his Time*, Oxford: Phaidon Press, 1978 (original title: *Rooted in the Soil: A Van Gogh Primer*. In response to the publisher's title they asked 'what artist isn't of their time'?) Fred Orton and Griselda Pollock, 'Memories Still to Come ... An Introduction', *Avant-Gardes and Partisans Reviewed*, Manchester University Press, 1996, pp. i–iv. Also: Griselda Pollock, 'Artists, Media and Mythologies; Genius, Madness and Art History', *Screen*, 21, 3, pp. 57–96 and the TV programme they produced together: Fred Orton and Griselda Pollock, 'Rooted in the Earth. Vincent van Gogh: The Potato Eaters', Open University/B.B.C.T.V., A315 Modern Art & Modernism (25 mins.), 1982.

life, which is an ideology generated from within that life.¹¹ However, Orton had taught art history in the art studio setting at Leicester Polytechnic before joining the Department in Leeds and Clark wanted him to teach a course for art students on post-war American art.¹² (Leeds is one of the few older universities in the UK to teach both art history and practising fine-art students). One way of accounting for Orton's rather particular orientation in Marxist art history is to note that his formation was in art practice and that he remained close to one of the most sophisticated critical-painting practices of the period after Conceptual Art, that of Art & Language. As it developed, Orton's art history involved a crossing of the Marxist critique of the discipline with the critical example of Art & Language and de Man's ethics of reading. Evidently, paths were converging, because Orton credits exhibition notes by Atkinson from 1976 with sparking his interest in Marx's *The German Ideology*.¹³

We get a sense of the programme for a Marxist art history developing at Leeds from an unpublished discussion paper for staff written by Clark in 1976, titled 'The Art History We Teach in the First Two Years'. Clark laid out questions for a non-celebratory art history. Citing his 'teacher and enemy', O.K. Werckmeister, he said, their guiding principle should be: 'Let us rob the student of the illusion of culture'. Clark called this a 'harsh instruction', but he said it was a 'dictum' he would rather have 'than most others on offer'. Clark listed 'Questions about the conditions of artistic production':

> what are works of art made *for*?
> Whom are they made for?
> To do what kind of job:
> How was this picture or this building understood by its maker, its owner, its first viewers?
> Where and how were works of art seen?
> who was their public?
> How were they bought and sold?
> What kind of relationship existed between artist and patron?

---

11 Fred Orton and Griselda Pollock, '*Les Données Bretonnantes: la Prairie de Représentation*', *Art History*, v. 4, n. 3, pp. 314–44, Sept. 1980. Orton's approach was to change markedly, but he remained committed to an investigation of 'discourse, meaning, ideology, and its critique': Fred Orton and Griselda Pollock, 'Memories Still to Come ... An Introduction': p. v.

12 At Leicester he taught a course on Duchamp with the composer Gavin Bryars, which stimulated his interest in collaborative work.

13 Terry Atkinson, *Notes*, Robert Self Gallery, 1976.

> How was the actual process of production – in studio or workshop or cloister or academy – organized?
> What kind of division of labour existed? (And how much room did it leave for 'individual creativity'?)[14]

He continued for another page with questions of this sort and ended by calling for a new *Grundrisse* for art history. This was to be an art history against the 'business as usual' manner of the discipline, whose modus operandi was to offer 'greatness', 'coherence' and 'complexity' as compensation for the 'charnel-house' of world history.[15] Orton took this lesson to heart and this programme remained, in essentials, the one he held to throughout his career.

There is a great deal of current talk in British universities about 'research-led teaching', but Orton's research has often been given direction by his teaching. The programme of study he developed focussed on Abstract Expressionism and the art that immediately followed as well as the related 'modernist' criticism of Clement Greenberg and Harold Rosenberg. What he carried over from his earlier work on Post Impressionism, particularly *Les Données Bretonnantes*, was a concern with meaning, ideology and ideology critique. Alongside this work, Orton engaged in an intensive reading of Marx. As noted, during the 1970s and 1980s, the Social History of Art developed in symbiosis with the study of French painting. There were many good studies produced, but this work easily tipped over into a new iconography, spotting the bourgeois in top hat or the prostitute or the factory chimney. American gestural abstraction and the work of the subsequent generation was not as easily amenable to this kind of iconographic-cum-semiotic treatment, demanding a different kind of attention and interpretation. At the same time, the stakes of this work were much higher in the art schools, where the legacy of this art was a key plank in ideology. Orton's art school background made him well prepared to think about these issues.

The predominant response to American abstract art from the radical left was to claim that it was a Cold War practice, promoted by the C.I.A., and associated bodies, working in conjunction with private museums, such as the Museum of Modern Art, in order to bypass the organised McCarthyite philistinism that risked tarnishing the international reputation of the U.S. Oper-

---

14 T.J. Clark, 'The Art History We Teach in the First Two Years', unpublished discussion paper, September 1976. I've retained the idiosyncratic format.
15 The argument, and certainly the tone, are close to better known interventions by Clark, such as 'The Conditions of Artistic Creation', *Times Literary Supplement*, May 24, 1974, pp. 561–2; and his unpublished paper presented at the Marxist Caucus of the College Art Association: 'Preliminary Argument: Work of Art and Ideology', Chicago, January 1976.

ating through covert channels, the secret state was said to have circumvented the dominant right-wing faction of U.S. capital, represented by the likes of Senator George A. Dondero, who believed modern art to be a communist plot, in order promote American liberal values abroad, while also displacing the legacy of New Deal social realism.[16] In this view, Abstract Expressionism is assimilated to support for the Congress for Cultural Freedom, *Encounter*, and the *Twentieth-Century*. These accounts went along with increasingly critical views of American formalist criticism. Orton and Pollock contributed to the critical assessment of American modernism, authoring a study of the depoliticisation of American art-criticism in the career of Clement Greenberg, who moved from Trotskyism to Cold War liberalism and formalism.[17] They also made an Open University T.V. programme on the politics of the Museum of Modern Art.[18] However, Orton subsequently wrote a critique of the supposed connection between the C.I.A. and Abstract Expressionism, pointing out that the artists in question barely appeared in the exhibitions at issue.[19] The story of the C.I.A.'s involvement in promoting this art has passed into folk wisdom, but it does not really survive Orton's scrupulous account. Instead, Orton offered a double move: in the first instance, he confronted the task of accounting for these works of art. Employing rhetorical analysis, he pursued a critique of modernist ideology on the surface of the paintings. Marx, Wittgenstein, Derrida and de Man were all put to work. In the process, he developed his account of the dialectic between 'surface matter' and 'subject matter'. His other line of attack was to switch attention from the critical explanations of this painting offered by Greenberg to those of Harold Rosenberg. At the time, Greenberg's work was undergoing something of a revival among British Social Historians or Marxists engaged with modern art, and Orton bucked this trend, insisting that Rosenberg offered a much more compelling and politicised version of Abstract Expressionism, which drew on his fascination with Marx's account of drama and the act in *The Eighteenth Brumaire*.[20]

---

16   The key texts are collected in Francis Frascina ed., *Pollock and After: The Critical Debate*, Harper & Row, 1985.
17   Fred Orton and Griselda Pollock, 'Avant-Gardes and Partisans Reviewed', *Art History*, Vol. 4, No. 3, 1983, pp. 305–27.
18   Fred Orton and Griselda Pollock, 'Art and U.S. Imperialism', Open University/B.B.C. Radio, A315 Modern Art & Modernism (25 mins.), 1983.
19   Fred Orton, 'Footnote One: The Idea of the Cold War' in *American Abstract Expressionism*, edited by David Thistlewood, Liverpool: Tate Gallery and Liverpool University Press, 1993, pp. 179–92.
20   Fred Orton, 'Action, Revolution and Painting', *Oxford Art Journal*, Vol. 14, No. 2, 1991, pp. 3–17.

For Rosenberg the proletariat embodied a unique capacity for action, and if the Stalinist counter-revolution produced a hiatus in history – a desolate lacuna – that potential was undimmed. For Rosenberg, in action painting the work of art was a pure event: stripped of content, it existed as absolute potential. As such, 'Action Painting wasn't revolutionary posturing. It was painting concerned with the dialectical possibility of revolution whose outlines could neither be defined nor denied' (p. 45). Acting is not 'acting out'. Orton reads the essay on Action Painting as a place holder for revolution, a practice that kept open possibilities and an openness to the future in a period of political defeat.

Rosenberg's essays of this period, including 'Character Change and Drama' (1932); 'The Fall of Paris' (1940); 'Resurrected Romans' (1948); 'The Pathos of the Proletariat' (1949); and 'The American Action Painters' (1952) are not only some of the most inventive and stimulating works of Trotskyist critical theory; they are also a major contribution to the interpretation of Marx.[21] Rosenberg was one of the first great readers of Marx's *The Eighteenth Brumaire*, who employed a legal-critical framework to develop a distinction between persons and identity, separating the ontological self from the formalised cluster of meanings that appear in representation. Rosenberg has undergone something of a revival, but the chapter included here is the best guide to his important contribution.[22]

While Orton published his significant critique of the standard radical account of Abstract Expressionism and essays on Greenberg (with Griselda Pollock) and Rosenberg, it is interesting that he did not publish on the work of the New York School.[23] Instead, he turned to their immediate successors, who picked up some of the mannerisms and problems raised by the work of Jackson Pollock, Mark Rothko and the others, but did so in a cooler, de-subjectified

---

21 All these essays appear in the collection *The Tradition of the New* (1959), New York: De Capo Press, 1994. Orton tells the story of Rosenberg's inability to secure a publisher, between 1949 and 1951, for his projected collection *Marx and the Drama of History*.

22 For recent writing on Rosenberg see: Elaine Owens O'Brian, *The Art Criticism of Harold Rosenberg*, unpublished PhD, New York: City University of New York; Nancy Jachec, *The Philosophy of Abstract Expressionism 1940–1960*, Cambridge: Cambridge University Press, 2000; Anika Marie, *The Most Radical Act: Harold Rosenberg, Barnett Newman and Ad Reinhardt*, unpublished PhD, Austin: University of Texas, 2006; Norman L. Kleeblatt ed., *Action/Abstraction: Pollock, De Kooning, and American Art, 1940–1976*, New Haven and London: Yale University Press, 2008; Robert Slifkin, 'The Tragic Image: Action Painting Reconfigured', *Oxford Art Journal*, 34, 2, 2011, pp. 227–46; and Christa Noel Robbins, 'Harold Rosenberg and the Character of Action', *Oxford Art Journal*, 35, 2, 2012, pp. 195–214.

23 The exception is a short piece on photographs of Jackson Pollock at work: Fred Orton and Griselda Pollock, 'Jackson Pollock, Painting and the Myth of Photography', *Art History*, 6, 1, 1983, pp. 114–22.

mode. In contrast to the rhapsodies associated with the reception of Abstract Expressionism, Orton focused on artists who challenged, or circumvented, 'expression claims'.[24] Orton presented admired public lectures on paintings by Frank Stella, Helen Frankenthaler and Larry Rivers, all of which remain unpublished and will sadly probably never be published. What did emerge was a series of studies of the artist Jasper Johns.

Jasper Johns was one of a number of American artists who, in the wake of Abstract Expressionism, reintroduced imagery into painting without abandoning the ambitious project of modernist painting. Drawing on Wittgenstein and Duchamp, Johns created a number of important works that appeared as pictorial conundrums. Examples might be his *Target With Four Faces* (1955); *White Target* (1957); or *Flag*. Orton famously asked of this latter work: was it a painting or a flag? Through a detailed examination of the surface, and by reading the rules for the manufacture of the U.S. flag, he showed that the painting was constructed in the same three sections. It was an aporia, at once painting and flag, yet never settling into the position of either.[25] His first published study of Johns, written with Charles Harrison, can be seen as emerging from concerns in Art & Language.[26] While the issues raised in that essay never disappear from view, his subsequent work drew on theories of allegory and rhetorical analysis, particularly the tropes of metonymy and synecdoche. Derrida was initially important, but increasingly Orton drew on Benjamin's *Origin of German Tragic Drama* and the essays of Paul de Man, alongside Marx.[27] There are two

---

24 According to Art & Language, expression claims block off causal explanations. See Art & Language, 'Abstract Expression', Harrison and Orton eds, *Modernism, Criticism, Realism*, pp. 191–204. The essay was published in 1982 and Orton had some input in this.
25 Orton, *Figuring Jasper Johns*.
26 Charles Harrison and Fred Orton, 'Jasper Johns: Meaning What You See', *Art History*, 6, 1, March 1984: 78–101.
27 Walter Benjamin, *The Origin Of German Tragic Drama*, Verso, 1979; Paul de Man's essays are collected in four volumes. Paul de Man, *Blindness and Insight: Essays in the Rhetoric of Contemporary Criticism*, Second edition, London: Routledge, 1983; *The Rhetoric of Romanticism*, Columbia University Press, 1986; *Romanticism and Contemporary Criticism: The Geuss Seminar and Other Papers*, Baltimore: The Johns Hopkins University Press, 1993; and *Aesthetic Ideology*, Minneapolis & London. University of Minnesota Press, 1996. For Orton's writing on Johns: Fred Orton, 'Present, the Scene of … Selves, the Occasion of … Ruses', *Block* 13, Winter, 1987, pp. 5–19; Fred Orton, 'On Being Bent Blue (Second State): An Introduction to Jacques Derrida/A Footnote on Jasper Johns', *Oxford Art Journal*, Vol. 12, No. 1, 1989, pp. 35–46; Fred Orton, 'J. Johns' Flag: A Different Kind of Beginning', *Over Here: Reviews in American Studies*, 11, 2, Winter 1991, pp. 64–84; Fred Orton, 'Figuring Jasper's Flag (First Draft): A Different Kind of Beginning' in *Kunstlerischer Autausch/Artistic Exchange, Akten des XXVIII Internationalen Kongresses für Kunstgeschichte, Berlin, 15–20 Juli 1992*, edited by Thomas W. Gaehtgens, Berlin: Akademie Verlag, 1994, pp. 703–11; Fred Orton,

points to be made here: first, he argued that while high modernism worked within the dominant aesthetic framework of the symbol (and in modernism the allied idea of metaphor), Johns was an allegorist, who cut against the idea of organic unity and immediacy central to aesthetic ideology. These themes run throughout the studies in this book: Orton is drawn to those artists who, he believes, occupy the alternative allegorical lineage. Secondly, through close attention to surface matter, he shows that while Johns's biography is present in these works, it always appears in dislocated or attenuated forms. Some of Johns's works include plaster casts and prints from the body: face, hands, breast, genitals, leg, foot. Objects are fixed to the surface, such as a plate, a chair, shovel or broom. There is evidently some relation to the artist's person in these paintings. Biographical explanation, and with it the key ideas of 'origin', 'intention' and 'expression', have been central to the dominant approach to artworks and are closely related to a symbolic conception. Orton, does not reject any of these themes outright, as did many post-modern critics, but he shows that they are always problematic and in need of sustained ideological scrutiny: he is 'cautious about the possibility of biographical narrative and also ... loath to abandon it'.[28] The artistic self appears on a painting's surface as metonymic trace or shadow, rather than the full and determining presence projected by modernist theorists. In the process of his investigation, the modernist self underwent a kind of defacement.[29] Rhetorical figuration unfixes meaning and calls into question any stable point of origin.[30] To put this another way, he wrote in a jointly authored text: 'there is no such thing as expression in art, only expression claims seemingly attached to a biography'.[31] He describes explanations of this kind as 'the dominant theory of modern art' and he usually cites Greenberg for his examples.[32] It is the role of curators, art historians and critics – 'cultural managers' – to stabilise such claims. The moments that an artist's biography

---

'Figuring Jasper Johns', in *Art Has No History! The Making and Unmaking of Modern Art*, edited by John Roberts, London: Verso, 1994, pp. 111–32; Fred Orton, *Figuring Jasper Johns*, Cambridge: Harvard University Press, 1994 and Fred Orton, *Jasper Johns: The Sculptures*, Leeds: The Henry Moore Institute, 1996.

28 J.R.R. Christie and Fred Orton, 'Writing on a Text of the Life', *Art History*, 11, 4, Dec. 1988, p. 555.

29 See: Paul de Man, 'Autobiography as Defacement', *The Rhetoric of Romanticism*, Columbia University Press, 1986, 67–82.

30 J.R.R. Christie and Fred Orton, 'Writing on a Text of the Life', *Art History*, 11, 4, Dec. 1988, 544–64. Though their essay is perhaps too textualist. This was Orton at his most structruralist or 'superstructuralist'.

31 J.R.R. Christie and Fred Orton, 'Writing on a Text of the Life', *Art History*, 11, 4, Dec. 1988, p. 560.

32 See: Clement Greenberg, 'Complaints of an Art Critic' (1967), John O'Brian ed., *The Col-*

appears most immediately accessible are those that need the most thorough investigation and doubt. Marxist art history of the period set itself against the monograph as an ideological form that cemented biography as explanation, offering a coherent life/oeuvre package in the service of auction house and museum. Orton's *Figuring Jasper Johns* was a kind of anti-monographic monograph, a 'certain kind of biograph'.[33]

Johns commented extensively, if elliptically, on his work and as with other 'wordy' artists, critics have leant heavily on interviews with him. In contrast, Orton decided not to speak to the artist, but to try to tease out meaning from the surfaces, testing his Marxist-rhetorical tools. Reportedly, Johns was astonished by what he was able to glean. In the essay included here, Orton focuses on intention and beginning and their relation to the resulting paintings. He does so through careful scrutiny of Johns's reports of a dream in which he was painting a flag of the United States. Tensions and contradictions are bought to the surface in a way that loop back to interrogate the dominant theory of modern art and its claims about an artist's intentions.

In the late 1990s, Orton again shifted focus and began writing about Anglo-Saxon Northumbrian sculpture: the Ruthwell Cross and the Bewcastle monument. There are precedents for this switch. The third great American Marxist art critic after Greenberg and Rosenberg, Meyer Schapiro, wrote studies of medieval sculpture and was also one of the first art historians to teach modern art in a university department (Columbia). The German Marxist O.K. Werckmeister has also written important studies of modern art and culture, as well as analyses of medieval art, including a brilliant study of ideology in the Bayeux tapestry.[34] Schapiro published on the Ruthwell Cross and it is likely that Orton first began puzzling over the monument while reading these works.[35]

---

lected Essays and Criticism: Modernism with a Vengeance, 1957–1969, Chicago: University of Chicago Press, 1993, pp. 265–69.

33 J.R.R. Christie and Fred Orton, 'Writing on a Text of the Life', *Art History*, 11, 4, Dec. 1988, p. 559. 'The project would thus remain one of attaining historicity through the realisation of human agency in the context of large-scale historical causes. Or, to put it somewhat differently, of combining structural and epochal causation and the historicity of the construction of the subject and subjectivity' (p. 559).

34 Meyer Schapiro, *Late Antique, Early Christian and Medieval Art: Selected Papers, Vol. 3*, Chatto, 1980. There are numerous examples by Werckmeister in German and English. For examples, see: O.K. Werckmeister, 'The Political Ideology of the Bayeux Tapestry', *Studi Medevali*, 3, 17, 1976, pp. 535–95; O.K. Werckmeister, 'The Islamic Rider in the Beatus of Girona', *Gesta*, 36, 2, 1997, pp. 101–6.

35 Meyer Schapiro, 'The Religious Meaning of the Ruthwell Cross', *The Art Bulletin*, 26, 4, Dec., 1944: 232–45; Meyer Schapiro, 'The Bowman and the Bird on the Ruthwell Cross and Other Works: The Interpretation of Secular Themes in Early Mediaeval Religious Art,' *The Art Bulletin*, 45. 4, 1963, pp. 351–5.

The acclaimed and controversial studies that resulted demonstrated that the current form of the Ruthwell Cross is a later construction, and offered a compelling account of time and power in eighth-century Northumbrian feudalism.[36] Orton's medieval work is not included in this volume, so I will leave it at that and suggest that interested readers should consult these studies firsthand.

It should be apparent that Orton sets great store by close reading (and looking). The resource for this work is the tradition of literary criticism from New Criticism to de Man, alongside Marxist ideology critique. Orton is an entertaining and impressive lecturer, but his most influential teaching has taken the form of intensive seminars involving detailed study of texts.[37] This work involves reading sentence by sentence, line by line, paying attention to figures and tropes. He carries over this practice of close reading/looking into his published writing. It is an approach that has resulted in some startling reevaluations of basic assumptions. For instance, it has always been assumed that Rosenberg's essay 'The American Action Painters' was an account of gestural abstraction in Jackson Pollock or Willem de Kooning, but Orton notes that neither are mentioned in the text, whereas Robert Rauschenberg's white canvases *are* cited.[38] In this version, that point is relegated to a footnote and he cites as his example Barnett Newman's *Onement I* (1948). This model of close reading is also a form of slow reading, giving the text or art work its due and trying to get the presentation right, rather than rushing to judgement. Some students loved this painstaking study, but it should be admitted, it drove some to distraction. Orton is not in a hurry. The essay on de Man and Marx in this volume has been worked and reworked for almost twenty-five years. Other major studies will never see the light of day.

---

36 Fred Orton, 'Rethinking the Ruthwell Monument: Fragments and critique; tradition and history; tongues and sockets', *Art History*, 21, 1, 1998, pp. 65–106; 'Northumbrian Sculpture (the Ruthwell and Bewcastle Monuments): Questions of Difference' in *Northumbria's Golden Age*, edited by Jane Hawkes and Susan Mills, pp. 216–27, Stroud: Sutton Publishing Ltd., 1999; Fred Orton, 'Rethinking the Ruthwell and Bewcastle Monuments: Some strictures on similarity; some questions of history' in *Theorising Anglo-Saxon Stone Sculpture*, eds. Catherine Karkov and Fred Orton, pp. 65–92, West Virginia University Press, 2003; 'Northumbrian Identity in the Eighth Century: Style, classification, class, and the form of ideology', *Journal of Medieval and Early Modern Studies*, pp. 95–145, Winter, 2004; 'At the Bewcastle Monument, In Place' in *The making of Place, Medieval to Modern*, edited by Clare A. Lees and Gillian R. Overing, Pennsylvania State University Press, 2006, pp. 29–66; and Fred Orton & Ian Wood with Clare Lees, *Fragments of History: Rethinking the Ruthwell and Bewcastle Monuments*, Manchester University Press, 2007. In 2002 he delivered the Tomás Harris Lectures on this material at University College London.

37 In the mid-1990s I participated in Orton's term long-seminar on de Man in Leeds.

38 Fred Orton, 'Action, Revolution and Painting', *Oxford Art Journal*, 14, 2, 1991, pp. 3–17.

The model of close reading finds its equivalent in detailed attention to the surface of a painting. I know few art historians who can match his sustained attention. Orton looks at paintings until they beg for mercy. One member of Art & Language told me that they placed 'Fred traps' in their paintings. These were impressions made from the base of tins or cups pressed into the surface of the paint, knowing that he alone was likely to look closely enough to find them and puzzle over them.[39] The results of this kind of study are evident in his examination of Johns's works, but the essay on Cézanne's painting of sensation in this volume is another excellent example. Cézanne is a pivotal figure in the story of modern art, but for all that Orton offers a distinct and compelling account of his work. Disentangling Cézanne from the right-wing thinkers who championed his art after his death for its supposed return to structure and 'order', Orton gives us a painter dabbing away, but unable to resolve his sensations as 'touch' on the canvas. Orton shows that Cézanne subscribed to a version of the dominant theory of modern art, intending to produce work with no gaps or slack links between experience, or sensation, and its embodiment on the canvas. Cézanne thought that even colour should give off an odour. Orton notes: 'That is to say, he seems to have thought that it was possible to achieve, in his pictures, the representation of a present. Yet even as he tried to do it [paint presence], he produced pictures that authentically declared the impossibility of being able to do it' (p. 35). He does not claim that Cézanne was a political radical (too often Marxist critics have projected their own values onto a canvas); instead he offers us a figure whose attention to his own perceptual experience resulted in pictorial fragmentation or irresolution 'to an art of painting slack links and admitting gaps'. His account undermines the modernist Cézanne as a painter of wholeness, immediacy and unity, which is to say a painter of the symbol.[40] In Orton's account, Cézanne is an unwilling allegorist. A lesser artist – his example is Claude Monet – 'might have faked the symbolic', but in Cézanne 'immediacy and wholeness give way to the fragmentary and fragmenting evidence of mediating memory and decision making' (p. 40). Cézanne's painted surface's can be seen as a critique of aesthetic ideology or, at least, a problem for

---

39 All that can be said about this bit of mischief is that it is altogether more benign than the words 'Hello Terry' visible beneath the surface of one of their versions of the *Origin de Monde*. Whether the Terry in question was Atkinson or Smith, I can't say.

40 Cézanne can be read as a double for Fred Orton himself, a figure who is rigorous, dogged, cussed and sometimes rude. For a serious study of Cézanne and symbolism, see Richard Shiff, *Cézanne and the End of Impressionism: A Study of the Theory, Technique and Evaluation of Modern Art*, University of Chicago Press, 1986. For a good short study of Cézanne and 'sensation' see: Paul Smith, *Interpreting Cézanne*, Tate Publishing, 1996.

the dominant theory of modern art. The artist's familiar and celebrated works emerge in Orton's account in an unfamiliar light, but they are more interesting for that.[41]

I have mentioned Paul de Man at various points in this introduction and something needs to be said in the light of his war-time writing for *Le Soir* and *Het Vlaamsche Land* and also his taste for fictionalising his own biography.[42] At least since the early 1990s Orton has been studying de Man alongside Marx, running seminars on both. One earlier incarnation of his Cézanne study was titled 'Cézanne/Medan/de Man'. Terry Eagleton presented probably the best-known Marxist critique of de Man in his essay 'Capitalism, Modernism and Postmodernism', arguing that de Man's work was quietist, depicting any political practice as necessarily self-blinding (and self-defeating). For Eagleton, there was a 'steady, silent anti-Marxist polemic' running throughout De Man's essays.[43] It should be noted that even this claim posits a back-handed political causality at the heart of the project. However, Orton was not alone in gravitating towards de Man's critical unravelling of the quick meaning fix. The critic John Roberts once described de Man as 'the "favourite" deconstructionist for historical materialists'.[44] Late in his life, de Man projected a sustained engagement with *The German Ideology*, but did not live to undertake that work.[45] Marxist critics as different as Frederic Jameson, Michael Sprinker, T.J. Clark and Gail

---

41   For a related account see: T.J. Clark, 'Phenomenality and Materiality in Cézanne', *Material Events: Paul de Man and the Afterlife of Theory*, edited by Tom Cohen et al., University of Minnesota Press, 2001, pp. 93–113. Clark was also seriously reading de Man at this point and organised a conference session in 1994 with the title 'A de Manian Art History?', to which Orton contributed.

42   For an extensive range of engagements with de Man's writings of the war years, see *Responses: On Paul de Man's Wartime Journalism*, edited by Werner Hamacher, Neil Hertz and Thomas Keenan, Lincoln & London: University of Nebraska Press, 1989; and for his biography – including political collaboration, embezzlement of family funds, faked qualifications, bigamy and reinvention of himself, see Evelyn Barish, *The Double Life of Paul de Man*, New York: W.W. Norton, 2015.

43   Terry Eagleton, 'Capitalism, Modernism and Postmodernism', *Against the Grain: Selected Essays 1975–1985*, London: Verso, 1986, pp. 131–47. The quotation is on p. 138. For an important response to Eagleton, see Michael Sprinker, 'Politics and Language; Paul de Man and the Permanence of Ideology', *Imaginary Relations: Aesthetics in the Theory of Historical Materialism*, Verso, pp. 237–66.

44   John Roberts, 'Introduction: Art Has No History! Reflections on Art History and Historical Materialism', *Art Has No History: The Making and Unmaking of Modern Art*, edited by John Roberts, London: Verso, 1994, pp. 28–9.

45   Stefano Rosso, 'An Interview with Paul de Man', in Paul de Man, *The Resistance to Theory*, University of Minnesota Press, 1986, p. 121.

Day, to name just a few, have all been drawn to de Man's work.[46] While Orton was drawn to Derrida and then de Man, his position has never has been a straightforward deconstructionism or post-modernism, not even anti-realism. Marx and Wittgenstein and Richard Wollheim have always been too present for that.[47] For Orton, these thinkers are guides to reading politically or ethically.[48] Briefly stated, what Marxist thinkers have found in his practice of close, rhetorical reading is a model for ideology critique, which undercuts false reconciliation in a society of social division. de Man coined the term 'aesthetic ideology' to describe that species of interpretation that finds meaning to be immediately accessible and untroubling. His central point is that close attention to the text reveals that such claims cannot be sustained. This is the case even, or perhaps especially, with those Romantic authors seemingly closest to symbolic presentation. In their work, de Man shows, the instantaneity and transparency of the symbol gives way to allegorical duration and a breakdown of coherence or emergence of undecidability. Orton demonstrates that de Man repeatedly engaged with Marx and Engels' critique of ideology, but that the engagement intensified later in his life. The chapter examines a range of essays by de Man, drawing out his largely ignored interest in Marx.

In modernist theory, whether aestheticist or formalist, the absolute autonomy and self-identity of art appears as the figure for that supposed cohesion, separating the artwork from history or society. A related ideology consists of treating authors or artists as autonomous selves, ontologically prior to the artwork. Breaking open the unity of the artwork, refusing the autonomous author and not allowing meaning to settle, Marxist critics have found fragmentation, negativity and temporality more amenable critical concepts with which to conduct critical work. Closure and fixity are enemies of dialectical

---

46   Frederic Jameson, *Postmodernism or, the Cultural Logic of Late Capitalism*, London: Verso, pp. 219–59; Sprinker, 'Politics and Language; Paul de Man and the Permanence of Ideology', and 'Art & Ideology: Althusser and de Man', *Material Events: Paul de Man and the Afterlife of Theory*, edited by Tom Cohen et al., University of Minnesota Press, 2001, pp. 32–48; T.J. Clark, 'Phenomenality and Materiality in Cézanne', *Material Events: Paul de Man and the Afterlife of Theory*, Tom Cohen et al., University of Minnesota Press, 2001, pp. 93–113; and Gail Day, *Dialectical Passions: Negation in Post-war Art Theory*, Columbia University Press, 2011, pp. 132–81.

47   Charles Harrison and Fred Orton (eds.), *Modernism, Criticism, Realism: Alternative Contexts for Art*, London: Harper & Row, 1984.

48   A link could be made here to Christopher Norris's attitude to deconstruction: *Paul de Man and the Critique of Aesthetic Ideology*, Routledge, 1988. Richard Wollheim, *Art and Its Objects*, New York: Harper & Row, 1968; *Painting as an Art*, London: Thames & Hudson, 1987. In this volume, Orton notes that his own aesthetic understanding is indebted to Wollheim.

thought and in their rejection Marxists might find many points of agreement with Paul de Man. Perhaps the best way to see de Man's textual criticism is as a more technically-linguistic version of T.W. Adorno's aesthetic philosophy, which refuses reconciliation.[49] In Adorno or de Man (or Orton) art cannot compensate for the wounds of social division and mass violence (Clark's 'charnel house') and any account of art as aesthetic balm is either inattentive or wilfully ideological. For Orton, this has always been allied to Marx's critique of ideological conjuring tricks, where false or bad totalities like the term 'population' make social class disappear from view.[50] Here self-deception or the 'false-consciousness' of *The German Ideology* is akin to mis-reading.[51] 'What is *The German Ideology*', Orton writes, 'if not an extended polemic against formalism, false historicism and Utopianism?' All are false reconciliations, in a hurry to arrive at the absolute. They make the 'unbearable bearable, the thinkable more or less unthinkable, the aberrant normal' (p. 135). Similarly, a de Manian criticism of the way the dominant theory of modern art treats the artwork as transparent, might be compared to Marx's critique of the supposed transparency of social relations. A further correspondence might be found in the link between the camera obscura of ideology and de Man's concern with seeing and knowing, blindness and insight.[52] There is an obvious appeal for a critic of the dominant theory of modern art in these tropes. In the famous passage on the camera obscura the ideologies of 'politics, laws, morality, religion, metaphysics, etc., of a people' take shape in language, even if it is 'life that determines consciousness'.[53] It is necessary to attend to both moments in this process and to develop a critique that attempts to unsettle the 'illusory correspondence or coincidence between sign and referent' (p.117). How this de Manian critique of immanence opens onto a positive conception of class in action is another matter. Orton seems to share de Man's tragic humanism. While Marx too draws on tragedy, he also has his pastoral moments, and the insistence on practice and production seem to open on to another conception of human life.[54] Perhaps,

49 Theodor Adorno, *Aesthetic Theory*, Athlone Press, 1997.
50 Karl Marx, *Grundrisse: Foundations of a critique of Political Economy (Rough Draft)*, Penguin, 1973, p. 100; 605–8.
51 Though, Orton always notes that Engels does not speak of 'false-consciousness', but sees ideology as 'a process accomplished by the so called thinker consciously ... but with a false consciousness'.
52 Marx & Engels, *The German Ideology*, MECW Vol. 5, London: Lawrence & Wishart, 1976, p. 36; De Man, *Blindness and Insight*.
53 Marx & Engels, *The German Ideology*, p. 36; 37.
54 For samples of a debate: S.S. Prawer, *Karl Marx and World Literature*, Oxford: Oxford University Press, 1978: 197–31; Raymond Williams, *Modern Tragedy*, Toronto: Broadview, 2006;

the problem is attempting too rapidly to reconcile the destructive tools needed for the critique of aesthetic ideology with those required for building socialism.

Though Fred Orton has written a number of important books, he is essentially an essay writer whose work takes shape over a long period of reading and looking. He probes, again and again, key ideological themes: biography, intention, the aesthetic self, immediacy and unity, developing a searching critique of the dominant theory of modern art. This book offers four still fecund examples of his sustained thinking about paintings, the attention required for their understanding, and the critique of ideological assumptions that attempt to secure their meanings.

> Terry Eagleton, *Sweet Violence: The Idea of the Tragic*, Oxford: Blackwell, 2003; *Why Marx was Right*, New Haven and London: Yale University Press, 2011; T.J. Clark, 'For a Left with No Future', *New Left Review*, No. 74, 2012, pp. 53–75; Raphael Hörmann, 'Social Tragedy and Political Farce: Marx's Poetics of History and Revolution', *Facing Tragedies*, edited by Christopher Hamilton, Otto Neumaier, Gottfried Schweiger & Clemens Sedmak, Vienna, Berlin and Munster: LIT Verlag. 2009, pp. 203–14; Alberto Toscano, 'Politics in a Tragic Key', *Radical Philosophy*, No. 180, July/August 2013, pp. 25–34; Jason Baker, 'Epic or Tragedy? Karl Marx and Poetic Form in the Communist Manifesto', *Filozofia 71*, 4, 2016, pp. 316–27. For Marxism and pastoral: William Empson, *Some Versions of Pastoral*, London: Penguin, 1995, pp. 9–26; and Steve Edwards, *Martha Rosler, The Bowery in two inadequate descriptive systems*, London: Afterall, 2013.

Publications by Fred Orton

Books

Fred Orton and Griselda Pollock, *Vincent van Gogh: Artist of his Time*, Oxford: Phaidon Press, 1978

Charles Harrison and Fred Orton, *A Provisional History of Art and Language*, Paris: Editions Fabre, 1982.

Charles Harrison and Fred Orton eds., *Modernism, Criticism, Realism: Alternative Contexts for Art*, London: Harper & Row, 1984.

Thom Mayne and Fred Orton, *Morphosis: Tangents and Outtakes*, London: Artemis, 1993.

Fred Orton, *Figuring Jasper Johns*, Cambridge: Harvard University Press, 1994.

Fred Orton, *Jasper Johns: The Sculptures*, Leeds: The Henry Moore Institute, 1996.

Fred Orton and Griselda Pollock, *Avant-Gardes & Partisans Reviewed*, Manchester: Manchester University Press, 1996.

Catherine Karkov and Fred Orton eds., *Theorising Anglo-Saxon Stone Sculpture*, Morgantown: West Virginia University Press, 2003.

Fred Orton & Ian Wood with Clare Lees, *Fragments of History: Rethinking the Ruthwell and Bewcastle Monuments*, Manchester: Manchester University Press, 2007

Book Chapters, Journal Essays and Catalogue Essays

Fred Orton, 'Vincent van Gogh in Paris 1886–1888', *Bulletin of the Rijksmuseum Vincent van Gogh*, Vol. 1, No. 3, Autumn 1971: 2–12.

Gavin Bryars and Fred Orton, 'Morton Feldman', *Studio International*, Vol. 192, No. 984, Nov–Dec. 1976: 244–8.

Republished as: Gavin Bryars and Fred Orton, 'Studio International Interview, Fred Orton and Gavin Bryars, 27 May 1976' in *Morton Feldman Says: Selected Interviews and Lectures 1964–1987*, edited by Chris Villars, London: Hyphen New Series, Hyphen Press, 2005: 63–73.

Gavin Bryars and Fred Orton, 'Tom Phillips', *Studio International*, Vol. 192, No. 984, Nov–Dec. 1976: 290–6.

Fred Orton, 'Vincent van Gogh and Japanese Prints: An Introductory Essay' in *Japanese Prints Collected by Vincent van Gogh*, edited by L. Couvée, pp. 14–23,

Amsterdam: Rijksmuseum Vincent van Gogh, 1978.

Fred Orton, 'A Little Art History', *Open Letter: A Canadian quarterly review of writing and sources*, ser. IV, No. 1–2, Spring 1978: 158–80.

Fred Orton and Griselda Pollock, '*Les Données Bretonnantes: la Prairie de Représentation*' *Art History*, Vol. 4, No. 3, Sept. 1980: 314–44.

Republished in *Modern Art and Modernism: A Critical Anthology*, edited by F. Frascina and Charles Harrison, London: Harper & Row, 1983: 285–304.

Fred Orton and Griselda Pollock, 'Avant-Gardes and Partisans Reviewed', *Art History*, Vol. 4, No. 3, Sept. 1981: 305–27.

Republished in *Pollock and After: The Critical Debate*, edited by F. Frascina, pp. 167–83, London: Harper & Row, 1985 and *Pollock and After: The Critical Debate Second Edition*, edited by Francis Frascina, London: Routledge, 2000: 211–26.

Fred Orton and Griselda Pollock, 'Cloisonnism?', *Art History*, Vol. 5, No. 3, Sept. 1982: 341–8.

Fred Orton and Griselda Pollock, 'Jackson Pollock, Painting and the Myth of Photography', *Art History*, Vol. 6, No. 1, March 1983: 114–22.

Michael Baldwin, Charles Harrison, Fred Orton, M. Ramsden (as Art & Language), 'A Cultural Drama: The Artists Studio', *Art and Language* (exhibition catalogue), Los Angeles Institute of Contemporary Art, Sept–Oct. 1983: 3–25.

Charles Harrison and Fred Orton, 'Jasper Johns: Meaning What You See', *Art History*, Vol. 6, No. 1, March 1984: 78–101.

Fred Orton, 'Art & Language', The Fifth Biennale of Sydney. *Private Symbol: Social Metaphor* (exhibition catalogue), April–June 1984: n.p.

Fred Orton, 'Reactions to Renoir keep changing', *Oxford Art Journal*, Vol. 8, No. 2, 1985: 28–35.

Fred Orton, 'Modernism, Postmodernism, and Art Education (English)', *Circa*, No. 28, May–June, 1986: 62–4.

Fred Orton, 'Present, the Scene of … Selves, the Occasion of … Ruses', *Block* 13, Winter, 1987: 5–19.

Republished in *Foirades/Fizzles: Echo and Allusion in the Art of Jasper Johns*, edited by James Cuno, pp. 167–92, Los Angeles: Wight Art Gallery, U.C.L.A. 1987, and Chicago: University of Chicago Press, 1988. Also in *The Block Reader in Visual Culture*, edited by the *Block* editorial board, London: Routledge, 1996: 87–114.

J.R.R. Christie and Fred Orton, 'Writing on a Text of the Life', *Art History*, Vol. 11, No. 4, Dec. 1988: 545–64.

Fred Orton, 'On Being Bent Blue (Second State): An Introduction to Jacques Derrida/A Footnote on Jasper Johns', *Oxford Art Journal*, Vol. 12, No. 1, 1989: 35–46.

Fred Orton, 'Action, Revolution and Painting', *Oxford Art Journal*, Vol. 14, No. 2, 1991: 3–17.

Republished in *American Abstract Expressionism*, edited by David Thistlewood, pp. 147–78, Liverpool: Tate Gallery and Liverpool University Press, 1993. Also anthologized in *Pollock and After: The Critical Debate Second Edition*, edited by Francis Frascina, London: Routledge, 2000: 211–26.

Fred Orton, 'J. Johns's Flag: A Different Kind of Beginning', *Over Here: Reviews in American Studies*, Vol. 11, No. 2, Winter 1991: 64–84.

Fred Orton, 'Footnote One: The Idea of the Cold War' in *American Abstract Expressionism*, edited by David Thistlewood, Liverpool: Tate Gallery and Liverpool University Press, 1993: 179–92.

In German as '*Footnote Eines: Die Idee das Kalten Krieg*' in *Abstrakte Expressionismus, Konstruktion eines Aesthetik*, edited by R. Breugel, Dresden: Verlag der Kunst, 2000.

Fred Orton, 'Figuring Jasper's Flag (First Draft): A Different Kind of Beginning' in *Kunstlerischer Autausch/Artistic Exchange, Akten des XXVIII Internationalen Kongresses für Kunstgeschichte, Berlin, 15–20 Juli 1992*, edited by Thomas W. Gaehtgens, Berlin: Akademie Verlag, 1994: 703–11.

Fred Orton, 'Figuring Jasper Johns' in *Art Has No History! The Making and Unmaking of Modern Art*, edited by John Roberts, London: Verso, 1994: 111–32.

Fred Orton, '(Painting) Out of Time', *Parallax: A journal of metadiscursive theory and cultural practices* 3, September 1996: 99–112.

Fred Orton, 'The Object After Theory (Figuring Jasper Johns – Supplement 1: Flag)', *de-, dis-, ex*, Vol. 1, Ex-cavating Modernism, 1996: 23–34.

Fred Orton, 'Rethinking the Ruthwell Monument: Fragments and critique; tradition and history; tongues and sockets', *Art History*, Vol. 21, No. 1, March 1998: 65–106.

Fred Orton, 'Northumbrian Sculpture (the Ruthwell and Bewcastle Monuments): Questions of Difference' in *Northumbria's Golden Age*, edited by Jane Hawkes and Susan Mills, Stroud: Sutton Publishing Ltd., 1999: 216–27.

Fred Orton, 'Beginning with Intention' in *The Dynamics of Now: Issues in Art and Education*, edited by William Furlong, Polly Gould and Paul Hetherington, London: Tate Gallery Publishing, 2000: 137–49.

Fred Orton, 'On the Intention of Modern(ist) Art' in *A Companion to Art Theory*, edited by Paul Smith and Carolyn Wilde, Oxford: Blackwell, 2002: 229–43.

Lisa Joyce and Fred Orton, '"Always Elsewhere": An Introduction to the Art of Jeff Wall (A Ventriolquist at a Birthday Party in October, 1948)' in *Jeff Wall: Photographs*, Köln: Verlag der Buchhandlung Walther König, 2003: 8–33.

Fred Orton, 'Rethinking the Ruthwell and Bewcastle Monuments: Some strictures on similarity; some questions of history' in *Theorising Anglo-Saxon*

Stone Sculpture, eds. Catherine Karkov and Fred Orton, West Virginia University Press, 2003: 65–92.

Fred Orton, 'Northumbrian Identity in the Eighth Century: Style, classification, class, and the form of ideology', *Journal of Medieval and Early Modern Studies*, Winter, 2004: 95–145.

Fred Orton, 'At the Bewcastle Monument, In Place' in *The Making of Place, Medieval to Modern*, edited by Clare A. Lees and Gillian R. Overing, Pennsylvania State University Press, 2006: 29–66.

Fred Orton, 'SUSPENSA VIX VIA FIT: Jasper Johns' catenary, the everyday self, the work of art/aesthetic self, and the art object', *Oxford Art Journal*, Vol. 27, No. 1, 2004: 79–93.

Television and Radio Programmes for the Open University

Fred Orton and Griselda Pollock, 'Rooted in the Earth. Vincent van Gogh: The Potato Eaters', Open University/B.B.C.T.V., A315 Modern Art & Modernism (25 mins.), 1982.

Fred Orton and Griselda Pollock, 'The Museum of Modern Art', Open University/B.B.C.T.V., A315 Modern Art & Modernism (25 mins.), 1983.

Fred Orton and Griselda Pollock, 'Peasants and Paintings of Peasants', Open University/B.B.C. Radio, A315 Modern Art & Modernism (25 mins.), 1983.

Fred Orton and Griselda Pollock, 'Art and U.S. Imperialism', Open University/B.B.C. Radio, A315 Modern Art & Modernism (25 mins.), 1983

Fred Orton, 'Jasper Johns' *Flag*', Open University/B.B.C.T.V., A316 Modern Art – practices and debates (25 mins.), 1993.

Fred Orton, 'Jasper Johns', Open University Video, A318 Art of the Twentieth Century, video, (30 mins.), 2003.

CHAPTER 1

Beginning ... with Intention

> Hamm: We're not beginning to ... to ... mean something?
> Clov: Mean something! You and I, mean something! [*Brief laugh.*] Ah that's a good one!
>
> SAMUEL BECKETT, *Endgame*

∴

> One of the crucial problems in art is the business of 'meaning it'. If you are a painter, meaning the paintings you make; if you are an observer, meaning what you see. It is very difficult for us to mean what we say or do.
>
> JASPER JOHNS to JOSEPH E. YOUNG, 1969

∴

'Intention' became something of a controversial concept in literary theory and criticism with the publication of W.K. Wimsatt and M.C. Beardsley's essay 'The Intentional Fallacy' in 1946.[1] Even now, it offers much food for thought, but it requires more careful reading than it perhaps received when it was first published. Wimsatt and Beardsley wrote in opposition to the legacy of Romantic

---

[1] The first version of this essay was given as a paper at 'What Do You Think You Are Doing? Intention in Making, Understanding and Teaching Art', February 1997, the third of four conferences organised by Wimbledon School of Art in collaboration with the Tate Gallery, London, and held at the Tate Gallery. It was published, as it was read, under the title 'Beginning with Intention' in William Furlong, Polly Gould and Paul Hetherington (eds.), *Issues In Art Education: the Dynamics of Now*, London, Wimbledon School of Art in association with Tate Publishing Ltd., 2000, pp. 137–49. Another version was included under the title 'On the Intention of Modern(ist) Art' in Paul Smith and Carolyn Wilde (eds.), *A Companion to Art Theory*, Oxford: Blackwell Publishing Ltd., 2002. Neither version was provided with footnotes. What's published here is a revised, amended and corrected, footnoted and referenced composite of those previous attempts to get to grips with intention. Inevitably, what I've come up with is not what I intended. Not exactly. As you'll see: One always does other.
Wimsatt and Beardsley 1946, pp. 468–88.

aesthetics, which, they claimed, privileged intention when it came to judging poetry, particularly lyric poetry. While they recognised that writing a poem is an intentional act, they argued that knowledge of the author's intentions should not be used as a standard with which to value his poem. Wimsatt and Beardsley also wrote in opposition to the emphasis on subjectivity that criticism had inherited from the Romantics. The procedures of literary criticism had to be disassociated from those of literary biography. As far as they were concerned, the critic's job was to value a poem, as far as possible, without reference to its author's life, psychology and historical context. 'The evaluation of the work of art', they wrote, 'remains public; the work of art is measured against something outside the author'.[2]

Rereading 'The Intentional Fallacy', I'm struck by how much Wimsatt and Beardsley's argument was about evaluation rather than meaning. At one point in the fourth section of the essay, where they engage with the idea that 'there is a difference between internal and external evidence for the meaning of a poem', they have interesting things to say about how poems might be interpreted but their main concern is with evaluation not interpretation.[3] The idea – it's almost conventional wisdom now – that interpretation should be concerned only with what can be read (or, in its extension to the visual arts, seen to be the case without reference to the author's purpose) came later. This was either, at worst, a careless reading of 'The Intentional Fallacy' or, at best, in the reading associated with so-called American New Criticism, an extension of a concern with value judgement to new ways of understanding balance, contrast, rhetorical structure and so on.

Whatever you might think about 'The Intentional Fallacy' and the arguments it provoked regarding the irrelevance or relevance of intention in the evaluation and interpretation of literary texts, for over half a century now the problem of intention has been a more or less big issue in literary theory and criticism in a way that it rarely has been in art theory and criticism. Indeed, it seems that intention hasn't been much of an issue at all for art theory and criticism. Which is not to say that art theorists and critics have been unaware of the 'intentional fallacy' or some extension of it, or that intention hasn't had its moments. But those moments have been few and far between. As we'll see directly, one such moment occurred in 1970. Another moment occurred in 1985 when, during a debate in *Artforum* about the *Primitivism* show at the Museum of Modern Art, New York, Thomas McEvilley took Kirk Varnedoe and William

---

2   Wimsatt and Beardsley 1946, p. 477.
3   Ibid.

Rubin back to school for a lesson on the 'intentional fallacy', intentionality and intention, and much more besides.[4] Another moment, also in 1985, was the publication of Michael Baxandall's book *Patterns of Intention: On the Historical Explanation of Pictures*, a work of high scholarship as remarkable for its seeming productive avoidance of saying anything about intention as it was disingenuous about the degree to which it was saying something about it.[5] Since then, with the exception of some passages in Richard Wollheim's *Painting as an Art* of 1987, which argues, contrary to the extended idea of the 'intentional fallacy', that the meaning of a work of art is to be properly identified with the intention of its author, little or nothing has been published on the issue.[6] In other words, though intention seems never to have been a vexed or vivid topic for art theory and criticism, it has occasionally floated onto the agenda only to be jettisoned almost immediately. There's no reason to suppose that this moment of thinking about intention won't go the same way.

As I understand it, 'intention' is the determining desire or force that, when acted on, makes an object what it is and gives it meaning. Intention is the emotions and desires, thoughts and beliefs that initiate an action to make, structure and form an object – my interest is in the work that results in the kind of object that we refer to as a work of art, of course – that will affect, in its beholder, an experience or feeling and occasion at least one interpretation of what it might mean. 'I am not merely saying this, I mean something by it'.[7] Intention is always directed towards meaning and meaning is always intentional.

Wimsatt and Beardsley's 'The Intentional Fallacy' was intended as a contribution to aesthetics. Richard Wollheim's *Painting as an Art* is surely that. Philosophy is unavoidable in talk about intention, and philosophy has always been concerned with it. But I am no philosopher. I went to college in the early 1960s with the intention of becoming an artist. I became an art historian in the late 1970s. So much for intention. I know very little philosophy, and when my art history has needed some aesthetics or philosophy of art I have usually appropriated it from Wollheim's publications, either *Art and Its Objects*, published in 1968, or his 1970 essay 'The Work of Art as Object', which I nodded

---

4 McEvilley, Thomas, 'Doctor Lawyer Indian Chief: "Primitivism" in 20th Century Art" at the Museum of Modern Art in 1984', *Artforum*, November 1984, pp. 54–61 and the subsequent exchange of letters in *Artforum*, February 1985 and *May* 1985. The full correspondence is published in *Uncontrollable Beauty: Toward a New Aesthetics*, edited by Bill Beckley with David Shapiro, New York, School of Visual Arts: Allworth Press, 1998.
5 Baxandall 1985.
6 Wollheim 1987.
7 Wittgenstein 1958, 139e see 507.

towards just a moment ago.⁸ That said, since my art student days, I have also, on occasion, turned to the philosophy of Ludwig Wittgenstein, to the *Tractatus Logico-Philosphicus* and, more often, to the *Philosophical Investigations*.⁹ Fragments of the latter and also of the *Lectures on Aesthetics* have their place here.¹⁰ But it is Wollheim, not Wittgenstein, who I turn to now for the beginning of 'The Work of Art as Object' serves me very well insofar as it sets down several givens about art and making a work of art and suggests a structure for what I want to say. Here it is:

> If we wanted to say something about art that we could be quite certain was true, we might settle for the assertion that art is intentional. And by this we would mean that art is something we do, that works of art are things that human beings make. And the truth of this assertion is in no way challenged by such discoveries, some long known, others freshly brought to light, as that we cannot produce a work of art to order, that improvisation has its place in the making of a work of art, that the artist is not necessarily the best interpreter of his work, that the spectator has a legitimate role to play in the organization of what he perceives.¹¹

If occasionally I have turned to Wollheim's writing on aesthetics for philosophical resources for doing art history, I have more often turned to the work of Jasper Johns for my objects of study.¹² I'm convinced that several of Johns's works are among the most exceptional – canonical – works of twentieth-century art. None more so than *Flag* (The Museum of Modern Art, New York), begun at the end of 1954 and perhaps worked on in 1955, an object that effects a knowledge about the self and the world that is difficult to accept and impossible to transcend. I believe that it has an extraordinary sensual and cognitive value. It has punctuated my progress as an art historian in much the same way that it has marked the progress of Johns's art. We continually return to it and some of what it established. I'm not going to break with that continual return now, for *Flag*, and Johns's story of how he came to make it, are such

---

8   Wollheim 1968, and Wollheim, 'The Work of Art as Object', *Studio International*, 180, 928, December 1970 republished in Richard Wollheim, *On Art and the Mind*, Harvard University Press, 1973, 112–19, and in Harrison and Orton (eds.) 1984, pp. 10–17.
9   Wittgenstein 1974.
10 Wittgenstein 1966.
11 Wollheim in Harrison and Orton (eds.) 1984, pp. 10–11.
12 See for example: Orton 1987, pp. 5–19; Orton 1989, pp. 35–46; Orton, 2004, pp. 79–93. See also Orton 1994 and Orton 1996.

exemplary objects with which to examine, illustrate and explain what's special about intention that I would be foolish to ignore them here.[13]

> What one sees one tends to suppose was intended by the artist. I don't know that that is so. I think one works and makes what one makes and then one looks at it and sees what one sees. And I think that the picture isn't pre-formed, I think it is formed as it is made; and might be anything.
> JASPER JOHNS to DAVID SYLVESTER[14]

> The experience of looking at a painting is different from the experience of planning a painting or of painting a painting. And ... the statements one makes about finished work are different from the statements one can make about the experience of making it.
> JASPER JOHNS to DAVID SYLVESTER[15]

To those people who asked him why he made *Flag* or how he came to make it or what it means, Johns first replied that he had 'no ideas about what the [*Flag*] paintings imply about the world' and that he 'intuitively likes to paint flags'.[16] Afterwards, he would reply, and thereafter would always reply along the same lines, that he 'dreamed one night of painting a large flag' or 'a flag of the United States of America' or 'a large American flag'.[17] It's worth noting that we're not told what kind of flag or what specific flag was in Johns's dream. Hindsight would suggest that the dream flag was the national flag of the United States of America but it could have been the flag of any one of the forty-eight states in the Union at that time or, indeed, any other flag. It seems that he told one or two close friends about his dream, and one or the other or both of them thought that it presented him with a good idea for a painting.[18] After that, he went out and bought the materials with which to begin. And began. 'Beginning' is important. In several additions to the story of the dream, Johns has said

---

13   What follows takes a lot from the discussion of *Flag* in Orton 1994, pp. 89–146.
14   Interview by David Sylvester with Jasper Johns, in Johns 1974, p. 18.
15   Interview by David Sylvester with Jasper Johns, in Johns 1974, p. 18.
16   Jasper Johns quoted in Johns 1958, p. 96. The paintings referred are not only *Flag* (1954–55) but also, for example, *White Flag* (1955), *Flag Above White* (1955), *Flag Above White with Collage* (1955), *Gray Flag* (1957), and *Flag on Orange Field* (1957).
17   Solomon 1964, in Jasper Johns 1964, New York, p. 6 and London, p. 7; Johns interviewed in 1966 by Alan R. Solomon, in Castleman 1986, p. 28; and De Antonio and Maurice Tuchman 1984, p. 97 (based on transcripts from the movie *Painters Painting*, directed by Emile de Antonio, 1972).
18   Tomkins 1980, p. 177 and Solomon 1988, p. 63.

that 'using the design of *the* [emphasis added] American flag took care of a great deal' for him because he didn't have to design it;[19] that 'it had a clearly defined area, which could be measured and transferred to canvas';[20] and that it would be something he could do that could be his.[21] When it came to turning the dream into actuality, the dreamed flag, which was 'a large flag' or 'a flag of the united States of America' or 'a large American flag', becomes not merely any flag or any unspecified American flag but *the* American flag, the national flag of the United States of America, the Stars and Stripes.

'If we wanted to say something about art that we could be quite certain was true, we might settle for the assertion that art is intentional. And by this we would mean that art is something we do, that works of art are things that human beings make' (Wollheim, 'The Work of Art as Object'). This makes a distinction between an intentional man-made object and a natural object, a distinction that could be applied, for example, to a sculpture by Henry Moore or Barbara Hepworth and any of the Norber Erratics near Austwick, North Yorkshire. Whereas poems, other literary texts, paintings and sculptures, music, and so on and so forth, are made of imagined form, time and place, natural objects have not been imagined and imaged into existence by man's invention; their material, formal, spatial and temporal characters are, as it were, given. Though according to the 'intentional fallacy', poems and works of art might be judged as if they were natural objects, they could only be so judged as meaningful by ignoring their intentional character. Paul de Man, discussing the relation between form and intention in American New Criticism, put the matter like this:

> Certain entities exist the full meaning of which can be said to equal the totality of their sensory appearances. For an ideal perception, entirely devoid of complications resulting from the interference of the imagination, the 'meaning' of 'stone' could only refer to a totality of sensory appearances. The same applies to all natural objects. But even the most purely intuitive consciousness could never conceive of the significance of an object such as, for instance, a chair, without including in the description an allusion to the *use* to which it is put; the most rigorous description of the perceptions of the object 'chair' would remain meaningless if one does not organize them in function of the potential act that defines the object; namely, that it is destined to be sat on. The potential act of sitting down is a constitutive part of the object. If it were absent, the object

---

19 Steinberg 1972, p. 31.
20 Hopps 1965, p. 177.
21 Crichton 1977, p. 28.

could not be conceived in its totality. The difference between the stone and the chair distinguishes a natural object from an intentional object. The intentional object requires a reference to a specific act as constitutive of its mode of being. By asserting ... that, in literary language, the meaning is equal to the sum of sensory appearances, one postulates in fact that the language of literature is of the same order, ontologically speaking, as a natural object. The intentional factor has been bypassed.[22]

What de Man says about the way a literary text and the language of literature are valued and understood according to the 'intentional fallacy' accords well with the way paintings and sculptures were valued and understood by those art theorists and critics who, at that time, held to what might be called the dominant theory of the expressive quality of the work of art as object. Even now, such theorists and critics see themselves as disinterested and evaluate the work of art as object by its effects as they feel them. This is Clement Greenberg, who, in a common variation on the belief in the expressive quality of the work of art, also held to the near ineffability of the work of art's emotional consequence: 'Whatever Dante or Tolstoy, Bach or Mozart, Giotto or David intended his art to be about, or said it was about, the works of his art go beyond anything specifiable in their effect. That is what art, regardless of the intention of artists, *has* to do, even the worst art ...'[23] This theory of the expressive quality of the work of art, like the intentional fallacy, is doubly fallacious because it holds not only that the expressive quality of the work of art can be felt and valued independent of any consideration of the artist's intention but also that what is expressed is a natural expression, is in and of itself expressed directly and immediately regardless of any intention.

Chairs and literary texts or, as Baxandall would have it, bridges and paintings are different kinds of intentional objects,[24] each with its own relation to intention, and to what Wollheim in 'The Work of Art as Object' referred to as a 'concept' or 'description'. Because works of art are things that human beings make, they must be made according to a concept or according to various descriptions of the qualities, features, characteristics, etc., that make the work of art – the painting or sculpture – what it is. There will be a hierarchy among these concepts or descriptions that regulates the production of the work of art. At different periods and under different conditions the relations that

---

22 De Man, Paul, 'Form and Intent in the American New Criticism', in De Man 1983, pp. 23–4.
23 Greenberg, Clement, 'Complaints of an Art Critic', in O'Brian 1993, p. 269.
24 See Baxandall 1985, ch. 1, 'The Historical Object: Benjamin Baker's Forth Bridge', pp. 12–40.

hold within the concept or description will be felt or thought to change. Modern works of art – by which I mean so-called Modernist works of art, broadly conceived – are somewhat different from pre-Modern works of art. According to the dominant theory of modern art – Modernist art as Wollheim understood it in 1970 – the material character of the work of art has to be emphasised. With regard to painting, the concept or description requires that the surface has to be asserted or insisted on – Wollheim took as his examples Henri Matisse's *The Open Window* (1913), Mark Rothko's *Red on Maroon* (1959) and Morris Louis's *Alpha Phi* (1962) – and used to effect in the beholder, a feeling and knowledge of what and how the painter felt and knew, or, for Wollheim, an expressive quality and a kind of beauty.

Works of art, especially works of modern art, are different from other things that human beings make. The act of making a work of art, especially the act of making a modern work of art, involves an intention and a concept very different from that of, to stay with Baxandall's *Patterns of Intention*, making a bridge where everything, including the designer's sense of expression and beauty, has to be subordinated to the intention of making a structure that will span and facilitate movement across a gap. Another example, directly relevant to Johns's *Flag*, is provided by the national flag of the United States of America, the Stars and Stripes, which is an intentional object whose manufacture is controlled under the United States Statutes at Large by a description of its proportions, size, situation of its elements and colours, and whose use is subordinated to the controlled intention of facilitating the demonstration, affirmation and celebration of citizenship, loyalty and patriotism. The work of art is an intentional act that produces an intentional object but it is not, as is the case with making a Stars and Stripes or a bridge, an act that is subordinated to another act that exists beyond the intention of making it and trying to make it, as far as possible, according to that intention. Here I come in line with those who have argued that the modern artist makes a work of art with no intention other than that of making it, where 'making it' constitutes a closed structure autonomous of whatever use might be made of it after it has been made; for example, selling it. The value of making a work of art as object is, for the artist, an experiential value. The value that a work of art as object has in the market economy is an exchange value. The artist may or may not have the intention of selling the work of art once it's made but that intention of exchanging it for hard cash exists beyond the intention of making it. Exchanging the work of art for money in the marketplace might well have helped the artist make it, and help make more works of art in the future, but that was not the intention, in-and-of-*itself*, when the artist began making it – not if what the artist was intending to make was a work of art. To understand the work of art in this way is not to insist, as

New Criticism insisted, on the idea of the 'self-sufficiency' or 'self-focusedness' of art. Rather, to insist on the way the artist works the sensuous materials – if it's a painting, by asserting and using the surface – of the work of art according to no other intention but to make a work of art is to insist that making and understanding a work of art enables an acute kind of coming to 'self-consciousness'.

The work of art is an intentional act and object of 'self-consciousness'. Making a work of art is an operation of a mind that would know itself. 'Self-conscious' then, but not 'self-sufficient' where 'self-sufficient' is taken as a metaphor for the belief that the production and consumption of a work of art is independent or autonomous of reference to the world outside its structure and form. And 'self-conscious' then, not 'self-focused', because there is no originary, ontologically prior or transcendental self that could be focused on and met with or matched in the making and understanding of the work of art. 'Self-conscious', then, because the intention to make a work of art is an intention to inaugurate a structuring process where some degree of self-consciousness comes into place only to be negated – it's not that, it's not that, it's not that – and then progressed, placed, negated, progressed, and so on. Seen and understood like this, the work of art appears as but one moment in the continuous process of desiring a self-identity whereby material signs – metaphors, metonyms, the full range of tropes and figures of speech or their visual equivalents – of that identity are found and lost, put in place and displaced, brought to practical consciousness and found wanting. Whatever the modern artist's intentions and whatever meaning was intended, the modern artist makes a work of art to know a self. The modern work of art comes in place of a self's yearning for knowledge of itself ... not to express its self for there is no self to express. Suffice it to say that the work of art cannot be reduced to the intention that brings it into being. The intention of making, sensing and making sense of, feeling and understanding a work of art maintains itself as a process of desiring self-consciousness.

When Johns first allowed his story of the dream and its relation of association with the object that became *Flag* into what would become published discourse, he did so in ways that suggest that he may not have been clear about what he saw himself doing in his dream. Remember, he said that he 'dreamed one night of painting a large flag', which suggests that he dreamt the intention to paint a large flag or was painting one, though it is not clear what flag or what kind of flag he might paint or was painting. Was he, in his dream, dreaming the intention of painting or was he already at work painting a ... whatever it was? Was he intending to make or was he making either a painting *of* a big flag or actually painting a large flag? Was it the same flag in both stories? Was the object he was dreaming of intending to make or was making a work of art, something insubordinate and self-conscious, or was it a flag, an object seemingly without self-consciousness and subordinate to another intention? The story effects an uncertainty, irresolvable by either grammatical or rhetorical analysis or by conversation with the artist about what the intention was and what kind of object it was that was there in the dream that, subsequently, was taken into the object that became *Flag*.

Awake and in the studio, making *Flag*, Johns blurred the distinction between making an object under the concept 'flag' (and making a large Stars and Stripes with paint and stuff) and making an object under the concept 'painting' (and making a work of art as object that could be referred to as a painting). From the moment he hit on the idea of having the Stars and Stripes provide the structure for the way he was to assert and use the surface of what it was that he was producing, making the one congruent with the other, the idea of making a work of art as object that could be seen and understood as a painting was compromised. It was further compromised, bearing in mind how the national flag of the United States of America is made, by his decision to follow the usual method of making a Stars and Stripes (the kind that's made to be displayed on and in government and public buildings) and use three separate panels, one canvas for the canton with the stars, one for the short stripes to its right, and one for the long stripes below. This will be important for those persons, especially citizens of the United States of America, who know the Stars and Stripes and how it's fabricated. What Johns was doing was more like making a Stars and Stripes than making a work of art as object that could be seen as a painting of one.

'A picture represents its subject from a position outside it. (Its standpoint is its representational form.) That is why a picture represents its subject correctly or incorrectly ... A picture cannot, however, place itself outside its representational form'. Wittgenstein pointed that out in his *Tractatus Logico-Philosophicus*.[25] But he hadn't seen Johns's *Flag*. The point I'm making here is that Johns's *Flag*, as a work of art, does not represent its subject from a position outside its representational form. It represents its subject and is the subject represented. In managing to do this, it shifts the conditions of 'outside' and 'inside', the Stars and Stripes and a work of art as object – though perhaps modern art had already shifted the conditions of 'outside' and 'inside' as meant by Wittgenstein and Johns is, as it were, only playing with them, albeit seriously and for high stakes.

The peculiar character of *Flag* is such that, wherever one looks, there is both flag and painting. *Flag* is neither flag nor painting but flag and painting. Neither the Stars and Stripes nor a painting of the Stars and Stripes, it is simultan-

---

25   Wittgenstein 1974, p. 10 see 2.173 and 2.174.

eously both the Stars and Stripes and a painting of the Stars and Stripes. The oppositional concepts that organise *Flag* merge in a constant and provocative undecidable exchange of attributes in a way that causes problems for anyone who is concerned to fix its meaning. Whether Johns intended this undecidability or whether it resulted as an unintended effect of how he recollected his dream and acted on it, that was what materialised when he decided to have the structure and formal elements of the object he was making congruent with the structure and form of the flag of the United States of America. However, whatever it was that Johns intended to make or saw himself making in his dream, he must have been intending to make it or was making it according to some concept or description of what painting was as an activity. He was, after all, dreaming of 'painting' something. And awake and in the studio, in so far as his intention was to make whatever it was that he intended to make or was making in the dream under the concept or description 'painting', perhaps according to the dominant theory of modern art with regard to painting, that intention was frustrated in practice.

'We cannot produce a work of art to order ... improvisation has its place in the making of a work of art' (Wollheim, 'The Work of Art as Object'). The intention that Johns dreamed or was acting upon with paint in his dream began, in actuality, in the studio, with paint also, but then that medium was abandoned in favour of another medium. Johns began making the object that would become *Flag* with what would then have been regarded as respectable avant-garde materials: enamel paints, probably on a bed sheet. In the mid 1950s both Willem de Kooning and Jackson Pollock were using household nitro cellulose lacquer and alkyd enamel paints to make their paintings. For them, it had the value of an artisanal material; it signified a travesty or negation of oil paint. And like them, it was important for Johns that traces of the creative process should be part of the finished object. Its past had to be there as an aspect of its visual appearance, visible its presented state. Johns wanted to show something of what had gone before and what had been done after. He wanted the process and history of the making of the object to be part of its meaning and affect. That was a conventional avant-garde strategy of art-making. But when Johns applied the enamel paint, the second brushstroke smeared the first brushstroke unless he waited until the paint dried; and the paint took too long to dry. He was a skilled draughtsman and worked very effectively with collage, and he had developed the knack of making plaster casts, but it's possible that he was not then as patient or as adept as a painter – as an avant-garde painter – to the degree that his intention demanded; which is to say that he was either too impatient or lacked the skill with enamel paint to assert and use the surface successfully according to the dominant theory of modern art. So, he stopped

working with enamel paint and changed to working with hot wax, which dries very quickly. As soon as one application of wax had hardened, he could add another without altering what had gone on before. Splashes, drips and dribbles of wax become round as they dry, like enamel paint does but more so, just like wax dribbles down the side of a candle. Johns found the medium very easy to control and adapted it to his way with collage where more or less rectangular, more or less regular-sized bits of paper, some printed, some plain, would be stuck down next to each other or slightly overlapping, here and there not quite adhering, standing proud at the corners, slightly curling at the edges. Here and there a bit of rag might be stitched to the fabric but, by and large, the process Johns developed while working on *Flag* involved dipping cut and torn pieces of newspaper and cloth into hot coloured wax – blue, white and red – and fixing them to the fabric before the wax cooled. This meant that the various textures, value contrasts and texts would remain visible at the same time that their individualities were subsumed and unified by the structure of the Stars and Stripes and the all-over surface gloss or sheen of the wax. In some places wax has dripped and dribbled across the edges of stars and stripes, but those drips and dribbles never disrupt, spoil or break the genuine flagness of *Flag*. Wherever the wax has run from a red stripe across a white stripe or from a white stripe across a red stripe, it has been painted over with either red or white wax or paint to preserve the colouration of the Stars and Stripes.

That mention of paint, just then, reminds me that some areas of *Flag*'s surface also include the use brush and oil paint: always a kind of sliding dab, for the brush stays too long on the surface to make a proper dab.

The two ways of applying colour, with collage material dipped into blue, white or red melted wax and with brushes and oil paint have equal value and follow no particular sequence. Everywhere there is something to see and make sense of, some texture and text, some touch and textuality. In coming to make *Flag* like this, in a way that was not quite painting yet not quite its travesty or negation, something happened to the surface – to the fact that, according to the dominant theory of modern art, a painting has a surface and that surface has to be both asserted and used – for the process that made *Flag* might best described not as a way of asserting and using a surface but, rather, as a way of making a surface ... a surface that made a flag. The fact of the bed sheet or canvas as ground or surface, as it undergoes the application of the wax, collage and oil paint, almost disappears as something prior that's been asserted. Here, wax, collage and oil paint make the shapes of the stars and the stripes in much the same way that discrete pieces of blue, white and red fabric get sewn into place to make the Stars and Stripes: the individual pieces of cloth don't assert the surface of a flag; they construct the national flag of the United States of America.

That was not all there was to making *Flag*, but that brief account is sufficient for this discussion of intention. Almost. I need to point to one more aspect of its making. A year or so after Johns had thought that he had finished working on *Flag*, he put it on display on a temporary wall in his studio, which someone, at a party in the studio, toppled. *Flag* was damaged and it had to be repaired. The repair was made with then current newspaper material. Begun at the end of 1954, *Flag* was completed – we know this by the date of the newspaper used for the repair – on or after 15 February 1956. The manner of *Flag*'s completion, far removed from the intention that brought it into being, was almost unforeseeable and thoroughly contingent.

It has been claimed that though intention is never inconsistent with method, it may well be in conflict or at variance with method. Johns's stories about his dream and what I've been able to theorise about how he made *Flag* seem to confirm that this is so. Leaving aside the question of whether, in his dream, Johns was intending to make with paint a flag or was making a work of art as object, when he began making the object that became *Flag*, his intention, as it turned out, was at odds with the intention of making it with enamel paint on fabric. The activity of making a work of art – the relationship between intention, method and object – depends not only on the foreseeable but also on a multiplicity of more or less unforeseeable actions, occurrences and events, affects and effects. If Johns intended to do so, he did not paint a picture of a flag. And though he began making *Flag* with enamel paint on fabric under the concept or description 'painting', he eventually made it with wax, collage material and oil paint and invented a new medium and also a new surface, something that evaded adequate description for many years. Then having made it, *Flag* was subsequently damaged and repaired in – for some persons – a significantly vivid and affective way. The intentional act that makes a modern work of art, unlike the act of making the national flag of the United States of America, is not one that produces its object according to a description or set of instructions that have the force of law.

Pictorial meaning is conveyed by its sensory appearance. The artist makes a work of art to produce an experience and meaning in the work's beholder. The artist is, of course, the work's first or primary beholder. *Flag* brings about the experience and the meaning not only of being a work of art as object but also of being an object that is the flag of the United States of America. That's its undecidability. That undecidable experience and meaning must be made to try to 'match' the artist's intention. As the work's first beholder, the artist must continually match his experience and interpretation of what he is doing and of what he is bringing into being against the intention that was acted on to inaugurate the work. He sees, feels, smells, hears and explains to himself what he is doing and tries to make sure that the experience – especially the visual and tactile experience – he has and the interpretation that he makes of the object while he is making it is attuned to the intention that was acted upon and is bringing it into being. Sense perception and cognition are in a reciprocal relationship with intention in the process of making a work of art, which is one of continuous adjustment and readjustment between the intention that began bringing it into being and what is being brought into being, between what was desired and what is being achieved.

Here is Johns telling David Sylvester something of what happens when an artist makes a work of art.

> JJ: ... You do something in painting and you see it. Now the idea of 'thing' or 'it' can be subjected to great alterations, so that we look in a certain direction and we see one thing, we look in another way and we see another thing. So that what we call 'thing' becomes very elusive and very flexible, and it involves the arrangement of elements before us, and the arrangement of our senses at the time of encountering this thing. It involves the way we focus, what we are willing to accept as being there. In the process of making the painting, all these things interest me ...
>
> DS: Obviously each new move is determined by what is already on the canvas; what else is it determined by?
>
> JJ: By what is not on the canvas.
>
> DS: But there are a great number of possibilities of what might go on the canvas.
>
> JJ: That is true, but one's thinking, just the process of thinking, excludes many possibilities. And the process of looking excludes many possibilities, because from moment to moment as we look we see what we see, at another moment in looking we might see differently. At any moment one can't see all the possibilities. And one proceeds as one proceeds, one does something and then one does something else.[26]

In the process of making *Flag* each added piece of collage material, each text and texture, each drip and dribble of wax, and each brushstroke of oil paint would have modified what was already in place and partly determined what could be put in place. Once in place, some matter would have been left there, other matter would have been removed. Or amended. And so on. Though, as we've seen, the process was somewhat serendipitous and contingent, accidents

---

26   Johns 1974, pp. 9–10.

did not make *Flag*. Yes, an accident damaged it but a repair made the object what it is. With each addition and subtraction and so on, *Flag* would have been a different thing with which Johns would have a different relationship. In other words, the intention that made the object that became *Flag* put in train an unforeseeable and unknowable number of developing sensual and cognitive moments of intention. The intention that makes the modern work of art as object is, in this sense, always an intention-in-progress until the moment when the artist decides, for whatever reason or reasons, that that the work is finished – when, according to Johns, the artist gets 'bored' and has 'no other suggestions to make in the painting; no more energy to rearrange things, no more energy to see it differently'.[27]

Niggling away at the back of my mind, however, there are the questions: Is something of the artist's intention assured actualisation in the work of art as object? And if so, how? And where? Johns gives us a clue to at least one answer. When Sylvester asked him whether he intended a painting to have a 'dominant emotional idea' or a 'mood', Johns replied:

> I think in my paintings it has evolved, because I'm not interested in any particular mood. Mentally my preference would be the mood of keeping your eyes open and looking, without focussing, without any constricted viewpoint. I think paintings by the time they are finished tend to take on a particular characteristic. That is one of the reasons they are finished, because everything has gone in that direction, and there is no recovery. The energy, the logic, everything which you do takes form in working; the energy tends to run out, the form tends to be accomplished or finalised. Then either it is what one intended (or what one is willing to settle for) or one has been involved in a process which has gone in a way that perhaps one did not intend, but has been done so thoroughly that there is no recovery from the situation. You have to leave that situation as itself, and then proceed with something else, begin again, begin a new work.[28]

Intention is always in the present and in closest connection to action;[29] though one might not be certain of what one is intending to do or of the consequence of such an act of intending.[30] And without intention the work of art as object

---

27 Johns 1974, p. 9.
28 Johns 1974, p. 11.
29 Wittgenstein 1958, 85e see 217: 'The intention with which one acts does not "accompany" the action any more than the thought "accompanies" speech'.
30 Wittgenstein 1958, 80e see 197.

would have no form, and the fact that it has the form that it has – that it is the work of art as object – is to some extent the result of the intention that brought it to its mode of being. And yes, the intention is there in the work of art as object, not dominating the surface but certainly there as an aspect of the way the surface was asserted and used as the work was brought to its mode of being. Does intention, then, have an actual duration? Or is it in a constant state of mutability and unrecoverabilty? And, if so, does it have a past tense? And *if* the intention that brought the work of art as object to its mode of being can be said, because it must be 'embedded in its situation',[31] to *lie* in the work of art as object then it *rests* there on, in and as the surface as a moment of *untruth* or *falsehood*. This is something that Johns's *Flag* might very well be making clear with regard to its own uncertain, equivocating and undecidable intention.

Would it help clarify matters if we asked the artist what his intention was in making the work of art or what it means? Probably not. It is unlikely that the artist would provide a reassuring answer to either question. As Wittgenstein pointed out, 'The most explicit expression of intention is by itself insufficient evidence of intention'.[32] If, for example, the artist had said, 'My intention was to do so and so', would he have necessarily meant that quite seriously?[33] Would he necessarily have meant it at all? Think of the way that Johns said that he 'intuitively likes to paint flags'. Would he necessarily know? The work of art might resist his best efforts to know it or the intention that was acted on to bring it to its mode of being. Sometimes, given the complex character of the move from intention to the completed work of art, the artist may be more or less nonplussed by what he has made. He may not know what it means. In which case a beholder or spectator other than the artist himself may well reach an understanding of the work that the artist may want to accept and go on with. This way of a modern artist coming to an understanding of his intention and the meaning of his work of art may well be more often the case than hitherto realised. Indeed, far from being exceptional, it may well be the usual way that artists come to understand their intentions and the meaning of what they produce. Wollheim is surely right when he says that *'the artist is not necessarily the best interpreter of his work, that the spectator has a legitimate role to play in the organization of what he sees'.*[34]

---

31   Wittgenstein 1958, 108e see 337.
32   Wittgenstein 1958, 164–65e see 641.
33   Ibid.
34   It's worth noting here what Marcel Duchamp said about this matter at the end of a talk he gave in Houston at a meeting of the American Federation of Arts, April 1957, first published in ARTnews, vol. 56, no. 4, summer 1957, and reprinted as 'The Creative Act' in Duchamp

There are artists. There are (conscious and unconscious) intentions. Artists can and do sometimes speak or write their intentions but, as I said, such statements are unlikely to be reassuring or sufficient for coming to terms with the work. Sometimes artists chose not to let us know their intention. Whether they do or not, close attention to the work of art, to the way that the surface has been asserted and used, will enable a glimpse of the intention that brought it to its mode of being. And that glimpsed intention, as it lies on the surface, can and must be placed in a relation of association with whatever the artist has said concerning his intention. Both intentions, the intention that's put into words, *as if* that's the intention that brought the work of art to its mode of being, and the intention that comes to 'lie' in it, stretched out over the surface in a dissembling way, are intentions after the fact. But not even all the details together – the words and surface elements – *show*, in any self-evident way, the artist's intention.[35]

It's here that I want to resume what I began to say about the self-consciousness of the modern work of art. If we theorise the 'self' as a product of a situated use of language and take Johns's *Flag* as if it is equivalent to a literary text – all representations are, after all, kinds of statements – then we will be able to grasp something of how the modern artist, when making a work of art according to the dominant theory of modern art, is involved in a process of moving towards acquiring self-consciousness. Here, the 'self' of self-consciousness is recognised as one of those totalising metaphors that always claims more authority than it has or can ever achieve. Consciousness, of course, must always be consciousness of something, and the consciousness that must always be possessed of a self must be a consciousness of its self. But, as I began saying at the beginning of this paper, that self-consciousness will always be only a partial consciousness of its self because the self is never in place, integral, whole, but is always in process of becoming, of being made and unmade, abandoned or lost, made and unmade, abandoned ... and so on and so forth. The intention to make a work of art is an intention to mean something. When one means something, whatever the meaning, it is one's self trying to mean its self. And 'if you say: "How am I to know what he means, when I see nothing but the signs he gives?" then I say: "How is he to know what he means when he has nothing but the signs either?"'[36]

       1975, pp. 138–40 at 140: 'All in all, the creative act is not performed by the artist alone; the spectator brings the work in contact with the external world by deciphering and interpreting its inner qualifications and thus adds his contribution to the creative act'.

35   Wittgenstein 1958, 163e see 635.
36   Wittgenstein 1958, 139e see 504.

So when the artist, making a work of art, senses and makes sense of what he is making, compares and contrasts it with his intention, he is also engaged in a process of sensing and making sense of signs of his self. A self experiences and interprets the work of art as it brings it into being. As it does so, and because it does so, a self comes to know itself, if only partially and temporarily. The process of making a work of art is a relation-in-process between the self of the artist and a modification of that self as it comes *to lie* in the work of art and effects a new self that demands further work. The process of making a work of art, and the process of making a self in that process, is an oscillating process that comes to an end, and then only provisionally, when, as Johns put it, the artist gets bored and has no other suggestions to make, no more energy to rearrange things or to see it differently.

The interpretation of an intentional act or an intentional object implies understanding the intention that brought it into existence by attending to the relations that are there in the object's sensory appearance, its material actuality, which exist not in and by themselves – as with a natural object – but for the artist and (because of and after him) for us. Coming across Johns's *Flag*, for example, we try to understand how it accords with the concept or description 'flag' and the concept or description 'painting', and realise that it fits neither and both. We read and try to make sense of its texts. We see and feel its textures and imagine the ways that Johns's fingers made contact with the surface he was making – the way a piece of collage material was put in place or the way a brush stroked some paint onto the surface – matching our sense of his touch to similar forms that we've experienced inside and outside painting. What did that feel like? What did it mean when we felt like that? And so on. The epistemological character of interpretation, by no means disinterested, implies and effects a need to understand the intention that brought the work of art into being, not by adding sets of relations to the work of art but always with regard to what has actually been brought into being by the artist, by what can be seen to be the case in the way he has asserted and used the surface.

The process of interpretation is fraught with difficulties and open to great abuse. We should be very worried that so much interpretation goes on by seeing and making sense of relationships that are *not* actually there in the work of art; that works of art are all too often made subject to various intentions that are quite unrelated to the intentions that brought them into being as they appear on the surface and in the way that that surface has been used. When it meets its public, a work of art can be appropriated by any number of interests, each for its own purpose and each unrelated to the intention that brought the work of art into being. That should trouble us: the way a work of art is *used*. It shouldn't trouble us that our interpretation will never accord with the complexity of the intention or meaning of a work of art. A work of art, especially a modern work of art, is one of the most complex objects that human beings make. It's made of an almost infinite richness of signs and meanings. It will always resist our best efforts to give an adequate interpretation of its intention, meaning and self-consciousness – and not only of its self-consciousness but ours also.

If we beholders and interpreters who are other than the artist who made it are going to come to terms with the self-conscious intended meaning of the work of art, we are going to have to put it in some kind of narrative sequence between the desire that motivated it (the intention) and the contingencies it encountered (the experiential and interpretive process of its making) and the effect it affected (its sensual and epistemological character), as it is very likely that the artist positioned it while he was making it – and it positioned him while making him the artist who made it. The beholder who is other than the artist who made it is engaged in a complementary process of self-understanding. For the beholder, as it was for the artist, every development in the interpretation of the work of art occasions a development in his and her introspective observing and 'observed' self. The oscillating process of trying to come to self-consciousness in the making and interpreting of a work of art cannot be brought to an end, and, indeed, can only be terminated by that which is beyond both interpretation and self-consciousness and which, as one commentator put it, is something of a 'linguistic predicament'.[37]

> What we call the beginning is often the end
> And to make an end is to make a beginning.
> The end is where we start from.
> T.S. ELIOT, 'Little Gidding'

Like Johns making a painting, I am now approaching the moment when I know that, in the present circumstances, I'll have no more suggestions to make, no more energy to rearrange things. In conclusion, I want to pick up something I mentioned in passing a while ago about the importance of 'beginning'. There is a relationship between *Flag* and Johns's beginning as an artist that makes it appropriate to conclude with some remarks about the relation between intention and beginning. Sometime in 1954 Johns 'decided to stop becoming and to be an artist'.[38] At that moment, perhaps it was just before he made or just after he'd made *Flag*, he deliberately and methodically destroyed whatever objects

---

37 De Man, Paul, 'Autobiography as Defacement' in De Man 1984, pp. 67–81 at p. 81.
38 Hopps, 'An Interview with Jasper Johns', in Johns 1965, p. 33.

he had in his possession that he'd produced before.[39] As far as Johns was concerned, and thereafter art criticism and art history also, 'Jasper Johns' begins as an artist with *Flag*.

Johns provides us with a very good example of an artist who was especially concerned with beginning, by which I mean that he was very aware of the need to establish the material and ideological point at which his art would depart from all other artists' work and establish relations of similarity and difference with that body of work in such a way that what he produced as his 'beginning' would provide the main entry for what he (as an artist) and his art would be. Continuity and difference. Continuity, because a work of art must be made under a concept or description of art for it to be recognised and used as art. Difference, because the artist must distinguish his work of art from all other works of art and to do this he must rethink and practically amend the description or concept with which he is working. Indeed, it seems that this is something that all self-consciously 'modern' artists must do to be recognised as 'modern artists'. Examples of other works of art that, like Johns's *Flag*, were taken as establishing a beginning by and for their artists are easy to point to. Ones that come immediately to mind include: Picasso's *Les Demoiselles d'Avignon* (1907) and Brancusi's *The Kiss* (1907–8); Barnett Newman's *Onement* (1948) and Helen Frankenthaler's *Mountains and Sea* (1952); Frank Stella's series of Black Paintings (1958–60), notably *Arbeit Macht Frei* (1959); and Anthony Caro's *Twenty Four Hours* (1960). Establishing a beginning involves designating a consequent intent that follows from an action or event, an occurrence or object. It establishes an intention-to-be-continued, a belief that it will go on, that it will enable a practice by being sustainable in practice. As Baxandall put it, 'Intention is the forward-leaning look of things'.[40]

A beginning is a project always already underway. It's begun before you've noticed it. Because of the close relation between beginning and intention, it might be the case that beginning is always already in progress before it is identified and acted upon. This seems to be something that Johns's story of his dream is telling us. In the story, Johns is either intending to paint or is at work painting a large flag or a flag of the United States of America or a large American flag. He is intending to make or is making the object that he will take as his beginning as an artist. The intention to begin is, in the dream, already in mind or has already been acted on and passed to its object. From the residue of a life and a day, some raw material was taken into and reworked in the dream that might have been

---

39   Crichton 1977, p. 26.
40   Baxandall 1985, p. 42.

Johns's motive for dreaming it in the first place. In other words, an intention was already present that gave the dream such vivid meaning for Johns that it was acted on and passed over into the object that became *Flag*. The intention to paint or the act of painting a large flag or a flag of the United States of America or a large American flag must have been present with Johns as raw material before it entered and was reworked in the dream. It could be that the raw matter of an intention is always already there to be moved into an intentional act or object. The complexity here, with regard to Johns's dream, if we follow Freud's theory on interpreting dreams, is that the dreamed act of intending to paint or painting a large flag or a flag of the United States of America or a large American flag was not about intending to paint or painting a large flag or a flag of the United States of America or a large American flag. Not in any very straightforward way. Let's say that Johns's dream was a rebus that concealed a desire or, its reverse, a fear. In so far as *Flag* is made out of that dream, is a kind of secondary revision of work going on in the dream and of the dream work, then it too is made of a secret discourse, where that desire or fear is rephrased and rhetoricised according to perspectives that are deceitful and where, in the way its surface is asserted and used, everything conceals something else. Almost.

All artists worth their salt have been concerned with beginning and intention. They've had to be. You can start from anything ... but you have to decide. That should be easy ... but it's the start that's difficult.[41] And because of that, and without a doubt, what's required is something of that 'cheerful confidence in things to come' that we read about at the beginning of Wordsworth's *The Prelude* (Book First, 58), albeit in the knowledge that, inevitably, what will come won't be what's intended.

---

41   See the exchange between Estragon and Vladimir, in Beckett's *Waiting for Godot*, Beckett 1956, p. 55.

CHAPTER 2

Painting Out of Time

> A minute in the life of the world passes. To paint that minute in its precise reality! Forgetting everything else for its sake. To become that minute.
>
> PAUL CÉZANNE in conversation with JOACHIM GASQUET

∴

> It's not easy bein' green
> Having to spend each day the colour of leaves
>
> JOE RAPOSA, *Bein' Green*

∴

Symbol and Allegory

In the literature on the symbol, reference is usually made to this passage in S.T. Coleridge's *The Statesman's Manual* of 1816:

> Now an Allegory is but a translation of abstract notions into picture-language which is itself nothing but an abstraction of objects of the senses; the principal being more worthless even than its phantom proxy, both alike unsubstantial, and the former shapeless to boot. On the other hand a Symbol … is characterized by a translucence of the Special in the Individual, or of the General in the Especial or of the Universal in the General. Above all by the translucence of the Eternal through and in the Temporal. It always partakes of the Reality which it renders intelligible; and while it enunciates the whole, abides itself as a living part in that Unity, of which it is the representative. The other are but empty echoes which the fancy arbitrarily associates with apparitions of matter, less beautiful but not less shadowy than the sloping orchard or hill-side pasture seen in the transparent lake below.[1]

---

1 The first version of this paper was presented at the College Art Association 82nd Annual

This note in the appendix is usually overlooked but is also presently to the point:

> The power delegated to nature is all in every part: and by a symbol I mean, not a metaphor or allegory or any other figure of speech or form of fancy, but an actual and essential part of that, the whole of which it represents.[2]

Coleridge stresses that allegory is a translation of rarefied ideas about things into arbitrary illustrations or decorative images. It is made of and appeals to our wildest imaginings and it provides an image of that process as well as the generalisations produced by it. The symbol, however, is unique and provides its own significance; it is an image alone; it is part of the whole that animates it; it is characterised by transparency or near transparency and it makes immediately intelligible what shines through it – that which is essentially unchanging, the Eternal.

Coleridge's discussion of allegory and symbol occurs in connection with an argument advocating the Bible as a practical handbook for anyone actively engaged in the business of a government or in shaping its policies. Coleridge thinks of the Bible as 'a system of symbols, harmonious in themselves, and consubstantial with the truths, of which they are the *conductors*'.[3] Later commentators took Coleridge's remarks to define the general nature of the symbol in literature and the arts. As such, his writing marks one moment in the general process of secularisation in the modern epoch when the theological symbol's indivisible unity of the material and transcendental object – that Christ is *of* the substance or essence of the Father – is distorted in a burgeoning aesthetics into 'the idea of the unlimited immanence of the moral world in the world of beauty'[4] and a perfect coincidence of material form with immaterial content.

Conference, New York, February 1994, in the session 'A de Manian Art History?' chaired by T.J. Clark. I'd like to thank T.J. Clark for the invitation to contribute to that session and for his conversation around the work of Paul de Man and Paul Cézanne. An amended and slightly extended version of that first paper was published as '(Painting) Out of Time', *parallax* 3, September 1996, pp. 99–112. What's published here is a revised and amended, much corrected and extended version of what was published in *parallax*. For a more considered and developed take on Cézanne's materialism, which is implied throughout this essay and becomes explicit at the end, see T.J. Clark, 'Phenomenality and Materiality in Cézanne', in *Material Events: Paul de Man and the Afterlife of Theory*, edited by Tom Cohen, et al., Minneapolis and London: University of Minnesota Press, 2001, pp. 93–113.

Coleridge 1816, pp. 36–7.
2 Coleridge 1816, Appendix, p. xix.
3 Coleridge 1816, p. 35.
4 Benjamin 1977, p. 160.

Whereupon, thus profaned, allegory comes in place as the symbol's 'speculative counterpart ... adapted so as to provide the dark background against which the bright world of the symbol might stand out'.[5] Walter Benjamin referred to this notion of the symbol as 'a romantic extravagance which preceded the desolation of modern art criticism'.[6] In his 1967 essay 'Art and Objecthood,' Michael Fried, by way of reference to Jonathan Edwards' philosophical theology, set Modernist painting and sculpture against Minimal Art, ABC Art, Primary Structures, Specific Objects in terms closely related to 'symbol' and 'allegory'.[7]

Modernist Painting

Although in Christian theology the symbol is taken to be a unity, in aesthetics as it develops in late Neo-Classicism and Romanticism the plastic symbol is not quite that. Rather, it is a necessary connection or relation between what it is as a sensory thing and the supersensory totality that it comes in place of.[8] In the modern epoch it becomes a work of art conceived as the image of organic totality that carries a feeling or a state of mind from its producer to its beholder. The Modernist or dominant theory of modern art insists that there's a vivid connection between visual form and expressive content, quality or effect. As it applies to fine art practice, it holds that Modernist painters 'get at the

---

5 Benjamin 1977, p. 161.
6 Benjamin 1977, p. 162.
7 Fried 1968, pp. 116–47. Jonathan Edwards (1703–58) was an American Protestant preacher, philosopher, and theologian. In his biography *Jonathan Edwards*, first published in 1949, Perry Miller takes the view that Edwards's writing is best understood in aesthetic terms, especially with regard to his thinking about 'beauty', which he understands as a wider notion religiously than 'truth' or 'goodness', especially with regard to God and nature. Miller takes the view that Edwards was a major artist whose medium was theology instead of poetry or the novel. Michael Fried, 'Art and Objecthood', sets this fragment from Miller's book as epigraph to introduce his thinking about art and objecthood: 'Edwards's journals frequently explored and tested a meditation he seldom allowed to reach print; if all the world were annihilated, he wrote ... and a new world were freshly created, though it were to exist in every particular in the same manner as this world, it would not be the same. Therefore, because there is continuity, which is time, "it is certain with me that the world exists anew every moment; that the existence of things every moment ceases and is every moment renewed." The abiding assurance is that "we every moment see the same proof of a God as we should have seen if we had seen Him create the world at first"'.
8 De Man, Paul, 'The Rhetoric of Temporality', in De Man 1983, p. 189.

very essence of painting as well as visual experience';[9] that they 'expand the expressive resources of the medium, not in order to express ideas or notions, but to express with greater immediacy sensations, the irreducible elements of experience';[10] and that they make paintings which 'become more completely nothing but what they do ... they *look* what they *do*'.[11] A Modernist painting exhausts itself in the 'visual sensation it produces': for its beholder 'there is nothing to identify, connect or to think about but everything to feel'.[12] That's Clement Greenberg, no straw-Modernist, consolidating his beginning as an art critic, writing about the 'merits' and 'present supremacy' of abstract art in 1940.

Critical judgement, which is matter of taste, values feeling, which is to say that it values the content, quality or effect of a work of art. That's what makes or breaks a painting. This is Greenberg, again, writing twenty-five years later, about some of the work – in this instance, abstract paintings – he valued, hinting at where the feeling is and where it is coming from:

> [Morris] Louis is not interested in veils and stripes as such, but in verticality and colour. [Kenneth] Noland is not interested in circles as such, but in concentricity and colour. [Jules] Olitski is not interested in openings and spots as such, but in interlocking and colour. And yet the colour, the verticality, the concentricity, and the interlocking are not there for their own sakes. They are there, first and foremost, for the sake of feeling, and as vehicles of feeling. And if these paintings fail as vehicles and expressions of feeling, they fail entirely.[13]

Clearly there is a difference between experiencing a painting as a vehicle of feeling and experiencing an artist's feelings but surely these are what are being conjoined here. The work of art as object is taken as an essential part of the whole it represents. The dominant theory of modern art establishes just such a perfect coincidence between the emotion felt by the beholder of the painting, the way the surface of the painting has been asserted and used by the artist, and the artist's feeling, psyche or self. As I read what Greenberg is writing here, the kind of painting he values – Modernist painting – affects in him an identification with something which and someone who is not him. This is why he values it. And how long does it take for this kind this kind of painting – this kind

---

9   Greenberg 1986, p. 29.
10   Greenberg 1986, p. 30.
11   Greenberg 1986, p. 34.
12   Ibid.
13   Greenberg 1993, p. 153.

of work of art as object – to achieve its effect? 'Esthetic judgements,' Greenberg said, 'are given and contained in the immediate experience of art'. And not only are they immediate, they are also 'intuitive, undeliberate, and involuntary,' and 'leave no room for the application of standards, criteria, rules, or precepts'.[14] This accords well with how Friedrich Creuzer in his *Symbolik und Mythologie*, which was published some three years after Coleridge's *The Statesman's Manual*, defined the essence of the symbol in terms of 'the momentary, the total, the inscrutability of its origins, the necessary' and 'brevity ... It is a force that seizes hold of our entire being'.[15]

Modernist painting is an art of radical purity that develops in the pursuit of the plastic symbol. It is in a moment of autonomy and self-sufficiency, spontaneity and transcendence of all commonplace limits of perception and thought that the Modernist work of art as object, understood as symbolic, asserts its affect and effect, content and quality.

On the Motif

> One day we were sitting under a tall pine on the edge of a green and red hill, looking out over the Arc valley. It was in the neighbourhood of Blaque, not far from Mille and three-quarters of an hour from Aix and the Jas de Bouffan. The sky was blue and the air fresh, with a first hint of autumn on that late-summer morning. Hidden behind a fold in the hills, the town could be located by its smoke. We had our backs to the ponds. On the horizon, to our right, lay Luynes and the Pilon du Roi, and a glimpse of the sea. Before us were the huge mass of Sainte-Victoire, hazy and bluish in the Virgilian sunlight, the rolling hills of Montaiguet, the Pont de l'Arc aqueduct, the houses, rustling trees and square fields of the Aix countryside.
>
> This was the landscape Cézanne was painting.[16]

Cézanne's pictures, especially his landscape paintings, have always provided Modernist artists, critics and historians with paradigm examples of the sym-

---

14   Greenberg 1993, p. 265.
15   Benjamin quoting Creuzer's *Symbolik und Mythologie der Alten der Völker, besonders der Griechechen* (1819), in Benjamin 1977, p. 163.
16   Gasquet, Joachim, '"*Ce qu'il m'a dit ...*" (extrait de Paul Cézanne)', in P.M. Doran (ed.), *Conversations avec Cézanne*, Paris: Macula, 1978, 107–61, see Gasquet 1991, 'What he told me', pp. 147–217 at p. 147.

bolic. He, more than any other modern artist it seems, managed to assert and the use the surface of the canvas in such a way that what was brought to form thereon is taken to effect in its beholder a feeling or experience equivalent to Cézanne's experience of a bit of nature. Which is to say that the sensory appearance of the picture, as the object of the beholder's perception and of Cézanne's making, effects a unifying experience that conjoins two selves across time and place.

Sensations

> What captures light belongs to what it captures
> THOM GUNN, 'Sunlight'

∴

Cézanne said: 'I paint as I see, as I feel, and I have very strong sensations'.[17] Sensation is a mental process (such as seeing, hearing, touching, smelling and tasting) resulting from the external stimulation of a sense organ and it is also the awareness of that external stimulation. As far as Cézanne is concerned sensation is primarily light – light reflected off objects in the motif onto the retina at the back of the eye and thence, as neural signals, to the brain for visual recognition. Perception is the ability to become aware of external stimuli by means of sensation. Sensation is *of* the world outside the body, there to be perceived, and it's *of* the inside of the body as a mental process or mental function such as, of course, perceiving, and not only perceiving but remembering, and so on

---

17   Quoted in Shiff 1984, p. 188, who takes it from Rewald 1961, p. 246. The idea also crops up between 1903 and 1905 in Cézanne's letters to Louis Aurenche, Charles Camoin, and Émile Bernard.
   I thank Richard Shiff for directing me to Joachim Gasquet's book on Cézanne. Gasquet was the son of one of Cézanne's old school friends who put together memories of conversations he had with Cézanne into quasi-dialogue form. He seems to have done this in 1912 but his text remained unpublished until 1921. While there must have been some elaboration on Gasquet's part, the authenticity of the ideas and peculiar turns of thought strike me as authentic. That's to say, taken alongside the paintings, Gasquet's Cézanne produces a powerful effect of the real that is worth going on with in this context. Shiff's 'Introduction', Gasquet 1991, pp. 15–24, provides a very interesting take on Gasquet's relationship with Cézanne.

and so forth. Sensation is, then, both sensing and making sense of some thing in the world. 'Sense' means both 'meaning' and 'sensation'. Simultaneously both inside and outside, sensation is *of* the subject and *of* the object. Indeed, it's the very unification of inside and outside, subject and object that's taken to constitute a self and the world.

In one of the best explanations we have of Cézanne's practice, the explanation he himself gave to his friend Joachim Gasquet, the work of art comes in place of the way he feels and perceives, senses and makes sense of the 'very strong sensations' that he has in front of the motif. Cézanne's painting from nature is about phenomenal perception in the process of taking on material form. However, as he explained it to Gasquet, on the motif, making a painting, it was even more than this. As he theorises it, in the passage quoted below, not only does he paint visual sensations of the landscape but also its odours and textures – and perhaps sounds and tastes. Gasquet's Cézanne is a synaesthete who perceives colours as smells and textures. He also suggests that, in bringing his perceptions to visual form on the canvas, he makes objective not only his own subjective consciousness *of* nature but also the subjective consciousness *of* nature 'itself'.

> Cézanne: The artist is nothing more than a receptacle of sensations, a brain, a recording machine ... A damned good machine, fragile and complex, above all in its relationship to other machines ... But if he intervenes, if he dares to meddle voluntarily with what ought merely to be translating, he introduces his own insignificance into it and the work is inferior.
>
> Gasquet: In short, you consider the artist inferior to nature.
>
> Cézanne: No, that's not what I'm saying. You're on the wrong track. Art has a harmony which parallels that of nature. The people who tell you that the painter is always inferior to nature are idiots! He is parallel to it. Unless, of course, he deliberately intervenes. His whole aim must be silence. He must silence all the voices of prejudice within him, he must forget, forget, be silent, become a perfect echo. And then the entire landscape will engrave itself on the sensitive plate of his being. After that, he will have to use his craft to fix it on canvas, to externalize it; but this craft, too, is always ready to obey, to translate automatically, familiar as it with the language, with the text to be deciphered, with the two parallel texts, nature as it is seen and nature as it is felt, the nature that is there ... (*he pointed toward the green and blue plain*) and the nature that is here (*he tapped his forehead*), both of which have to fuse in order to endure, to

live that life, half-human and half-divine, which is the life of art or, if you will ... the life of God. The landscape is reflected, humanized, rationalized within me. I objectivize it, project it, fix it on my canvas ... You were talking to me the other day about Kant. It may sound like nonsense, but I would see myself as the subjective consciousness of that landscape, and my canvas as its objective consciousness. My canvas and the landscape are both inside me, but while the one is chaotic, transient, muddled, lacking in logic or rational coherence, the other is permanent, tangible, classifiable, forming part of the world, of the theatre of ideas ... of their individuality [...]

He had become gloomy. He was often depressed like this after an excited outburst. And it was no good trying to cheer him up. That only made him furious. He felt bad ... There was long silence. He picked up his brushes again, looking in turn at his canvas and his motif.

No. No. Just a moment. That's not it. There is no overall harmony. The canvas has no smell. Tell me what scent it gives off. What odour? Go on. ...

Gasquet: The odour of pine trees.

Cézanne: You say that because of the two large pines whose branches are counter-balancing one another in the foreground. But that's a visual sensation ... Besides, the pure blue smell of pine, which is sharp in the sun, ought to blend with the fresh green smell of meadows in the morning, and with the smell of stones and the distant marble smell of Sainte-Victoire. I have not achieved that effect. It must be achieved, and achieved through the colours, not by literary means. As Baudelaire and Zola succeed in doing, mysteriously perfuming a whole verse or phrase by the simple juxtaposition of words [...][18]

'Some things, by their affinity light's token, Are more than shown'.[19]

Paul Gauguin would have had Camille Pissarro drug Cézanne to get the 'prescription' for how Cézanne managed to compress 'the intense expression of his sensations into a single unique procedure'.[20] Though they don't provide a

---

18 Gasquet 1991, pp. 150–1.
19 Gunn 2017, p. 98, 'Sunlight'.
20 See Paul Gauguin's letter to Camille Pissarro, summer 1881, as quoted in Rewald 1961, p. 458.

prescription, the pictures, which Gauguin didn't really understand, provide the best evidence of the procedure – a procedure that Gasquet's Cézanne put into words thus:

> All right, look at this ... (*He repeated his gesture, holding his hands apart, fingers spread wide, bringing them slowly, very slowly together again, then squeezing and contracting them until they were interlocked*). That's what one needs to achieve ... If one hand is too high, or too low, the whole thing is ruined. There mustn't be a single slack link [*une seule maille trop lâche*], a single gap [*un trou*] through which the emotion, the light, the truth can escape. I advance all of my canvas at one time, if you see what I mean. And in the same movement, with the same conviction. I approach all the scattered pieces ... Everything we look at disperses and vanishes, doesn't it? Nature is always the same, and yet its appearance is always changing. It is our business as artists to convey the thrill of nature's permanence along with the elements and appearance of all its changes. Painting must give us the flavour of nature's eternity. Everything, you understand. So I join together nature's straying hands ... From all sides, here, there and everywhere, I select colours, tones, shades; I set them down, I bring them together ... They make lines. They become objects – rocks, trees – without my thinking about them. They take on volume, value. If, as I perceive them, these volumes and values correspond on my canvas to the planes and patches of colour that lie before me, that appear to my eyes, well then, my canvas 'joins hands'. It holds firm. It aims neither too high nor too low. It's true, dense, full ... But if there is the slightest distraction, the slightest hitch, above all if I interpret too much one day, if I'm carried away by a theory which contradicts yesterday's, if I think while I'm painting, if I meddle, then whoosh!, everything goes to pieces.[21]

A Dabbing Sensation

Each coloured dab, which seems intended to represent a sensation, is made, usually, with a 6mms or 12mms brush that touches the surface without sliding or trailing across it; the dab doesn't linger; it seems to come in place quickly – which doesn't mean that the process of painting moves along quickly. (Gasquet recorded that Cézanne sometimes waited twenty minutes between two

---

21 Gasquet 1991, p. 148.

brush strokes.)²² The dab is direct and decisive and doesn't distinguish between things and non-things, beings-in-the-world and beings-in-consciousness, solids and voids, near and far, surface flatness and illusionistic depth, and so on. Each dab is *of* nature and *of* Cézanne and *of* the forming process understood in the post-Romantic world of Modernist painting as a 'single and unique procedure' of seeing and feeling, dabbing and seeing and feeling, seeing and feeling and ... until what's achieved is, according to Greenberg's thinking about Cézanne:

> That fullest, triumphant unity which crowns the painter's work, which arrives when the ends are tightly locked into the means, when all parts fall into place and require and create one another so that they flow inexorably into a whole, when one can, as it were, experience the picture like a single sound made by many voices and instruments that reverberates without changing, that presents an enclosed and instantaneous yet infinite variety.²³

Here ends and means, parts and wholes, a single sound and many voices and instruments, presentness and infinity become one.

Gasquet's Cézanne says:

> Wherever sensation is at its fullest, it harmonizes with the whole of creation. Nature's stirrings are resolved, deep down in one's brain, into a movement sensed equally by our eyes, our ears, our mouth and our nose, each with its special kind of poetry ... And art puts us, I believe, in a state of grace in which we experience a universal emotion in an, as it were, religious but at the same time perfectly natural way.²⁴

It's this notion of temporality and, closely associated with it, the belief that one experiences a quasi-religious state of grace in front of it, that characterises the aesthetic ideology of Modernist painting. At the end of Fried's 'Art and Objecthood' – the essay I take as effecting or marking the complete desolation of Modernist art criticism, albeit in a supernova-like moment of blindness and insight – it's what distinguishes art from objecthood or 'literalist' work.

---

22   Gasquet 1991, p. 167.
23   Greenberg, Clement, 'Cézanne and the Unity of Modern Art', *Partisan Review*, vol. 18, no. 3, May–June, 1951, pp. 323–30, in Greenberg 1993, pp. 82–91 at p. 89.
24   Gasquet 1991, p. 151.

The latter '*persists in time*';²⁵ it affects a 'presentment of endless, or indefinite, *duration*', of 'time both passing and to come, *simultaneously approaching and receding*, as if apprehended in an infinite perspective'.²⁶ Whereas one's experience of the former, Modernist painting and sculpture,

> *has* no duration – not because one *in fact* experiences a picture by Noland or Olitski or a sculpture by David Smith or Caro in no time at all, but because *at every moment the work itself is wholly manifest* ... It is this continuous and entire presentness, amounting, as it were, to the perpetual creation of itself, that one experiences as a kind of *instantaneousness*: as though if only one were infinitely more acute, a single infinitely brief instant would be long enough to see everything, to experience the work in all its depth and fullness, to be forever convinced by it ... I want to claim that it is by virtue of their presentness and instantaneousness that modernist painting and sculpture defeat theatre [literalism or objecthood]. In fact, I am tempted far beyond my knowledge to suggest that ... it is above all to the condition of painting and sculpture – the condition, that is, of existing in, indeed of secreting or constituting, a continuous and perpetual *present* – that the other contemporary modernist arts, most notably poetry and music, aspire ... We are all literalists most or all of our lives. Presentness is grace.²⁷

Cézanne's painting from nature appeals to organicist notions of the ultimate, transcendent rapport between a consciousness and its objects *as if* his was a vision and practice in which ends were inseparable from means and parts from wholes, where the individual unit contains an infinite variety, and the instantaneous (present) is constantly repeated (for eternity); *as if* it facilitates the reconciliation of all antinomies and evokes a whole world of feeling and cognition untouched by the contingencies of human existence. In particular, the symbol is taken to give immediate access to a realm of intuitive or visionary insight where thought overcomes the time of material existence, contingency and change. The measure of time for the experience of the symbol is 'the mystical instant' in which is revealed a 'momentary totality'.²⁸

---

25   Fried 1968, p. 144.
26   Fried 1968, p. 144, p. 145.
27   Fried 1968, pp. 146–47.
28   Benjamin 1977, p. 165.

As If. As If.

The belief in a practical fiction is crucial. Here it is the belief in an ultimate, transcendent rapport between subject and object (a consciousness and its objects), between a pure ocular vision and a concrete representation of that vision. This belief is based on some very questionable presuppositions, not least that language – and I'm thinking of painting as a language, as did Cézanne also – or any concrete representation can actually represent an experience (of whatever kind), even the perception of a sensation. For while it can be said that one perceives sensations, as we'll see directly, the concrete representation of those perceptions encounters considerable difficulties.

At issue here is the high valuation of artistic creativity vested in the privileged tropes of symbol and metaphor that supposedly transcend the order of everyday language and perception.

Paul de Man, 'The Rhetoric of Temporality'

Paul de Man usefully reconsidered the relations between symbol and allegory in the modern epoch in his 1969 essay 'The Rhetoric of Temporality'.[29] In order to disclose how, as he theorised it, the former was falsely set in dominant opposition over the latter, he analyses that passage in *The Statesman's Manual* wherein Coleridge asserts that the symbol is characterised by 'translucence' and allegory is referred to as a 'phantom proxy' or reflexion. De Man points out that the distinction, as Coleridge has written it, disappears when read attentively. Allegory thought of as a 'phantom proxy' or reflection is something 'unsubstantial' and 'shapeless,' but the symbol, understood as something 'translucent,' must also be unsubstantial and shapeless. Both allegory and symbol, then, have the same relation to a transcendental origin 'beyond the world of matter'.[30] And it's this transcendental source that those critics who value the symbol concentrate on and not the material substantiality – for example, the actual words used in a poem – that effects it. 'Starting out from the assumed superiority of the symbol in terms of organic substantiality, we end up', he says, 'with a description of figural language as translucence, a description in which the distinction between allegory and symbol has become of secondary

---

29   De Man, Paul, 'The Rhetoric of Temporality', in De Man 1983, pp. 187–208.
30   De Man, 'The Rhetoric of Temporality', in De Man 1983, p. 192.

importance'.[31] Having pointed this out, de Man then attends to the materiality of the symbolic text and how it effects its seemingly transcendent vision. Wordsworth's sonnets on the River Duddon and the passages in *The Prelude* on crossing the Alps and a night-time ascent of Snowden provide him with several examples that literary criticism has continually misread as unifying the antimonies of inner and outer experience, mind and nature, subject and object, time and eternity. De Man demonstrates that these texts, when read attentively, turn out to be as much allegorical as they have been taken to be symbolical. In each case, Wordsworth, according to the canonical reading, has communicated a moment of pure perception but, as de Man demonstrates against the canonical reading, he can only be said to have done so by ignoring or making obscure the operations that make the text what it is as writing.[32]

De Man shows that symbol and allegory ought to be understood not as two distinct orders of language but as two ways of making sense of figurative language, two ways in which language is used – figured and troped – to achieve meaning and effect. As far as he's concerned, the Romantic and post-Romantic symbol appears more and more as a special case of figurative language in general, a trope or figure integrated with other tropes and figures. The symbol is, as it were, self-consciously figured and troped to affect us *as if* it isn't – it tries to efface, obscure or deny its mediating character as language. Allegory, however, is self-consciously figured and troped to make us aware that it is just that, figured and troped. There's also a temporal distinction to be made between language figured and troped to effect the symbol and allegory. The former tries for immediacy and simultaneity; whereas the latter progresses in a series of moments. Moreover, symbol and allegory are in an almost dialectical relation. The symbol always resolves into the figured and troped language of allegory. It cannot contain the linguistic feint that makes it what it is, and this occasions a negative moment that effects a hermeneutics of suspicion. This hermeneutics works against the symbolic effect, and against the claims made by critics in virtue of the symbol's transcendence, by bringing to mind the constitutive gap that's there in language between any instance of language use and the reality it's trying to evoke.

---

31   De Man, 'The Rhetoric of Temporality', in De Man 1983, pp. 192–93.
32   De Man, 'The Rhetoric of Temporality', in De Man 1983, p. 206.

Slack Links and Gaps

The plastic symbol is made of a peculiarly Modernist desire to close the gap between experience and the representation of experience.[33] Charles Baudelaire talks about it in 'The Painter of Modern Life' in terms of 'The pleasure we derive from the representation of the present,' which is 'not merely due to the beauty it may display, but also to the essential "present-ness" of the present'.[34] But, as de Man, engaging with Baudelaire here, points out in 'Literary History and Literary Modernity', 'The paradox of the problem is potentially contained in the formula "représentation du présent", which combines a repetitive with an instantaneous pattern without apparent awareness of the incompatibility',[35] This seems to help explain the look of Cézanne's paintings. As I see and make sense of them, Cézanne is aware of this paradox, perhaps even aware of it in Baudelaire's terms, and presents it in the way he asserts and uses the surface of his paintings.

The desire to close the gap between experience and the representation of experience manifests itself in the practice of Modernist painting as the persistent effort to assert and use the surface in such a way that the resulting painting will fulfil itself in a moment of brevity and clarity, immediacy and completeness. As far as Cézanne was concerned that meant closing the gap between nature and himself, which is to say between the phenomenal qualities of nature and his phenomenal perception and consciousness of those qualities, between his phenomenal perception and consciousness and that consciousness as it was put in place on and as the surface of a painting, and between the sensory appearance of that surface as it was perceived and brought to consciousness by its beholder. The theory of the symbol holds that *that* gap – those *several* gaps – can be closed. And Gasquet's Cézanne and Cézanne's pictures seem to effect a Cézanne who held to the theory. That is to say, he seems to have thought that it was possible to achieve, in his pictures, the representation of a present. Yet even as he tried to do it, he produced pictures that authentically declared the impossibility of being able to do it. Cézanne wants to make a painting *of* his experience *of* the sensation of nature's changing appearance and, at the same time, its essential permanence, and so on; and he wants to do this – indeed, must do it – without there being, on the surface of the painting, 'a single slack link, a single gap through which the emotion, the light, the truth can escape'. But slack links – places or moments in the picture that have the undecidability

---

33   De Man, Paul, 'Literary History and Literary Modernity' in De Man 1983, p. 156.
34   Ibid.
35   Ibid.

or uncertainty of slack water – and gaps are just what Cézanne can't avoid and doesn't deny. Indeed, the more his art progresses the more it becomes an art of painting slack links and admitting gaps.

The picture begins with line, but not with outlines. Cézanne seems loath to project outlines onto and around external objects and where an outline appears in a painting it does so, as Joachim Gasquet's Cézanne said, as the result of the way he brought together his perceptions as colours, tones, shades. Line, a point moving in space, usually made with a pencil or a fine brush charged with blue paint, has its places in Cézanne's paintings. It's there at the beginning of the process where it implies aspects or moments of the length of the major elements of the motif: its geological and orohydrographical givens; its 'structures,' 'strata', and 'main planes' but not their breadth. Drawn or brushed line is there indicating, for example, Mont Sainte-Victoire 'pale and trembling' against the sky, and where sky becomes sea or sea becomes land, and so on, not so much establishing a schematic picture of things to come but more as an aid to responding to the material complexities that the motif presented to phenomenal perception. Though it does both, of course. Where it's remained visible, more often than not, placed finely, it occurs broken and severally; it's never continuous and single; but nor, in Cézanne's hand, does it seem to falter or make mistakes. Rather, it marks Cézanne's certain uncertainty of not being able to or not wanting to establish the sensuous appearance of the limit or extremity – the outline – of a thing.

Rereading *Joachim Gasquet's Cézanne* and looking at Cézanne's pictures, it becomes apparent that as work on a painting progresses it becomes more and more difficult for Cézanne to bring his sensations to the canvas as dabs. Seeing and feeling nature *and* seeing and feeling the picture gets more and more difficult as more and more sensations get dabbed into place. Things get difficult. But do things get distorted? Merleau-Ponty pointed to what he called 'the famous distortions' that appear in the pictures Cézanne painted between 1870 and 1890:[36] cups, vases, and jugs that are asymmetrical around the vertical axis; elliptical saucers; tables that stretch and seem to warp; limbs with articulations and lengths that seem almost independent of the bodies to which they are attached; whole forms that seem dis-located in space; the horizontal and vertical infrastructure of architectural form that seems often to go out of kilter; and so on and so forth. But these are not really distortions for, in Cézanne's own account, what he was painting were not forms but sensations – primarily

---

36 Merleau-Ponty, Maurice, 'Cézanne's Doubt' (1945), in Maurice Merleau-Ponty, *Sens et nonsens*, Paris, 1948, translated by Hubert L. Dreyfus and Patricia Allen Dreyfus, Evanston: Northwestern University Press, 1961, excepted in Wechsler (ed.) 1975, pp. 120–4 see p. 122.

intensities and complexities of light – that, as he brought them to the canvas as dabs of colour, took on volume, value, and became objects.[37] There are no 'distortions' in Cézanne's paintings from nature. No thing has been distorted, for nothing was already in place – either in the way he perceived his motif or on his canvas – that could be pulled or twisted out of shape.

Ambiguities there are; and 'ambiguity is always the opposite of clarity and unity of meaning'.[38] But the ambiguities in Cézanne's pictures are ambiguities beyond even the seventh type – they're hardly ambiguities at all.[39] Rather, they are moments or places on the canvas and in the picture that mark Cézanne's rigorous certainty about what he's seeing, feeling and dabbing but which simultaneously bring about moments of rigorous uncertainty about, above all, whether the correspondence of mind and nature that he desired could be presented on canvas with paint. Here and there, we are presented with moments or places that are simultaneously neither foreground nor background but both foreground and background, neither solid nor void but both solid and void. And here and there, increasingly after 1890, so certain was his uncertainty, that he leaves us with bare canvas or paper, moments or places where the material basis for the way he tried to represent the presentness of his perceptions had to be presented untouched by representation.

As we noted a while ago, Gasquet's Cézanne, taking his metaphor from photography, says that the entire landscape will 'engrave itself on the sensitive plate of his being': the retina as it receives light, without which there is no colour or shape; the retina *as if* it were capturing the fact that he *is*.[40] The white canvas or paper ground – the surface that has to be asserted and used in practice – is surely the metaphor for that essential internal surface ready to receive 'nature as it is seen and nature as it is felt'. Remember, he then says: 'After that, he will have to use his craft to fix it on canvas, to externalize it; but this craft,

---

37 Gasquet 1991, p. 148.
38 Benjamin 1977, p. 177.
39 See Paul de Man, 'The Dead-End of Formalist Criticism', in De Man 1983, pp. 236–7, re Empson 1947: 'But as Empson's inquiry proceeds, there occurs a visible increase in what he calls the logical disorder of his examples until, in the seventh and last type of ambiguity, the form blows up under our very eyes. This occurs when the text implies not merely distinct significations but significations that, against the will of their author, are mutually exclusive'. De Man points out that Empson has a note here: 'It may be said that the contradiction must somehow form a larger unity if the final effect is to be satisfying. But the onus is of reconciliation can be laid very heavily on the receiving end'. To which de Man adds, 'that is, on the reader, for the reconciliation does not occur in the text. The text does not resolve the conflict, it *names* it'.
40 Gasquet 1991, p. 150.

too, is always ready to obey, to translate automatically, familiar as it is with the language'.[41] The painter mustn't 'intervene' or 'meddle voluntarily' in the activity of painting. Language guides seeing and feeling, gives us a chance to have perceptions that can be called our own. Without its mediation, alone directly confronting a world of sensations, we would be too much *of* the Real – infantile or insane. But painting, as an art, is never automatic. It is always, as Cézanne knew, a translation. And in a sense, as when we bring any perception to practical consciousness, it is not we who use language but language that uses us.[42] The slack links and gaps in the pictures mark the paradoxes and incompatibilities in Cézanne's practice. They give us a glimpse not only of the originary metaphor but also of the fact that, no matter how skilled you are as a language-user, language will never come directly and precisely in place of what you want it to, when you want it to.

In her book *On Not Being Able To Paint*, the psychoanalyst Marion Milner recorded some of the difficulties that she experienced while painting from nature.[43] Milner tried to teach herself to paint and, in trying, came to believe that she had 'discovered in painting a bit of experience that made all other experiences unimportant by comparison'.[44] She believed that

> when painting something from nature there occurred, at least sometimes, a fusion into a never-before-known wholeness; not only were the object and oneself no longer felt to be separate, but neither were thought and sensation and feeling and action. All one's visual perceptions of colour, shape, texture, weight, as well as thought and memory, ideas about the object and action towards it, the movement of one's hand together with the feeling of delight in the 'thusness' of the thing, they all seemed fused into a wholeness of being ...[45]

---

41 Gasquet 1991, p. 150.
42 See Paul de Man, 'Conclusions: Walter Benjamin's "The Task of the Translator"', in De Man 1986, p. 96, where he points to 'linguistic structures, the play of linguistic tensions, linguistic events that occur, possibilities which are inherent in language' and are there 'independently of any intent or drive or any wish or desire we might have'; and p. 101, where 'language does things which are so radically out of our control that they cannot be assimilated to the human at all, against which one fights constantly'.
43 Milner 1957. For a discussion of Milner's book in the context of psychoanalysis, her interest in Cézanne, and much interesting matter on Cézanne's landscape painting, see Podro 1990.
44 Milner 1957, p. 142.
45 On the irrationality here and how Milner tries to negotiate it, see Milner 1957, pp. 160–1: 'Perhaps the solution of the controversy over where the deepest meaning of art lies, can

Milner asks:

> How exactly does the capacity to make a whole picture in which every part is related connect with the capacity to be a whole person? Is the striving for one perhaps partly based on the striving for the other? And when, with infinite labour, such unity is achieved in a picture do we recognise it at once as something of unique value because it expresses one of the most fundamental urges of the force by which we are lived, the urge to form, to wholeness of pattern within ourselves? When we look at such a picture do we get a temporary glimpse of what it would be like to be a truly whole person?[46]

'And when, with infinite labour, such unity is achieved in a picture': thus isolated, the contradiction is obvious. The desired wholeness or unity in the picture, or in the activity of painting a picture, and the wholeness or unity in the person or self can never be achieved because the labour involved is infinite, with out bounds.

---

only be found through a fuller understanding of the differences between the kind of thinking that makes a separation of subject from object, me from not-me, seer from seen, and the kind that does not. We know a lot about the first kind of thinking, we know its basis in the primary laws of logic, which say that a thing is what it is and not what it is not, that it cannot both be and not be. We know also that these laws of reasoning work very well for managing the inanimate material environment. We divide what we see from ourselves seeing it, and in certain contexts this works very well. But it does not work so well for understanding and managing the inner world, whether our own, or other people's. For according to formal logic, all thought which does not make the total separation between what a thing is and what it is not is irrational; but then the whole area of symbolic expression is irrational, since the point about the symbol is that it is both itself and something else. Thus, though separation of the seer from what is seen gives a useful picture in some fields it gives a false picture in others. I think that one of the fields in which formal logic can give a false picture is aesthetics; and that the false picture is only avoided if we think about art in terms of its capacity for fusing and con-fusing subject and object, seer and seen and then making new division of these. By suffusing, through giving it form, the not-me objective material with the me – subjective psychic content, it makes the not-me "real", realisable'.

46   Milner 1957, p. 111.

Allegory

> Whereas the symbol postulates the possibility of an identity or identification, allegory designates primarily a distance in relation to its own origin, and, renouncing the nostalgia and the desire to coincide, it establishes its language in the void of this temporal difference. In so doing, it prevents the self from an illusory identification with the non-self, which is now fully, though painfully, recognised as a non-self.
>
> PAUL DE MAN, 'The Rhetoric of Temporality'

∴

Cézanne's is paradigmatic Modernist painting brought to form by a rigorous uncertainty with regard to its project. Success was dependent on there being not 'a single slack link, a single gap through which the emotion, the light, the truth could escape' but that seems to be where we have to locate 'the emotion, the light, the truth' of Cézanne's paintings and, as Milner would have it, his striving to be 'a whole person' – between the slack links and in the gaps, in those very moments and places in the picture 'where everything goes to pieces'. In these uncertain and undecidable places, immediacy and wholeness give way to the fragmentary and fragmenting evidence of mediating memory and decision-making. The gaps and slack links make us aware of the difference between the time of the sensations and the time of the painting. The slack links and gaps effect their undecidability and uncertainty and prevent the picture, both in practice and perception, achieving that wholeness and unity so valued by the likes of Milner, Greenberg, Fried, and all those persons who are persuaded by the aesthetic ideology of Modernist painting and sculpture. A lesser artist – Claude Monet comes to mind – might have faked the symbolic. But not Cézanne.

'The *sensations colourantes* that create light are the reason for the abstractions that do not allow me to cover my canvas', he wrote in a letter to Émile Bernard, 'nor to pursue the delimitation of objects when their points of contacts are subtle, delicate; the result is that my image or painting is incomplete'.[47] Though he deferred to 'nature', believing that by consulting it he would gain 'the

---

47 Paul Cézanne, letter to Émile Bernard, 23 October 1905, Danchev, 2013, p. 355.

means of achieving his goal',[48] he was too much of a materialist, too true to the phenomenal materiality of his sensations and to the material phenomenality of painting as an art, to succumb to the ideology of the aesthetic with its vaunted coincidence between the phenomenal perception of nature and the way it was represented in and by the work of art as object. And this he declared with a kind of persistent dignity in the way he asserted and used the surface of a picture to give colour and shape, volume and value to his sensations. As Cézanne himself pointed out, the slack links and gaps are there in the picture. We don't add them. In a way, as the space that exists between natural reality and the reality of a work of art as object, they determine the picture from the outset and, once in place, signify that very space, the originary space, the time and place that exists between phenomenalism and reference. As Merleau-Ponty put it, Cézanne's difficulties were those of 'the first word'.[49] These difficulties were those of moving from phenomenal perception and cognition to linguistic conceptualisation. Following de Man's reading of Jean-Jacques Rousseau's explanation of how man came up with them, man's first words were not 'literal denominations' but words 'effected by "an exchange or substitution of properties on the basis of resemblance" without declaring the comparisons that made them possible'.[50] The gaps and slack links come to Cézanne's picture by way of just such a process of exchange or substitution ... and are left in place, not as places where 'the light, the truth can escape' but as collective moments of almost Heideggerian *aletheia*: places where the, as it were, unexperienced and unthought that underlies our notion of truth or sense of correctness is unconcealed.[51] For they, along with the dabs that Cézanne substituted or exchanged for his sensations, clue the delusion of the work's trumpeted value, content, quality or effect as Modernist painting. The symbolic, thus disturbed and disrupted, discloses the allegorical. As it must. Because 'where man is drawn towards the symbol, allegory emerges from the depths of being to intercept the intention and triumph over it'.[52] Each picture becomes an allegory of the impossibility of the symbol, a Modernist allegory of the impossibility of Modernism's own ambitious project. It's this aspect of Cézanne's art that gives his paintings their value: aesthetic; moral; and political.

48 Ibid.
49 Merleau-Ponty 1975, 124.
50 De Man, Paul, 'Metaphor (*Second Discourse*)', in De Man 1979, p. 146.
51 See, for example, Heidegger 1971, p. 52.
52 Bejamin 1977, p. 183.

CHAPTER 3

Action, Revolution and Painting (Resumed)

> It is a psychological law that the theoretical mind, having become free in itself, turns into practical energy. Emerging as *will* from Amenthes's shadow-world, it turns against worldly actuality which exists outside it.
>
> KARL MARX, *Difference between the Democritean and Epicurean Philosophy of Nature*, Notes to the Doctoral Dissertation (1839–41)

∴

> Almost fifteen years ago Harold Rosenberg challenged me to explain what one of my paintings could possibly mean to the world. My answer was that if he and 267 others could read it properly it would mean the end of all state capitalism and totalitarianism. That answer still goes.
>
> BARNETT NEWMAN (1962)

∵

There was a time, in the 1950s and early 1960s, when explainers of Abstract Expressionism valued Harold Rosenberg's writings and took them into account. After that, he was increasingly marginalised, unreferenced or ignored, misunderstood or knowingly or unknowingly misrepresented. One reason for this misunderstanding, misrepresentation and marginalization might be that his writing on art uses a specialised language that is bound up with the terminology of modern culture, with experience and poetry, with history and politics. It is especially bound up with the history and politics associated with Marx and Marxism and deploys a terminology not specifically related to painting except insofar as painting is a creative activity. Bluntly, the criticism levelled at Rosenberg that he doesn't understand or look at pictures in 'visual terms' and that his writing is 'ideological' is, of course, the joint-stock in rhetorical-trade of any visually impaired, topsy-turvy critic who is frightened by art writing that's informed by a commitment to Marx and Marxism. Another not unrelated reason why he became marginalised was the increasing – and what came to be almost exclusive – admiring attention that was paid to the much easier to read and comforting essays of Clement Greenberg. This is not to say that that attention was misdirected, for Greenberg is a necessary if insufficient text. Critical art history needs him, but if it is not to rehearse its histories of Abstract Expressionism exclusively with reference to his ideas about the triumph of a depoliticized art practice, apolitical painting, and art for art's sake, then Greenberg's should not be taken as the only story. This is precisely where Rosenberg takes on importance. Rosenberg's writings on art and culture give us another necessary but insufficient corpus enabling a knowledge of Abstract Expressionism. Many of the Abstract Expressionists – most of the Irascibles and others – regarded their work as having a social and political content that Rosenberg, as close as anyone to the studio talk and closer than more or less anyone to its politics, was committed to explaining. This he did consistently and more vividly than any other explainer of Abstract Expressionism, not as an apologist, opponent, or aesthete but as someone keeping his preoccupations up to date and well-oiled.

This essay brings Rosenberg in from the margins and writes against the grain of those bits of conventional wisdom that represent his ideas as naïve, romantic, pseudo-philosophical, theatrical, and as reconciling an avant-garde ideology with the ideology of post-war liberalism. It situates Rosenberg in relation to the changes in New York Leftism in the 1930s and 1940s and uses his writing on the proletariat and on what he refers to as 'the drama of history' to explain what he meant by 'Action Painting' in his essay 'The American Action Painters', *ARTnews*, December 1952, one of the first published attempts to endow Abstract Expressionism with meaning.

'Drama': the term, as Rosenberg uses it, is heavily resonant of its origin in the Classical Greek word δρᾶμα (*drama*), meaning 'action', which is itself derived from δράω (*drao*), meaning 'to do' or 'to act'. 'History' from the Greek ἱστορία (*historia*), meaning 'inquiry, knowledge acquired by investigation', but now: 'A relation of incidents (in later use, only those professedly true); a narrative, tale, story' (*The Shorter Oxford English Dictionary*). History holds within it two meanings: the study of events or occurrences that have happened in the world, in real life, perhaps to oneself and the people around us; and any narrative of events or occurrences, real or imagined. There are two main parts to the structure of *drama* and of the drama of *history*: the sequence of events or plot will be marked by conflict, hardship, difficulty and pain; and the way that sequence of events or plot unfolds and is resolved will move one to pathos, will touch one in some emotional way. This essay stays with the *drama* and offers a politicised *history* of 'The American Action Painters' in place of those lazy conventional dismissals mentioned in passing a moment ago and alongside some recent serious commentary that either takes an existentialist-humanist tack or would explain Rosenberg's essay as evidencing a turn away from Marxist politics.[1]

You will see from what follows that the significance of 'The American Action Painters' has, in part, to be located in the way that Rosenberg shows that the political impasse, which many commentators on the Left in the 1990s regarded, and still regard, as uniquely 'post-modern', was already inscribed within the modernism that emerged in the United States circa 1940, and that this sense of impasse was international and not solely an American phenomenon. As far as Rosenberg was concerned, Action Painting was painting about the possibility of radical change that had not happened in the 1930s and 1940s – far from it – and could not happen in the 1950s. It was a possibility that neither he nor the 'American Action Painters' could afford to abandon. No more can we, now.

The politics of Action Painting were determined by the demise of the proletarian revolution and its continuing regeneration within capitalism as a mode

---

1 Note these abbreviations used throughout the main text and footnotes:

AA – Harold Rosenberg, *Act and the Actor, Making the Self*, New York: World Publishing Co., 1970; Chicago: The University of Chicago, 1983.

DP – Harold Rosenberg, *Discovering the Present/Three Decades in Art, Culture and Politics*, Chicago: The University of Chicago, 1973; Chicago: The University of Chicago, Phoenix Edition, 1976.

TN – Harold Rosenberg, *The Tradition of the New*, Chicago, New York: Horizon Press, 1959; Chicago: The University of Chicago, Phoenix Edition, 1982.

Rosenberg, Harold, 'The American Action Painters', *ARTnews*, vol. 51, no. 8, December 1952, pp. 22–3, pp. 48–50, in TN, pp. 23–39. Rosenberg's essay was discussed at the Club on 16 January 1953, more or less immediately after its publication – see warholstars.org/abstract-expressionism/abstractexpressionism.html

The first version of 'Action, Revolution and Painting' was published in the *Oxford Art Journal*, vol. 14, no. 1, 1992, pp. 3–17, some seven years before Harold Rosenberg's papers were released by the Getty Institute for the History of Art and the Humanities in 1999. At the time, I was unaware of their existence. I am pleased that they confirm what was then achieved by an attentive reading of essays that had long been in the public domain. This version of that essay has been rewritten for its inclusion in this collection, hopefully improving it by making certain passages less opaque and by adding some new material.

Mention needs to be made of three studies that either use or abuse the *Oxford Art Journal* essay, each of them, in whole or in part, offering a serious scholarly account of Rosenberg's writing, especially his art criticism and, in particular, 'The American Action Painters': O'Brien 1997, who had privileged access to Rosenberg's papers while researching and writing her Ph.D.; Jachec 2000; and Marie 2006. Marie's dissertation, which relates Rosenberg's idea of 'action' to Marx's notion of 'praxis' – free creative and self-creative activity through which man makes and changes the world and himself – more directly than did I, is the only one to keep faith with the revolutionary politics that writes 'The American Action Painters'. For a recent essay on the way that Rosenberg read Marx and how that reading informed his idea of action and Acton Painting see Robbins 2012.

of production. They acted out the possibility of radically transforming the situation, while continually failing to do so. As this essay proceeds, it will become clear that the negation of negation played out in Action Painting could never effect the redefinition of identity that would negate the negative identity given to the proletariat in capitalism. The Action Painter could not succeed in art where the proletariat had failed in politics. Action Painting could not compensate at the symbolic level for the fact that, at that moment, the political action that would redefine the proletariat did not seem available to it as a class. Action Painting was caught up in the failure of the proletariat. Nevertheless, the Action Painter glimpsed that that failure was not – or need not be – total.

In this reading of Rosenberg's 'The American Action Painters', the Action Painter was no middle-class artist playing with symbolic or surrogate revolutionary gestures, merely 'acting out', in art, the 'drama' of political agency and identity that no social class was able to do at the time. Action Painting wasn't revolutionary posturing. It was painting concerned with the dialectical possibility of a revolution whose outlines could neither be defined nor denied.

I

> who thrust his fist into cities
> arriving by many ways
> watching the pavements, the factory yards,
> the cops on the beat
>
> walked out on the platform
> raised his right arm, showing the fist clenched
> 'comrades, I bring news'
>
> came back then skies and silhouettes,
> facing the bay, of sailors
> who no longer take the sea
> because of strikes, pay-cuts and class-unity
>
> 'comrades, I bring news'
>
> of the resistance of farmers
> in Oneida county on a road
> near a small white cottage
> looking like a Xmas card,

4 shot, the road was blocked
glass to blow their tires

there was one guy we grabbed
some bastard of a business man
learning to play State Trooper
one of the boys tackled him neat as he ran

Behold my American images get it straight
a montage of old residences bridges shops freights
Xmas, the millions walking up and down
the tables where applications are received
the arguments that will yet get down to something

in the center of this a union-hall
and on the platform he
with right arm crooked, fist clenched
'comrades, I bring news'

That poem by Rosenberg was published in the January–February issue of *Partisan Review*.[2] Titled 'The Front', it refers to the life circumstances of millions of Americans around Christmas 1934, some five months into the sixth year of what is euphemistically called the 'Great Depression', to capitalism in the prolonged crisis that affected every part of the United States of America: mass unemployment and applications for benefits; strikes; organised labour; and the class struggle in town and country. At the centre is a union hall; and out on to its platform walks someone who raises his right arm, fist clenched, and addresses the assembly: 'comrades. I bring news'. I cannot describe the specific circumstances of the poem's making or limit the excess of meaning available for its references to strikes, pay cuts, and so on, nor specify the particularity of that event in Oneida County, New York State. What can be said – leaving aside a discussion of its structure and the momentum of its syntax – is that Rosenberg's poem, dedicated by its title to the United Front, was meant to participate in winning the workers' support for revolutionary organisations and for an agreement on action of some kind: resistance and insurrection, if not revolution.

Aged twenty-eight when he wrote 'The Front', Rosenberg had already earned himself something of a reputation as a poet and intellectual. *The Symposium*,

---

2   Rosenberg, 'The Front', *Partisan Review*, vol. 2, no. 6, January–February 1935, p. 74.

edited by James Burnham and Philip Wainwright and described as a journal of philosophical discussion, had published several of his essays, including, in 1932, the seminal 'Character Change and the Drama', which will be considered in a moment.[3] He had also edited with H.R. Hays an 'experimental quarterly' called *The New Act*.[4] Harriet Moore's *Poetry: a Magazine of Verse*, which published all kinds of poetry, conventional, unconventional and innovative, had regularly included his poems and commissioned book reviews from him, and would continue to do so throughout the 1930s and 1940s.[5]

In 1936 William Phillips and Philip Rahv reckoned Rosenberg as one of those who had achieved 'the much desired integration of the poet's conception with the leading ideas of the time' – a 'desired integration' that was achieved by way of his awareness that the necessary revolt was aesthetic as well as social and that, as such, it was 'a revolt within the tradition of poetry rather than against it'.[6]

If 'The Front', as the editors of *Partisan Review* were keen to point out, was the first of Rosenberg's poems to be published in a 'proletarian magazine',[7] 'The Men on the Wall', one of four poems by Rosenberg that were published in *Poetry* magazine, April 1934, some eight months before, may have been the first or, if not the first, one of the first of his poems to make reference to the historically specific social circumstances of its writing. It's wholly different from the other poems by Rosenberg that were published along with it. Does 'The Men on the Wall' evidence the 'integration' required by Williams and Rahv? As this extract shows, the appropriate stereotypical metaphors are certainly all there:

---

3 Rosenberg, 'Character, Change and the Drama', *The Symposium*, vol. 3, no. 3, July 1932, pp. 348–69, in TN, pp. 135–53. See also his other work for *The Symposium*: 'Myth and Poem', vol. 2, no. 2, April 1931, pp. 179–91; a review of William Empson's *Seven Types of Ambiguity*, vol. 2, no. 3, July 1931, pp. 412–18; a review of Kenneth Burke's *Counter Statement* and Montgomery Belgion's *The Human Parrot and Other Essays*, vol. 3, no. 1, January 1932, pp. 116–18; and a review of Jules Romaine's *Men of Good Will*, vol. 4, no. 4, October 1933, pp. 511–14.

4 Rosenberg and Hays published three issues of *The New Act*, 1, January 1933; 2, June 1933; and 3, April 1934. It was referred to as an 'experimental quarterly' by *Poetry: A Magazine of Verse*, vol. 45, no. 6, March 1935, p. 357. *The New Act* published articles by René Daumal, Paul van Otayen, Henry Bamford Parkes, George Plekhanov, Ezra Pound, Samuel Putman, and Parker Tyler. For Rosenberg's contributions see 'Note on Class Conflict and Literature', *The New Act*, no. 1, January 1933, pp. 3–10, and 'Sanity, Individuality and Poetry', no. 2, June 1933, pp. 59–75, two essays in which he developed ideas that he had first published the previous year in 'Character Change and the Drama'.

5 Rosenberg's contributions are indexed in *Thirty Years of Poetry: A Magazine of Verse*. Index to Volumes 1–60, October 1912–September 1942 (inclusive) and Index to *Fifty Years of Poetry: A Magazine of Verse*, Volumes 1–100, 1912–1962, New York: AMS Reprint Company, 1963.

6 Phillips, William, and Philip Rahv 1936, p. 104.

7 'Contributors', *Partisan Review*, vol. 2, no. 6, January–February 1935, p. 2.

> A raised arm has many meanings.
> Convictions falter with desire; the arm remains.
>
> You have seen a sword
> in the hand of the arm
> flower from a sleeve of gold brocade;
> you have seen in the pearl of dawn the arm
> ascend from sleeping oyster-vagues,
> rising to ripple the silent threats
> of your old interior myth of arms.
>
> And the future myth of avenues
> is also yours; and that arm's fist,
> whose khaki cuff is stained with grease,
> is yours, and clasps the hammer of your resolve.
> And whose contending tendons flex with threat
> Against the background factories and glass?
>
> Pace quietly on the walls
> while the wind still affirms
> the faces of ruminants with folded arms,
> the men below, divining peace before their doors;
> the azure casings of whose blood are torn
> by no quick hemorrhage of indissoluble event;
> whose ecstasy, despair and rage
> are hidden escapades that lift no arms.[8]

Unlike 'The Front', 'The Men on the Wall' seems more symptomatic than critical of the context that inscribes it, while textually its language is not yet positively the language of unrest, still less of revolution. It's a poem with a social conscience but one that has a tendency to leave some of its characters thinking that taking action isn't or won't be necessary, while others amble half-asleep up and down deliberating about it. Only one of them, the one bearing the clinching metaphor of the hand clasping the hammer, seems about to act or is threatening to act. By the end of 1934, when Rosenberg wrote 'The Front', that tendency

---

8   Rosenberg, Harold, 'The Men on the Wall', *Poetry: A Magazine of Verse*, April 1934, vol. 44, no. 1, pp. 3–4.

had changed, or been clarified: the workers recognise their alienation for what it is; they are unemployed and angry, awake, politicised ... and taking action.

Unlike 'The Men on the Wall', which seems uncommitted and full of suppressed action, 'The Front' is a clearly a committed poem full of exactly the kind of action that would appeal to the editors of *Partisan Review*, the then year-old journal of the John Reed Club of New York. The John Reed Club was founded in 1929, the year the Great Depression began and the year Stalin's first Five Year Plan was adopted. Initiated by and affiliated to the International Union of Revolutionary Writers, it was, from the outset, influenced by the Proletcult movement, led by members of the Communist Party, and dedicated to the idea of art as a weapon for informing, educating and radicalising the worker. It had branches in most large cities in the USA and many of them, like the New York branch, published their own periodical of literature and art.[9]

The 'Harold Rosenberg' of 'The Front' is a Marxist and probably a fellow traveller of the CPUSA, a poet and critic committed to the artist's capacity to participate in the class struggle.[10] But this 'Harold Rosenberg' was short-lived. The authorial 'I' that 'The Front' had introduced in *Partisan Review* was put in the position of having to change tack when, in July–August 1935, the Seventh Congress of the Third International, the Communist International or Comintern, turned away from the United Front to promote 'the establishment of a unity front with social and democratic reformist organisations ... with mass liberation, religious-democratic and pacifist organisations, and their adherents ... for the struggle against war and its fascist instigators'.[11] Unlike the United Front that it replaced, this 'Popular Front' was not a strategy of class struggle but of class cooperation. And one immediate effect of that cooperation was that the Proletcult movement was abandoned.

---

9   For still recommended reading on the John Reed Club and *Partisan Review* see Aaron 1968; Pells 1973; Wald 1974; and Homberger 1986.

10 Considering the secrecy that continues to surround membership of the Communist Party, and which the CP deliberately fostered, it's very difficult to know who was and who was not a member of the CPUSA. It seems that being a member demanded a kind of discipline that most writers and artists could not accept. One has to remember that the CPUSA was partly committed to a form of democratic centralism and to the strategic use of writers and artists. Because it could not tolerate any criticism from its members at local levels of organisation, it would not accept into its ranks any really independent figures, and they, in turn, could not accept its dictates. It's my guess that Rosenberg was a fellow traveller, not a member of the CPUSA.

11 Degras 1965, Jane (Tabrisky), *The Communist International 1919–1943: Documents Vol. 3*, London and New York: Oxford University Press, 1965, p. 375, quoted in Halas 1985, which provides an excellent discussion of the Comintern's revolutionary period.

Coming events cast their shadows before. The idea of the Popular Front was there, for example, at the moment *Partisan Review* published 'The Front', in January 1935, when, under instructions from the CPUSA, the National Committee of the John Reed Clubs called for an American Writers' Congress to undertake an 'exposition of all phases of a writers' participation in the struggle against war, the preservation of civil liberties, and the destruction of fascist tendencies every where'.[12]

The American Writers' Congress met at the end of April, and Rosenberg reported on its proceedings in the July issue of *Poetry*.[13] He was obviously impressed by the representative of a group of Pennsylvania miners who were prepared to print and circulate 10,000 copies of any poem that they could recite or sing together and by an appeal on behalf of 300 workers' theatres for material to perform.[14] Here 'it became possible to see how poetry might step forth from the little magazines ... and walk once more upon the stage and the street'.[15] How, in other words, art might achieve a valid constituency and a valid agency. Nevertheless, it was clear to him that, faced with the dangers presented by fascism and war, the writer was forced to play his part not by revolution but in the effort to protect peace, freedom and progress.[16] The questions were: what was the role of the writer in the social movement, and what was the best mode of performance?[17] The answers were provided by Earl Browder, national spokesman and General Secretary of the CPUSA, in his opening address: one could not be converted automatically into a literary genius merely by calling oneself a 'Marxist'; revolutionary art could succeed 'only through achieving superiority as art, not through politics'; 'the socially conscious writer need not engage in organisational activity at the expense of his writing'. The attitude of the Party was: 'better a good writer than a bad organiser'.[18] After quoting Browder, Rosenberg made a point of mentioning Waldo Frank who also attacked 'leftism' and

---

12　See the 'call to participate' in 'The Coming Writers' Congress', *Partisan Review*, vol. 2, no. 6, January–February 1935, pp. 94–6 at p. 95. The Congress, it was announced, would also 'develop the possibilities for wider distribution of revolutionary books and the improvement of the revolutionary press, as well as relations between revolutionary writers and bourgeois publishers and editors'. It was clear from this that when the Congress met at the end of April it would not be concerned with revolution but with establishing good relations with the literary bourgeoisie and with fighting fascism.

13　Rosenberg, Harold, 'The American Writers' Congress', *Poetry: A Magazine of Verse*, 46, 4, July 1935, pp. 222–7.

14　*Poetry*, vol. 46, no. 4, p. 226.

15　*Poetry*, vol. 46, no. 4, pp. 226–7.

16　*Poetry*, vol. 46, no. 4, p. 225.

17　Ibid.

18　Ibid.

those who would 'capitulate easily to dogma, outside control'.[19] Frank, one of the editors of *New Masses*, the cultural magazine of the CPUSA, would go on to represent the League of American Writers, the organisation that came out of the Congress at the Popular Frontist First International Congress of Writers for the Defense of Culture that met two months later in Paris. Rosenberg, writing in the liberal-democratic *Poetry*, pointed out, reassuringly, and following Browder's line, that though the American Writers' Congress 'turned its face left it donned no red uniform'.[20]

Later that year Rosenberg became active in Popular Front politics through his involvement with *Art Front*, the official publication of the Artists' Union, the militant trade union that had emerged from the Unemployed Artists Group set up by the John Reed Club of New York in 1933 and which, in 1935, came to represent the interests of artists employed on the Federal Art Projects. This was a moment in the history of American art and culture when artists were classed as and classed themselves as wage-labourers. *Art Front*'s political orientation was, of course, never in doubt. Dominated by the Communist Party, it was committed to art as propaganda, and to guiding its members in their role as revolutionary artists. Even so, it was always prepared to debate whether the art they were to produce should be social realist or modernist, realist, expressionist, surrealist, abstractionist, etc., for, at that time, there was no party-line on art, not even in the Soviet Union. In a sense, *Art Front* was the New York art communist and Left art community's public conversation. Moreover, it was, at that time, the only periodical in the United States that was primarily concerned with art and politics. At the end of 1935, the editors of *Art Front* signified the journal's sympathetic attitude to modernist art by bringing onto the board Joseph Solman and Max Spivak, along with the assistant who'd been assigned to Spivak, working in the Mural Division of the Federal Arts Projects – Harold Rosenberg.[21]

---

19   Ibid.
20   Presumably Browder's mention of 'uniforms' would have been taken as a clear reference to Max Eastman's *Artists in Uniform*, New York: Alfred A. Knopf, 1934.
21   Here I've relied on Monroe 1973. The editorial board's shift towards modernism was made partly as a result of pressure that had been brought to bear by some modernist members of the Union – Solman, Ilya Bolotowsky, Balcomb Greene, Mark Rothkowitz [Mark Rothko], Byron Browne, George McNeil, and others – and partly because the Popular Front made it necessary to open the editorial board to modernism. The move did not go uncontested. Rosenberg's place was secured only on the advice of a visiting official of the French Communist Party who sat in on a crucial board meeting.

  In *Poetry*, vol. 52, no. 4, January 1938, Rosenberg is referred to as a 'poet, critic, and painter of murals'.

Rosenberg's first efforts as a practising art critic were published in *Art Front*:[22] a translation of a lecture titled 'The New Realism' that Fernand Léger gave at the Museum of Modern Art;[23] reviews of the Museum of Modern Art's *Van Gogh* and *Cubism and Abstract Art* shows;[24] several book reviews, including one of Salvador Dali's *Conquest of the Irrational*;[25] and a review of William Gropper's painting at the A.C.A. gallery in which he stated that 'the revolutionary painter, far from being a grim specialist of a world seen in concentrated focus, is precisely the major discoverer of new pictorial possibilities as well as new uses for the old ... by his easy and graceful mastery of the materials of social struggle, by his presentation of it, as it were, from the inside, without strain, [the revolutionary painter] carried forward the possibility of technical discovery in revolutionary art'.[26]

The history of American art has produced several accounts of how artists on the Left were affected by the Russian-French Non-Aggression Pact of 1935 and the end of the United Front, by the three show trials of prominent intellectuals, Party leaders and activists in Moscow during August 1936, January 1937 and March 1938, by the signing of the Russian-German Non-Aggression Pact and the Soviet invasion of Finland in 1939.[27] Large numbers of intellectuals who began the decade in support of the Communist Party lost faith in it at some point, abruptly, reluctantly and with such disillusion that they could not be reconciled to it. As we've seen, Rosenberg's support for the Party survived the shift from the United Front to the Popular Front. It also survived the Moscow Trials of 1936 and 1937 but was abandoned sometime before the events of 1939, probably early in 1938.[28] The moment of one's move away from the Party, early

---

22 Rosenberg's first piece for *Art Front* was a report of an Artists' Union demonstration outside the CAA on 15 August 1935, at which 83 W.P.A. artists and art teachers were arrested: see 'Artists Increase their Understanding of Public Buildings', *Art Front*, November 1935, p. 6.
23 See Léger 1935.
24 Harold Rosenberg, 'Peasants and Pure Art', *Art Front*, January 1936, pp. 5–6, and 'Cubism and Abstract Art', *Art Front*, June 1936, p. 15.
25 Rosenberg, Harold, 'Book Reviews', *Art Front*, March 1936, p. 14.
26 Rosenberg, Harold, 'The Wit of William Gropper', *Art Front*, March 1936, pp. 7–8.
27 See, for example, Serge Guilbaut 1983, Chapter One, 'New York, 1935–1941: The De-Marxization of the Intelligentsia', pp. 17–47.
28 In 1937 Rosenberg published several things in the CPUSA magazine *New Masses*, which affirmed the validity of the Moscow Trials and the Party line. 'Portrait of a Predicament', his very hostile review – in the context of *New Masses* it couldn't have been anything but hostile – of William Saroyan's *3 Times 3* appeared in the same issue as 'The Moscow Trials: An Editorial', *New Masses*, 9 February 1937, see p. 24. See also: 'What We May demand', *New Masses*, 23 March 1937, pp. 17–18, an article on literature and major political writing

or late, and in Rosenberg's case it was quite late, is an important indicator of the intensity – as a fellow-traveller or otherwise – of one's commitment to and subsequent disillusion with the Party and with the model of Soviet communism as dictated by Stalin. It is to the point that Rosenberg did not publish in *New Masses* after July 1937 and did not put his name to 'The Moscow Trials: A Statement by American Progressives' endorsing the Trials, *New Masses*, May 1938.[29]

For Marxists like Rosenberg, who were disillusioned with the Party but who remained committed to Marxist politics and to the revolutionary function of the artist and intellectual, it must have seemed inevitable that they should be attracted by the character and writings of Leon Trotsky – not to the Trotsky of the Civil War and Red Army but to the outlawed, hunted and peripatetic Trotsky of the 1930s, moving from Turkey to France to Norway and then to Mexico, analysing fascism and Stalinism and still committed to keeping the radical Marxist project going.

Trotsky held that revolution and art were, in certain respects, alike as forms of human activity. This was clearly stated in his letter of 1 June 1938, to the founding conference on the Fourth International, which was called on his initiative in opposition to the Comintern:

> I have always forced myself to depict the sufferings, the hopes and struggles of the working classes because that is how I approach life, and therefore art, which is an inseparable part of it. The present unresolved crisis of capitalism carries with it a crisis of all human culture, including art ... Only a new upsurge of the revolutionary movement can enrich art with new perspectives and possibilities. The Fourth International obviously cannot take on the task of directing art ... give orders or prescribe methods. Such an attitude towards art could only enter the skulls of Moscow bureaucrats drunk with omnipotence. Art and science do not find their fundamental nature though patrons; art, by its very existence, rejects them ... Poets, artists, sculptors, musicians will themselves find their paths

---

(i.e., 'But the least we may demand from literature is that it equal the best political and historical writings of our time in the consciousness of its own subject matter. Only thus can it probe the wound of humanity which the act of thinking and of political combination is part of the effort to cure ... no poem or novel of the past few years can equal as a literary expression of modern human consciousness the Communist Manifesto or Marx's Eighteenth Brumaire'); 'Aesthetic Assault', a review of Jules Romains's *The Boys in the Back Room*, *New Masses*, 30 March 1937, p. 25; and a poem, 'The Melancholy Railings', *New Masses*, 20 July 1937, p. 20. Rosenberg's contributions to *New Masses* indicate that he was not yet sympathetic to Trotsky.

29 Arent (and 137 other signatories) 1938, p. 19.

and methods, if the revolutionary movement of the masses dissipates the clouds of skepticism and pessimism which darken humanity's horizon today ...[30]

Two weeks later Trotsky expanded on what he'd written to the Fourth International in a letter to the editors of the still Marxist but, by then, anti-Stalinist *Partisan Review*. This letter was subsequently published in the August–September issue of the journal under the title 'Art and Politics'.[31] In the autumn, *Partisan Review* made its relations with Trotsky more secure by publishing the manifesto of his International Federation of Revolutionary Writers.[32]

It was at this juncture that Rosenberg reconnected with *Partisan Review*, just at the moment when it was courting Trotsky and identifying itself with Trotskyism. He reentered it in the winter issue with a long critical discussion of Thomas Mann's idealistic, anti-radical anti-fascism, which he titled 'Myth and History'.[33] To the summer issue he contributed replies to a questionnaire-symposium on 'The Situation in American Writing',[34] and a commentary on Arthur Rosenberg's *Democracy and Socialism*: 'By his sly shifts in historical meanings' this author converted the [i.e. Trotsky's] 'principle of "permanent revolution" into that of the coalition governments of the Popular Front'.[35] Rosenberg also signed the statement issued by the Trotskyist League of Cultural Freedom and Socialism with its demand: 'COMPLETE FREEDOM FOR ART AND SCIENCE. NO DICTATION BY PARTY OR GOVERNMENT'.[36] The next year *Partisan Review* published Rosenberg's essay 'On the Fall of Paris', an essay that is thoroughly Trotskyist in its art and politics, which will be considered directly.[37]

---

30   Trotsky 1970, pp. 351–2.
31   Trotsky 1938, pp. 3–10.
32   See Breton and Trotsky 1938, pp. 49–53 – it's generally agreed that this text is substantially Trotsky's but that he asked that his name be left off the by-line.
33   Rosenberg, Harold, 'Myth and History', *Partisan Review*, vol. 6, no. 2, winter 1939, pp. 19–39.
34   Rosenberg, Harold, contribution to 'The Situation in American Writing', *Partisan Review*, vol. 6, no. 4, summer 1939, see pp. 47–9.
35   Rosenberg, Harold, 'Marx and "The People"', *Partisan Review*, vol. 6, no. 4, summer 1939, p. 124.
36   Rosenberg, Harold, (with other members of the League for Cultural Freedom and Socialism), 'Statement of the LCFS', *Partisan Review*, vol. 6, no. 4, summer 1939, pp. 125–7, see p. 127. Rosenberg also signed the League's manifesto 'War Is the Issue!', see *Partisan Review*, vol. 6, no. 5, fall 1939, pp. 125–7. See also Rosenberg on the L.C.F.S. in 'Couch Liberalism and the Guilty Past', *Dissent: a Quarterly Review of Socialist Opinion*, II, autumn 1955, reprinted in TN, pp. 221–40.
37   Rosenberg, 'On the Fall of Paris', *Partisan Review*, vol. 7, no. 6, December 1940, pp. 440–8, reprinted under the title 'The Fall of Paris', in TN, pp. 209–20.

The foregoing describes part of the historical matrix that produced 'Harold Rosenberg'. It enables a reading of 'The American Action Painters' as a text situated in and inscribed by a particular Marxist tradition, by the mutation and modification of New York Marxism with regard to the CPUSA, by the setbacks of the 1930s, and by the espousal of Trotsky's ideas about agency and the freedom of art. Rosenberg's Marxist beginnings were in the early and mid-1930s, in the art and politics of the Great Depression and the New Deal, the union movement, strikes and resistance against repressive state authorities, the move from the United Front to the Popular Front, and from the Third International to the Fourth International. The encounter with Marxism and Marxist politics was significantly different for him and for many of his comrades than it was for those persons who began with Marx around 1939, never having embraced but already disenchanted with Soviet Communism and the Communist Party. This 'Harold Rosenberg' was not the kind of commentator on art and culture who, in the late 1930s and early 1940s, would quote Marx word for word to get noticed by New York's Left intelligentsia only to jettison that Marxism once it had served its purpose. In the 1950s this 'Harold Rosenberg' was scathing about those persons of what he called the 'turning generation', 'couch liberals' with regard to their 'guilty past'.[38]

II

Another clenched fist begins 'The Fall of Paris', which was published in *Partisan Review*, December 1940. This time it's the 'rapping of the soldier's fist' that announces the German army's unopposed entry into the city on 14 June 1940. Rosenberg's focus, however, is not on the demise of Paris as the capital of France but as 'the laboratory of the twentieth century' or the 'Paris "International"', the place that had attracted artists from all over the continents of Europe and America and had become the site of their collective practice producing new ways of seeing, showing and telling. Rosenberg, like Trotsky, thought that the continuity of culture mattered, even through revolutions and periods of social upheaval. As far as he was concerned, despite a degree of continuity, the Paris International had not been working very effectively for ten years or so. However, with the fall of Paris, it was closed down for good and all.[39]

---

38   Rosenberg, Harold, 'Couch Liberalism and the Guilty Past', in TN, pp. 221–40.
39   TN, p. 209.

Rosenberg thought that twentieth-century Paris was to the intellectual what the United States of America had been in the nineteenth century to the immigrant and pioneer. It was a place where no one class was able to its impose its purpose and its representations on artistic creation, where individual nationalities and cultures were blended, and yet where what was alive in various national cultures might be discerned or discovered. Paris stood for the opposite of individualism and nationalism in art because in it and through it the art of every individual and nation was increased. At the end of the 1930s and the beginning of the 1940s, with Europe at war with itself, and when cultural production was being directed by state bureaucracies in the United States and the Soviet Union, what had been achieved in Paris provided evidence for Rosenberg that artistic and cultural internationalism was possible as a creative communion that could sweep across national boundaries.[40] In effect, the Paris International was a 'No-Place'.[41]

Rosenberg's Paris was a material place with a particular physiognomy and a lot of ideology. It was the French capital at a particular moment, say 1907–29, and the artists who gathered there. It was also the style that was produced there: 'Modernism' or 'the Modern', 'the Paris style' or 'the Paris Modern': a style that was based on the 'assumption that history could be entirely controlled by the mind'; and, in as much as it was that, the Paris Modern was as far as humankind had 'gone toward freeing itself from its past'.[42] The Paris Modern had produced a 'No-Time'.[43]

Rosenberg, of course, realised that the Paris International was not entirely 'the actual getting together of peoples of different countries'. And he also realised that the Modern 'was an inverted mental image ... with all the transitoriness and freedom from necessity of imagined things. A dream living-in-the-present and a dream of world citizenship – resting not upon a real triumph, but upon a willingness to go as far as was necessary into nothingness in order to shake off what was dead in the real. A negation of the negative'.[44] Leaving aside any discussion of the intended Zen connotations that attach to that use of 'nothingness' – which also attach to the references to 'No-Place' and 'No-Time', designations that seem informed by what he knew of the Zen state of 'no-mindedness' and which will be redeployed in 'The American Action

---

40   TN, pp. 209–10.
41   TN, p. 214.
42   Ibid.
43   Ibid.
44   TN, pp. 212–13.

Painters'⁴⁵ – it is important to notice that, in this instance, Rosenberg is following Marx and Engels following Hegel with regard to the negation of the negation as a dialectical process of development effecting a positive change.⁴⁶

Rosenberg saw the Modern as 'the style and tempo of our consciousness', of 'the contemporary as beginning in 1789',⁴⁷ and by referring to it as 'a negation of the negative' he pointed to its critical, resistive and emancipatory potential in the development of an advanced, liberating, revolutionary consciousness. Paris had been central to the Modern as the site of the International of culture but not to the modern as a temporality because 'the social, economic and cultural workings which define the modern epoch are active everywhere'.⁴⁸

And just as the International of culture had a capital, Paris, so in the 1920s the political international, the Third International, had a capital: Moscow. 'It is a tragic irony', writes Rosenberg, 'that these world centers were not brought together until the signing of the Franco-Soviet pact [in 1935] when both were

---

45   Rosenberg derives the idea of 'no-place' and 'no-time' from 'no-mindedness', a state of mind essential to Zen Buddhism. 'No-mindedness' is a state of mind that is present everywhere because it is nowhere attached to any particular object. In so far as the Paris International was a 'no-place', it grasped nothing of Paris as the capital of France yet refused nothing from any other place. In so far as the Paris Modern was a 'no-time' it was an emptying or a negation of history and so was completely open to the future. In a state of 'no-mindedness' an individual holds to no preconceptions: he just acts. Nothingness is the negation of all qualities as a vital part of the process of cognition. It's likely that Rosenberg derived his knowledge of Zen 'nothingness' and 'no-mindedness' from reading either Suzuki 1934, or Watts 1936, which were the first books to introduce Zen Buddhism to English-speaking readers, or both. See also note 59 below.

46   Wilczynski 1981, p. 382, gives this succinct explanation: 'The old quality is negated by its opposite [...] thus constituting the first negation. However, the superceded quality does not remain in its original form but, by another process of negation develops into the next stage, the negation of the negation. Marx, Engels and other classical Marxist philosophers developed the concept from Hegel, but gave it a materialist content and stressed its dynamic aspect of development. However, as Engels and Lenin insisted, neither negation nor the negation of the negation in dialectics amounts to the total denial or rejection of the old. Thus socialism is basically a negation of capitalism, yet the former also embodies the best elements of the latter ...'

For the exemplary formulation of the negation of the negation see Marx 1976, p. 929: 'The capitalist mode of appropriation, the result of the capitalist mode of production, produces capitalist private property. This is the first negation of individual private property, as founded on the labour of the proprietor. But capitalist production begets, with the inexorability of a law of Nature, its own negation. It is the negation of the negation. This does not re-establish private property for the producer, but gives him individual property based on co-operation and the possession in common of the land and the means of production'.

47   TN, p. 214.
48   TN, p. 215.

already dead. Then the two cadavers of hope embraced farcically, with mutual suspicion and under the mutually exclusive provincial slogans: DEFENSE OF THE USSR and FRANCE FOR FRENCHMEN'.[49]

And what happened to the formulae perfected by Paris and Moscow that were discarded after the French-Russian Non-Aggression Pact and the inauguration of the Popular Front? They were taken over by Germany and adapted to its particular aims. 'In that country politics became a "pure (i.e., inhuman)" art, independent of everything but the laws of its medium ... Against this advanced technique, which in itself has nothing to do with revolutionary change, the Paris of the Popular Front compromise was helpless'.[50] The demise of the Paris Modern and the Paris International was inseparable from revolutionary defeat and the defeat of the idea of revolution, i.e., from the rise of Stalinism and fascism, the rehegemonisation of nationalism and individualism, and the working class's loss of political independence. The German occupation of Paris merely made it definitive.

Despite this double defeat, Rosenberg managed to bring his essay on the fall of Paris to an optimistic end. Against 'Fascism's modernist mysticism, dreaming of an absolute power to rearrange life to any pattern of its choice', Rosenberg glimpsed the possibility of 'other forms of contemporary consciousness, another Modernism'.[51] But he could not predict where or when this new Modernism might come into being.

III

By the late 1940s to early 1950s, it had become possible for Rosenberg to identify the new International of culture – though not the International of politics – and to discuss the significance of the style associated with it. This he does in 'The American Action Painters'. Like 'The Front' and 'The Fall of Paris', 'The American Action Painters' begins with a gesture or, more accurately, several gestures, set epigraphically as a line taken from Apollinaire's poem 'Merlin et la Vieille Femme' (Alcools, 1913): 'J'ai fait des gestes blancs parmi les solitudes': gestures – 'tournoiements' – that express 'les beatitudes qui toutes ne sont rien qu'un pur effet de l'Art'. That quotation was set above another, this time a sentence, slightly modified, taken from Wallace Stevens's 1942 essay 'The Noble Rider and the Sound of Words': 'The American will is easily satisfied in its efforts to realize

---

49   Ibid.
50   TN, p. 214.
51   TN, p. 220.

itself in knowing itself'. Or, as it is in Stevens's essay, with the elision reinstated: 'it is obvious that the American will as a principle of the mind's being is easily satisfied in its efforts to realize itself in knowing itself'.[52]

One thing that needs to be established immediately is what Rosenberg thought was 'American' about 'American Action Painting'. He was certainly trying to write something about a kind of collective identity but there is not anything nationalistic, patriotic or chauvinistic about it or about his idea of what kind of 'American' the 'American' Action Painter might be. In this context, 'American' has to be understood as meaning a kind ethnic diversity and cosmopolitanism.[53] You only have to read his 1959 essay 'Tenth Street: A Geography of Modern Art' to see how clearly the material and ideological space of the American Action Painters was, in Rosenberg's scheme of things, related to the International of culture that he'd described nineteen years before in 'The Fall of Paris'.[54] In this essay, 'the new American "abstract" art' is the kind of painting made around Tenth Street, New York, by displaced persons, immigrants, the sons and daughters of immigrants, and by Americans who have 'moved' there[55] maybe for reasons similar to those of the artists, writers, etc., who travelled from all over the world to Paris and who, once there, made works that presented or represented the Modern.

In 'The American Action Painters' the artist is figuratively and literally a pioneer and an immigrant. And just as the earlier International of culture was determined partly by the physical character of Paris and by the qualifying and blending of nationalities and class positions which was possible there, so 'Tenth Street' was determined not only by its physical geography – Rosenberg writes that it 'has not even the picturesqueness of a slum', it is 'devoid of local color'[56] – but also by the unfixing and mixing of nationalities, races, classes, and ideologies that occurred there.[57] I have already mentioned that in 1940 Rosenberg

---

52   Stevens 1951, pp. 3–36 at p. 11. Rosenberg was very taken with this essay and with 'The Figure of the Youth as a Virile Poet' (1944), which was also included in *The Necessary Angel* and from where he came by Stevens's notion of poetry as a 'process of the personality of the poet' (see TN, p. 29). Stevens means by this that what keeps 'poetry a living thing, the modernizing and ever-modern influence' is 'not the poet as subject' or ego but a series of actions that are *of* the poet's distinctive character.
53   See Hollinger 1975, especially with reference to Rosenberg pp. 146–7.
54   Rosenberg, Harold, 'Tenth Street: A Geography of Modern Art', *ARTnews Annual*, vol. 28, 1959, pp. 120–37, p. 184, p. 186, p. 190, p. 192, reprinted with slight modifications in DP, pp. 100–9.
55   DP, p. 102.
56   DP, pp. 103, 104.
57   DP, p. 106.

had had recourse to the Zen state of 'nothingness' and, drawing on the Zen of 'no-mindedness', had described the Paris International as a 'No-Place' and the Paris Modern as a 'No-Time'. In 1959 he described the area around Tenth Street, New York, as a 'no environment':[58] it was a location or situation that was, as it were, everywhere because it was nowhere attached to any particular situation or location.[59] More than that, as the new site of cultural internation-

---

58   DP, p. 104.
59   See Rosenberg, DP, p. 104: 'Identical with rotting streets in Chicago, Detroit, and Boston, Tenth Street is differentiated only by its encampment of artist. Here de Kooning's conception of "no environment" for the figures of his Women has been realized to the maximum with regard to himself'. According to Hess 1968, pp. 78–9, Willem de Kooning came up with the idea of 'no-environment' while he worked on *Woman I* (1950–2) to refer to 'the American urban scene and its lack of specificity ... Everything has its own character, but its character has nothing to do with any particular place'. Rosenberg 1973, p. 15, refers to de Kooning coming up with the idea 'no-style' as an aspect of 'the act of painting': 'transient and imperfect as an episode in daily life, the act of painting achieves its form outside the patterning of style. It cuts across the history of art modes and appropriates to painting whatever images it attracts into its orbit. "No Style" painting is neither dependent upon forms of the past nor indifferent to them. It is transformal ...'

As we have seen, Rosenberg had become aware of Zen Buddhism probably in the 1930s and had used it as a resource when he wrote 'The Fall of Paris' in 1940. In this respect, he seems to have been unusual for appropriations of Zen did not become common around Tenth Street until 1948 when The Philosophical Library republished D.T. Suzuki's *An Introduction to Zen Buddhism*, with a preface by Carl Jung, and Suzuki himself began teaching at Columbia University.

John Cage may also have been familiar with Zen Buddhism since the 1930s but he had little use for it in his work until, along with several other figures in the New York vanguard art community, he attended the twice-weekly open lectures that Suzuki gave at Columbia between 1949 and 1951 – see John Cage 1961, 'Foreword', xi and Kostelanetz 1971, 'Conversation with John Cage', p. 23. The references in Cage's writing to 'nothing', and so on, date from this time. The first version of his 'Lecture on Nothing' was given at the Artists' Club in November 1949 to be followed by 'Something and Nothing' in February 1951 – see warholstars.org/abstract-expressionism/abstractexpressionism.html

According to Hellstein 2011, the Club considered Zen Buddhism in one way or another 'on at least ten separate evenings' between 1949 and 1955; it was discussed 'more than any other single topic'.

At this juncture it's worth recalling part of the statement that Cage wrote to accompany Robert Rauschenberg's *White Paintings* (1951) when they were exhibited at the Stable Gallery in 1953, see Kostenanetz 1971:

To Whom:
No subject
No image
No taste
No object
No beauty

alism, 'Tenth Street' transcended the Paris International not only in terms of its unfixity of nationality, race, class, ideology and age[60] but also in terms of its modernism, which went beyond 'the bellicose verbal internationalism of the thirties'.[61] I will consider this double 'going beyond' later. For the moment I want to stay with Rosenberg's idea of 'American' and 'Americanness' and how it relates to his thinking about identity and action.

One of Rosenberg's most interesting considerations of 'Americanness' occurs in his 1949 essay 'The Pathos of the Proletariat'.[62] This was the second of two essays on class and class struggle that Rosenberg wrote at a time when he was concerned with 'the drama of modern history as conceived by Marx – a drama in which individual identity and action are replaced by collective actors formed out of historical processes and myths'.[63] The first of these two essays was 'The Resurrected Romans' of 1948, an extended engagement with Marx's *The Eighteenth Brumaire of Louis Bonaparte*.[64] Together, they provided the core of a book of essays that Rosenberg offered to several publishers in 1949–51

No message
No talent
No technique (no why)
No idea
No intention
No art
No feeling
No black
No white (no and)

After careful consideration, I have come to the conclusion that there is nothing in these paintings that could not be changed, that they can be seen in any light and are not destroyed by the action of shadows.

It's possible that Rosenberg had Rauschenberg's *White Paintings* in mind when he wrote in 'The American Action Painters', TN, p. 26: 'the new American painting is not "pure" art, since the extrusion of the object was not for the sake of the esthetic. The apples weren't brushed off the table in order to make room for perfect relations of space and color. They had to go so that nothing would get in the way of the act of painting. In this gesturing with materials the esthetic, too, had been subordinated. Form, color, composition, drawing, are auxiliaries, any one of which – or practically all, has been attempted logically with unpainted canvases – can be dispensed with'.

60 DP, p. 106.
61 DP, p. 104.
62 Rosenberg, Harold, 'The Pathos of the Proletariat', *The Kenyon Review*, vol. 11, no. 4, autumn 1949, pp. 595–629, in AA, pp. 2–57.
63 AA, p. 206.
64 Rosenberg, Harold, 'The Resurrected Romans', *The Kenyon Review*, vol. 10, no. 4, autumn 1948, 602–20, in TN, pp. 154–77.

under the title *Marx's Drama of History*, none of whom would take it on.[65] Both essays, but particularly 'The Pathos of the Proletariat', are significantly inscribed by ideas that Rosenberg had first published in 'Character Change and the Drama'.[66] We need to look at that essay, which also had its place in the book on Marx, before we consider how 'Americanness' is represented in 'The Pathos of the Proletariat', for it's in this early essay that Rosenberg develops the ideas on 'identity' and 'action' that become so central to his politics and his writing about art and culture in the 1940s and 1950s.

It is germane that what Rosenberg wrote in 'Character Change and the Drama' with reference to Shakespeare's *Hamlet* and Dostoevsky's *The Brothers Karamazov*, to name two of his case-study examples, was informed as much by his studies at the Brooklyn Law School, 1924–7, as by his interest in the poetics of drama.[67] Legal definitions were important for his argument. The law defines an individual by his 'overt actions', by what an individual did in a particular circumstance or particular set of circumstances. The law does not recognise 'personality', a person with a history and psychology. It's only interested in a person's actions, as an 'identity' to which its judgements are applied.[68] Rosenberg goes on to argue that, in *Hamlet*, the Prince is transformed from a 'personality' (a thoroughly naturalistic, self-analytical, non-active psycho-biographical character) into a dramatic 'identity' (a character relevant to and able to perform the role required by the interrelationship of the main events in the play).[69]

---

65   Proposed under the title *Marx's Drama of History*, the book was rejected by Alfred A. Knopf (1949), Pantheon Books (1950) and Beacon Press (1951) – see Marie 2006, p. 68, p. 324 notes 166, 171, 172, 173. Paul de Man, with whom Rosenberg was acquainted during 1949–51, while de Man was teaching at Bard College, Annandale-on-Hudson, New York, 1949–50, knew of this project; see Marie 2006, p. 324 note 176, quoting a letter to Rosenberg from de Man, 5 November 1949: 'This book of yours on Marxism is an event of the first importance and let no publisher tell you otherwise. I mean it'. De Man's acquaintance with Rosenberg (and Mary McCarthy) is touched on in the disparaging and misleading essay on de Man's time at Bard by Lehman 1992, p. 9.

66   Rosenberg, Harold, 'Character Change and the Drama', *The Symposium*, vol. 3, no. 3, July 1932, pp. 348–69, in TN, pp. 135–53. This issue of the journal also contained a lengthy review by Jack Burnham of the first volume of Trotsky's *History of the Russian Revolution* (1930).

67   Born in New York in 1906, Rosenberg attended College of the City of New York (City College), 1923–4, and then Brooklyn Law School from which he graduated in 1927 with a degree conferred under St Lawrence University's state charter to educate attorneys.

68   TN, p. 138. A tangential gloss on this point of law can be read in Mantel 2012, p. 369: 'Gregory [Cromwell] nods. He seems to understand, but perhaps seeming is as far as it goes. When Gregory says, "Are they guilty?" he means, "Did they do it?" But when he [Thomas Cromwell] says, "Are they guilty?" he means, "Did the court find them so?" The lawyer's world is entire unto itself, the human pared away'.

69   TN, pp. 146–9.

Hamlet is built on its hero's hesitations in fulfilling the task that is assigned to him by the drama.[70] Why doesn't Hamlet act? Students of the play have tried to answer this question since Goethe first asked it in his *Wilhelm Meister's Apprenticeship* of 1795–6. As Rosenberg puzzles it, Hamlet has all the qualities required for action but lacks the identity structure necessary to his character in the drama, a oneness with the role originating in and responding to the dramatic laws of his diegetic world. The change occurs when, on his return from England after having escaped death at the hands of the pirates, he acquires a certainty with regard to his feelings and a capacity for action that is no longer an expression of his 'personality' but is in accord with the dramatic rules of the situation in which he finds himself. Regenerated, he breaks with one character and transforms himself into another: 'This is I, Hamlet the Dane' (*Hamlet*, Act 5, Scene 1, 242). From that moment – from the moment he jumps into Ophelia's grave[71] – when, as Marx might have put it, 'his mind, having become free in itself, turns into practical energy', emerges 'as *will*' and 'turns against worldly actuality which exists outside it', Hamlet's 'action hustles the play to its tragic close and the apparently accidental character of his revenge serves to emphasise that he is controlled at the end not by the conflicting intentions of a self but by the impulsions of the plot'.[72] Transformed, 'all at once, in a leap',[73] from the image of a 'personality' to that of an 'identity', Hamlet 'has found at last his place in the play' and, having vacillated for so long, performs the actions required of him by the plot.[74]

Here, in Rosenberg's legalistic thinking about how dramatic thought required that the character of Hamlet had to be changed from a 'personality' to an 'identity' for the play to become a tragedy and to excite pathos,[75] we find a key for understanding his reading not only of Marx on class and class struggle but also of the American Action Painters and Action Painting. This paragraph near the end of 'Character Change and the Drama' is crucial:

---

70 Though he makes no obvious reference to it, I guess that Rosenberg must have been familiar with and was engaging with Freud's Oedipal interpretation of Hamlet's 'hesitations over fulfilling the task of revenge that is assigned to him'; see Freud 1976, pp. 366–7. Perhaps it's just a coincidence – which, after all, is sometimes a messenger sent by certitude – that the third edition of the first English translation of Freud's *The Interpretation of Dreams*, London: Allen & Unwin, New York: Macmillan, was published in the same year as Rosenberg's 'Character Change and the Drama', 1932.
71 AA, p. 143.
72 AA, p. 149.
73 AA, p. 143.
74 TN, p. 149.
75 TN, p. 148.

> Individuals are conceived as identities in systems whose subject matter is action and judgment of actions. In this realm the multiple incidents in the life of an individual may be synthesized, by the choice of the individual himself or by the decision of others, into a scheme that pivots on a single fact central to the individual's existence and which, controlling his behavior and deciding his fate, becomes his visible definition. Here unity of the 'plot' becomes one with unity of being and through the fixity of identity change becomes synonymous with revolution.[76]

There can be no doubt that here, in 1932, Rosenberg has in mind that bit of Marx's third thesis on Feuerbach that goes: 'The coincidence of the changing of circumstances and of human activity or self-changing can be conceived and rationally understood only as *revolutionary practice*'.[77]

Fifteen years later, in 'The Pathos of the Proletariat', the change from 'personality' to 'identity' that becomes synonymous with revolution is the crucial change required of 'the hero of Marx's drama of history' whose 'action is to resolve the tragic conflict and introduce the quiet order of desired happenings'.[78] This hero is not to be an individual but a particular kind of collective identity, a social class: the proletariat.[79] But for an American radical like Rosenberg, four or five years after the Second World War, the social revolution seemed unlikely: though crisis-ridden, capitalism seemed in good health; its internationalism well advanced; the revolutionary processes within it had not genuinely illuminated the worker about himself or united him with other workers.[80] Existence had not effected a revolutionary consciousness. In Germany and Italy the proletariat had been 'driven off the stage of history by the defeat of the Communist Party – in Russia it was driven off by its victory',[81] leaving the Party 'absolute with regard to class' and 'history'.[82] In 'The Pathos of the Proletariat', the problem of the agency of revolutionary change that Rosenberg had previously theorised in terms of individual character change is theorised in terms of class. Knowing full well that the drama of history is discontinuous with 'long intermissions in which the proletariat vanishes from the stage',[83] the

---

76   TN, p. 152.
77   See Karl Marx, Karl, *Theses on Feuerbach*, in Marx and Engels 1976, pp. 6–8 at p. 7; this translation taken from Marx 1975, pp. 421–3 at p. 422.
78   AA, p. 14.
79   AA, p. 15.
80   AA, p. 43.
81   AA, p. 56.
82   AA, p. 55.
83   AA, p. 50.

question that concerned Rosenberg in 'The Pathos of the Proletariat' was how, at that historical moment, in 1949, the proletariat, which had neither chosen nor been compelled to change itself,[84] might change its character and gain its revolutionary 'identity'.

The proletariat had been brought into existence by the industrial revolution. It is an 'invention of modern time'.[85] It is *of* 'the Modern'.[86] As a social class, the proletariat is 'a materialist connection of men with one another' formed 'to carry on a common battle with another class'[87] – so, from the moment of its birth it 'begins its struggle with the bourgeoisie'.[88] The proletarian, having no means of production of his own, lives entirely and solely from the sale of his labour-power and not from the profit derived from any capital. But, if the individual capitalist and proletarian as 'the principle agents' of the capitalist mode of production, writes Rosenberg quoting the 'Preface' to *Capital*, are 'individuals ... only in so far as they are personifications of economic categories, embodiments of particular class-relations and class-interests',[89] individuals whose definite social characters are assigned to them by the process of social production, then what did it mean to speak of the proletariat as revolutionary?[90] Rosenberg finds answers, or partial answers, to this question in Marx's *The Class Struggles in France*, *The Civil War in France* and especially in *The Eighteenth Brumaire*. In these 'historical-literary' writings, class transcends its economic form and given function and 'expresses its collective personality and acts with an intelligence and spirit peculiar to itself'.[91] It is clear to Rosenberg that, in these texts, 'the essence of class definition consisted for Marx in this active character-shaping spirit'.[92] In 'Character Change and the Drama', Hamlet stopped being a 'personality' described by his psychobiography and gained an 'identity' defined 'by the coherence of his acts and with a fact in which they ... terminated'.[93] Without effecting a like change of character and transforming itself from a 'personification' to an 'identity', the proletariat will not be able to act with an intelligence and spirit peculiar to itself and so become 'the future hero' who will 'resolve the tragic conflict and introduce the quiet order

---

84   AA, p. 56.
85   AA, p. 24.
86   AA, p. 25.
87   AA, p. 15.
88   AA, p. 21.
89   AA, p. 17. Marx 1976, 'Preface', p. 92.
90   AA, pp. 17–18.
91   AA, p. 19.
92   Ibid.
93   TN, p. 136.

of desired happenings' into the 'drama of history'.[94] Since Rosenberg, following Marx, believes that the proletariat is destined to alter completely the conditions that created it, the proletariat must undergo that character change from 'personification' to 'identity'.[95] Since its very existence presupposes a revolutionary consciousness and its own decision to act (and not decisions or acts taken on its behalf) must be taken as the basis of any change that might be considered to be socialist, Rosenberg argues that the self-consciousness that converts the proletariat from 'personification' to 'identity' must be an aspect of revolution and revolutionary practice.[96] The proletariat must come to realise itself through its own self-understanding and its own action, its own mindful active response to the structural contradictions of capitalism. Its collective consciousness must become free and issue as action in order for it to overthrow all existing social conditions. 'Both class awareness and class identity arise out of class action'.[97]

Rosenberg finds an answer to how the proletariat's social character might be transformed in that part of *The Eighteenth Brumaire* where Marx writes that the proletarian revolution will be effected by its total abandonment of the past:

> The social revolution cannot draw its poetry from the past but only from the future. It cannot begin with itself before it has stripped off all superstitions in regard to the past. Earlier revolutions required world-historical recollections in order to drug themselves concerning their own content; the revolution of the nineteenth century must let the dead bury the dead. There the phrase went beyond the content; here content goes beyond the phrase.[98]

Whereas the bourgeois revolutions had been performed in costumes borrowed from the past with ghosts presiding over events – like the ghost of Hamlet's father – the proletarian revolution has to be without recourse to myth and must be clear with regard to its content. The proletariat, called into existence by modern industry against the bourgeoisie, is without a past. Its revolution 'is to owe nothing to that repertory of heroic forms out of which history had supplied earlier revolutions with the subjective means for meeting their situation'.[99] Pastless, the proletariat must begin its revolution by becoming at one

---

94   AA, pp. 19, 21, 14.
95   AA, p. 19.
96   AA, p. 22.
97   AA, p. 22.
98   AA, p. 23.
99   AA, p. 23.

with the dramatic narrative of history, and, with a profound asceticisation of mind, understand itself for what it is – not anything more nor less than, as Marx put it – the aforementioned 'wretched personification of wage labour',[100] the 'personification of exploitation and misery'.[101] In other words, there will come a moment when the proletariat will abandon its given character and function under capitalism. In the words of the 1848 *Manifesto*, 'The proletarians have nothing to lose but their chains'. The proletariat will understand itself for what it is and initiate the action necessary to fulfil its historical role for it has a world to win.

The pastlessness of the proletariat is key to its character and its revolutionary role. Likewise, the 'American'. It was in 'The Pathos of the Proletariat' that Rosenberg developed the idea that the proletariat and the American – a citizen of the United States of America, that is – are alike with regard to their pastlessness and their capacity for action. As an immigrant or a descendent of immigrants, the American is detached or estranged from his origins – the culture, traditions, places, things, even human relations of Europe or wherever – and this constitutes a kind of pastlessness: the 'American' exists 'without the time dimension'.[102] Moreover, 'the American does not meditate, he acts'.[103] And what 'self-consciousness' he has is effected through 'practical movement',[104] an action or series of actions that 'For the American ... is a natural response to need or desire (whether his action can satisfy that need is another question)'.[105]

That Rosenberg sees the proletarian and the American as similar might strike one as a bit flim-flam now but the resemblance would have seemed less forced in the 1940s when Lenin's and Trotsky's views on US agriculture and industry were better known than they are today.[106] That's to say that, in the context of use in which that assimilation was effected, the qualities that, in 1949, make the 'American' similar to the proletarian, and vice versa, would have been effective: 'Many of the attributes of the proletarian as the potential embodiment of the spirit of the modern are, inescapably, attributes of the

---

100 AA, pp. 20, 23.
101 AA, p. 52.
102 AA, p. 27.
103 AA, p. 28.
104 Ibid.
105 AA, p. 31.
106 On the place that the United States of America had in Lenin's thinking see Lenin 1970. Trotsky's most extended discussion of the economy – and politics – of US monopoly capitalism is to be found in the introduction to Trotsky 1947, which was published separately as *Marxism in the United States*, New York: Workers Party Publications, 1947.

American,[107] unquestionably the best available model of the new-fangled; from Marx to Lenin and Trotsky, American practices have been cited to illustrate qualities needed under socialism'.[108] However, though he is 'a natural representative of the modern', the American, immigrant or descendant of immigrants, is no revolutionary.[109] Pastless, in so far as the American has a history that 'history has been one of setting limits to his revolutionising'.[110] Nevertheless, speaking 'half-figuratively',[111] to become a human being the proletarian must '*Americanize*' himself by overcoming the void that is his past and making a new self through his actions.[112] 'Yet all the relations of capitalist society forbid the work-

---

107 Rosenberg has a note here: 'In comparing the American and the proletariat we are thinking of them, of course, not as categories, where they overlap (since many Americans are wage workers), but as collective entities or types – the first actual, the second hypothetical'.

108 AA, p. 29. See, for example, this fragment from Trotsky's 'Europe and America' (1926), here taken from James Cannon, 'Trotsky on the United States', *International Socialist Review*, vol. 21, no. 4, fall 1960, reprinted in Hansen 1969, pp. 87–8: 'we do not at all mean thereby to condemn Americanism, lock, stock, and barrel. We do not mean that we abjure to learn from Americans and Americanisms whatever one can and should learn from them. We lack the technique of the Americans and their labour proficiency … to have Bolshevism shod in the American way – there is our task! … If we get shod with mathematics, technology, if we Americanise our frail socialist industry, then we can with tenfold confidence say that the future is completely and decisively working in our favour. Americanised Bolshevism will crush and conquer imperialist Americanism'.

109 Ibid.

110 AA, p. 30.

111 AA, p. 32. Rosenberg has a note here: 'Only *half* figuratively, since becoming Americans has been the actual salvation chosen by millions of workingmen from older nations. With the proletariat there is more to the impulse to become an American than the desire for economic opportunity, flight from oppression, etc. Primarily, it is a will to enter a world where the past no longer dominates, and where therefore that creature of the present, the workingman, can merge himself into the human whole. Thus proletarians immigrate to America in a different spirit from middle-class people or peasants, who from the moment they enter "American time" experience it as something disconcerting or even immoral, and whose nostalgia for their homelands and customs is often communicated from one generation to the next. But America's thin time crust, that seems so desolate to immigrants from other classes, is precisely what satisfies the proletariat and has provided so many workers with the energy to become leaders of industry. Becoming an American is a kind of revolution for foreign proletarians, though it is a magical revolution rather than a revolutionary act. It alters the workingman's consciousness of himself; like a religious conversion it supplies him with a new identity. But this change does not extinguish his previous situation as a character in the capitalist drama; he is still in the realm of economic personifications. As an American, too, a social-economic role will be assigned to him: worker, farmer, capitalist. The elimination of these abstract types continues to call for a transformation of the historical "plot"'.

112 AA, p. 32.

ing class to act except as a tool. Hence its free act must be a revolutionary act, one that must subdue "all existing conditions" and can set itself no limits'.[113] It must 'continue to create itself in revolutionary action' for 'at rest it has no identity'.[114]

At which juncture it is worth recalling what Wallace Stevens said about how 'obvious' it is that 'the American will as a principle of the mind's being is easily satisfied in its efforts to realize itself in knowing itself', which Rosenberg set as one of two epigrams above his essay on the kind of painting being made by the artists who gathered around Tenth Street, New York, in the late 1940s–50s. What, at that time, was impossible for the proletariat became possible for the American Action Painters, artists who were less easily satisfied in their efforts to realise themselves in knowing themselves than was Stevens's generalized American with an 'American will', for what is 'will' if not the faculty by which one decides on and initiates action?

IV

It should be clear from the foregoing that the writings of Marx were the major resource for Rosenberg's thinking about 'action', about action as a necessary way of coming to a proper awareness of one's self, one's identity, one's role in the drama of history, and about what was special about the kind of painting he called 'American Action Painting'. But they would not have been his only resource. According to Robert Motherwell, for example, Rosenberg was taken by something he read in the proofs of an essay by Richard Huelsenbeck, written in 1920, that Motherwell included in his 1951 collection *The Dada Painters and Poets: An Anthology*.[115] Rosenberg lighted on the passage, in what was eventually set under the title 'En Avant Dada', where 'Huelsenbeck violently attacks literary esthetes, and says that literature should be action, should be made with a gun in the hand, etc.'[116] In Berlin, 1918–20, this is revolutionary art. No wonder the passage caught Rosenberg's eye. The appropriation of Marx as a resource aside, it's certainly possible that Rosenberg also paid attention to Huelsenbeck's essay, which he and Motherwell had known since at least 1947 when, as editors along with John Cage and Pierre Chareau, they included some

---

113 Ibid.
114 AA, p. 37.
115 Motherwell (ed.) 1951.
116 Motherwell 1956, p. 37 – see Robert Huelsenbeck, 'En Avant Dada' (1920) in Motherwell (ed.) 1951, pp. 22–48.

fragments from it in the one and only issue of *Possibilities* that came out in the winter of 1947–8.[117] In one of those fragments you can read: 'The Dadaist should be a man who has fully understood that one is entitled to have ideas only through action, because it holds the possibility of achieving knowledge'.[118] That seems compatible with what Rosenberg took from his reading of Marx.

At which juncture it has to be said, with regard to Action Painting, as such, that I doubt that Rosenberg found much that was useful in what he knew about Jackson Pollock's way of painting, either at first hand or by what he could have seen in Hans Namuth's photographs of Pollock painting, which appeared in *ARTnews*, May 1951 – which is not to say that he did not find something.[119] Some commentators have claimed that Rosenberg was thinking of Pollock when he wrote 'The American Action Painters' but this seems unlikely,[120] and, anyway,

---

117 Motherwell and Rosenberg, et al. (eds.) 1947, pp. 41–3.
118 Huelsenbeck (1920) in Motherwell 1965, p. 28.
119 Goodnough 1951.
120 See Harold Rosenberg 1961, his review of Bryan Robertson's *Jackson Pollock*, New York: Abrams, 1961: 'according to Robertson ... "during a conversation in 1949 with Harold Rosenberg, Pollock talked of the supremacy of *the act of painting* as in itself a source of magic. An observer with extreme intelligence, Rosenberg immediately coined the new phrase: Action Painting". The aim of this sentence is obviously to present Pollock as the originator of Action Painting in theory and practice, if not in name ... The statement is, of course, entirely false, and whoever informed Mr Robertson that this conversation took place knew it was false. Pollock never spoke to Rosenberg about the "act of painting", of its "supremacy" (to what?) or of any "source of magic" in it. This can easily be demonstrated. The concept of Action Painting was first presented in the December 1952 *Art News*, so that if the conversation described by Robertson had taken place in 1949 Rosenberg did not produce the phrase "immediately" but waited three years. It may have taken him that long to penetrate the depths of Pollock's observation, but in that case one would be justified in questioning his "extreme intelligence". On the other hand, Rosenberg had published writings on the subject of action as constitutive of identity as far back as 1932. In 1948, a year before the alleged tip-off, he further elaborated the topic in an essay in *The Kenyon Review* entitled "The Resurrected Romans", which may have something to do with "magic" but nothing to do with Pollock or with painting. A conversation between Pollock and Rosenberg did occur in 1952, immediately preceding the composition of "The American Action Painters" but in this talk Pollock said nothing about action. He spoke of identifying himself with a tree, a mode of self-stimulation not unknown in the tradition of which we have been speaking and more relevant to the paintings for which he is famous. He also attacked a fellow artist for working from sketches, which in Pollock's opinion, made the artist "Renaissance" and backward (the point was reported in the "Action Painters" essay, though without mentioning names). In the last years, Robertson informs us that Pollock liked to refer to the canvas he was working on as "the arena" – this term was garnered from "The American Action Painters", which says, "At a certain point the canvas began to appear to one American painter after another as an arena in which to act". Apparently, Pollock, or someone presently speaking for him, wished to acquire this thought for himself exclus-

he didn't need to see – or see photographs of – Pollock or any of the artists he might have had in mind actually painting to write what he saw the paintings as *of*. He didn't think of himself 'as a critic writing about specific painters or sculptors' or about 'problems that are distinctly – or let's say, exclusively – restricted to painting'; rather, he saw himself as 'dealing with the condition of some creative act on the part of an individual or a group, even ... a pervasive spirit'.[121] If Rosenberg had the work of anyone in particular in mind as evidencing the kind of action he associated with Action Painting, it was probably the work of Barnett Newman: specifically, perhaps, *Onement 1*.[122] This was the painting that Newman made on 29 January, 1948, his birthday, by fixing a piece of tape down the vertical centre of a canvas that he'd painted cadmium dark red and, after that, smearing some cadmium light red over it to test the colour. Newman then studied what he had produced for some eight or nine months, figuring out what precisely he had done – 'What was it?' – and what he might do, before definitively abandoning it as complete[123] and, having 'affirmed himself ... freed himself' and moved on with a 'totally new vision'.[124]

We can now start reading 'The American Action Painters' and answer the question posed about Action Painting in the first section of the essay: 'Modern Art? Or an Art of the Modern?' For Rosenberg, writing in 1952, Modern Art is painting that has caught up with, or is catching up with, what was produced by the 'School of Paris', the moribund Modernism of the late 1920s to 1930s. Modern Art is painting that is secure in the knowledge of what it is, practising its immediate past, enabled and supported by a stable structure. As Wallace Stevens might have phrased it: it puts things together by choice, not of the will; it selects from among objects already supplied by association; it's a selection

---

      ively, although Rosenberg told Pollock, in the presence of a witness, that the article was not about "him", even if he had played a part in it ...'

      Despite this, the idea that Pollock's practice was somehow what Rosenberg had in mind as 'Action Painting' or that Pollock provided him with the concept, or that Namuth's photographs of Pollock painting did, persists. See, for example, the letters exchanged between Rosenberg and William Rubin in *Artforum*, April, pp. 6–7 and especially that of May 1967, p. 4, concerning Rubin's 'Jackson Pollock and the Modern Tradition', *Artforum*, February 1967, pp. 14–22. For some more examples, not involving Rosenberg, see: Barbara Rose 1979, pp. 112–13; Solomon 1987, p. 210; Landau 1989, *Jackson Pollock*, New York: Abrams, 1989, pp. 85–6; Naifeh and Smith 1989, pp. 703–07.

121   See Gruen 1972, pp. 172–8 at p. 173.
122   Hess 1972, p. 30, for one, thought that this was the case.
123   Newman interviewed by Emile de Antonio in the movie directed by de Antonio, *Painters Painting: The New York Art Scene 1940–1970*, 1972, transcript published in De Antonio and Tuchman 1984, see p. 306.
124   Hess 1972, p. 30.

made from what's in place and available and for purposes that are not then and there in the process of being shaped. Modern Art has to be negated: an Art of the Modern will be the negation of that negative.[125]

But Modern Art isn't only painting. As Rosenberg points out, the category could also include architecture, furniture, household appliances, advertising 'mobiles', a three thousand year old mask from the South Pacific, and even a piece of wood found on a park bench.[126] Modern Art has little or not anything to do with style or with when or why something was produced, by whom it was produced or for whom it was produced, etc., and more or less everything to do with those persons who are socially and pedagogically empowered to designate it as 'psychologically, esthetically or ideologically relevant to our epoch'.[127] It is part of a 'revolution of taste' conducted by those persons who value it and contested by those who do not. Responses to it represent 'claims to social leadership'.[128] In other words, Rosenberg recognised that what was being done with art was but an aspect of the struggle for leadership within the US ruling class that, during the 'Cold War', was contested with opposing claims about the value of Modern Art. On one side there was that fraction made up of internationalist-multinationalist business liberals that valued it, collected it and made it available to the public in those bits of what C. Wright Mills would call 'the cultural apparatus' that they owned and controlled – the Museum of Modern Art, New York, which Rosenberg has in his sights in 'The American Action Painters', was a prime site in this regard – and for whom Modern Art had 'a supreme Value [...] the Value of the NEW'.[129] On the other side there was that fraction made up of isolationist-nationalist 'practical conservatives' that regarded Modern Art as un-American, subversive, 'snobbish, Red, immoral, etc.'[130] and whose views were represented by the likes of Congressman George A. Dondero.[131] Rosen-

---

125 TN, pp. 23–4.
126 TN, p. 35.
127 TN, p. 36.
128 Ibid.
129 TN, p. 37.
130 TN, p. 36.
131 On the internationalist 'business-liberals' and the old-guard, 'America First' isolationists as fractions of the US ruling class, see for example the books of Domhoff 1967 and Domhoff 1978.
   In 'Revolution and the Idea of Beauty', *Encounter* vol. 1, no. 3, December 1953, revised and reprinted as 'Revolution and the Concept of Beauty', in TN, pp. 74–83, Rosenberg discusses how (without mentioning him by name, see especially pp. 74–5, 77–8) Alfred H. Barr Jr., Director of Collections at the Museum of Modern Art, New York, responded to Dondero's attacks on Modern Art in his belated 'Is Modern Art Communistic?', *New York Times Magazine*, 14 December 1952, pp. 22–3, pp. 28–30. No doubt Rosenberg would have

berg, who understood how Modernism – or those aspects of Modern Art that were synonymous with the Art of the Modern – put the cultural politics of both fractions at risk, regarded this struggle, restricted to 'weapons of taste', and at the same time addressed to the masses, as a 'comedy of revolution'.[132] In other words, it was a farce.

The professional enlighteners of Modern Art use Action Painting in their political struggle with those who oppose their view of the world not only for ideological purposes but also as a way of making money.[133] But they don't understand it. Their value judgements are based in identifying 'resemblances of surface' and on the perpetuation of beliefs about what is 'modish'.[134] Which is why they have failed to grasp 'the new creative principle' that sets Action Painting apart from twentieth-century picture making.[135] Action Painting has not anything to do with taste or with 'the mode of production of modern masterpieces', which 'has been all too clearly rationalized'.[136] It is a very different kind of practice to that of the earlier abstractionists of the Paris Modern or, as it is called in 'The American Action Painters', the 'Great Vanguard'.[137] The Modern or the Great Vanguard was historically and culturally specific to the Paris International, 1907–29. Action Painting was historically and culturally specific to the community associated with Tenth Street, New York, 1945–52. It was that community's response to the unevenness and discontinuity of history and to what Rosenberg regarded as a break in and with the Modern. Not surprisingly – or illogically according to what Rosenberg had written in 'The Fall of Paris' – the Action Painters regarded the style of the Great Vanguard as dead or as something that had to be transcended. Though it is possible to see a cutaneous similarity between their work and previous abstract painting, the two kinds of painting are crucially different with regard to their intention and function. Because of this, the work of the American Action Painters had to be seen as different and separate from the painting of the Great Vanguard and from what the taste bureaucracies and formalist critics had designated as

---

chuckled when it came out in *The New York Times*, 27 April 1966, that *Encounter* had been funded by the Central Intelligence Agency (CIA).

On the Abstract Expressionists' relation to the struggle between the business-liberals and isolationists see Orton 1991, pp. 3–17.

132   TN, p. 36.
133   TN, p. 37.
134   TN, p. 38.
135   TN, p. 39.
136   TN, p. 34.
137   TN, p. 24.

Modern Art.[138] Rosenberg's use of 'the Modern' had remained consistent since 'The Fall of Paris' and continued to mean – as it did in 'The Pathos of the Proletariat', where he talked about 'the spirit of the modern'[139] – the style of an epoch's progressive consciousness. Action Painting is not 'Modern Art'. It is an 'Art of the Modern'.

Rosenberg points out that most of the artists he's writing about were over forty years old when they became Action Painters. Before then, many of them had been '"Marxists" (W.P.A. unions, artists' congresses) ... trying to paint Society. Others had been trying to paint Art (Cubism, Post-Impressionism)'.[140] It amounted to the same thing. They had been trying to paint the Modern. By 1940 both Art and Society – the art of the Paris International and the aspirational politics of the Communist International – as the necessary form and dynamic principle of the immediate future were dead. It is in this double demise, not in 'the war and the decline of radicalism in America', that Rosenberg locates the beginnings of Action Painting.[141] 'At its centre the movement was away from, rather than towards. The Great Works of the Past and the Good Life of the Future became equally nil'.[142]

Wallace Stevens, thinking about the period from the French Revolution to 1942, a moment in the War when the defeat or triumph of Hitler was still undecided, wrote about 'the pressure of reality, a pressure great enough and prolonged enough to bring about the end of one era in the history of the imagination and, if so, then great enough to bring about the beginning of another'.[143] In a sense that's the moment of Rosenberg's 'grand crisis',[144] the moment when the two Moderns became 'nil': the moment when it became possible to make an Art of the Modern again. But with what? The ideas, beliefs, theories, practices, materials and methods of Art and Society that survived were deemed useless as resources for those artists who were compelled to deal with the crisis and work it out in practice. 'Value – political, aesthetic, moral' had to be rejected.[145] But

---

138 TN, p. 24.
139 AA, p. 29.
140 TN, p. 30.
141 TN, p. 30.
142 Ibid.
143 Stevens 1951, pp. 21–2.
144 TN, p. 30.
145 See the note that Rosenberg added in *The Tradition of the New*, 1965, and subsequent reprints, TN, pp. 33–4: 'As other art movements of our time have extracted from painting the element of structure or the element of tone and elevated into their essence, Action Painting has extracted the element of decision inherent in all art in that the work is not finished at its beginning but has to be carried forward by an accumulation of "right" ges-

ACTION, REVOLUTION AND PAINTING (RESUMED)

this rejection did not take the form of condemnation or defiance, as it had done with Dada and Surrealism after the 1914–18 War. This time, owing no political, aesthetic, or moral obligation to a past-dominated present but trying presently to paint the Modern, the artist's reaction was one of diffidence:[146] the artist was not so much excessively modest and reticent as distrustful and uncertain about what constituted and might yet constitute 'art', 'creation', 'creativity', 'individuality' and the 'identity' of the artist.

In becoming 'nil', the two Moderns had provided artists with a major resource for any vanguard practice: 'nothingness'. In a state of nothingness or with the experience of nothingness, the Action Painter 'decided to paint ... just TO PAINT'.[147] There was no intention 'to reproduce, re-design, analyse or "express" an object, actual or imagined. What was to go on the canvas was not a picture but an event. The painter no longer approached his easel with an image in mind; he went up to it with material in his hand to do something to that other piece of material in front of him'.[148] The image that was produced by 'staining' the canvas or by 'spontaneously putting forms into motion upon it'[149] was the indexical – and occasionally iconic – mark or trace of those actions.[150] Initially that was all there was to it. But subsequently the painter began to take stock of the way that the surface was marked, started to attend to the 'act of painting', to what might be learned about painting and art and about himself: 'what matters always is the revelation contained in the act'.[151]

Action Painting, as Rosenberg sees it, is painting at the point of formation, when everything has to be redone. It is Ur-painting at the point of thematisation; but it is not yet, and may never become, painting as an art.[152] *As if*. In redoing everything from scratch the Action Painter relies on an '*as if*'. In our life circumstances we behave *as if* our world is as we know it, we live our lives often according to ideas and models that we know to be untrue but take for granted *as if* they are true. The *as if* is a fiction that we find useful for going

---

tures. In a word, Action Painting is the abstraction of the *moral* element in art; its mark is moral tension in detachment from moral or esthetic certainties; and it judges itself morally in declaring that picture to be worthless which is not the incorporation of a genuine struggle, one which could at any point have been lost'.

146 TN, p. 30.
147 TN, p. 30.
148 TN, p. 25.
149 Ibid.
150 For an interesting discussion of the indexical and iconical in Abstract Expressionism see Richard Shiff 1978, pp. 94–123.
151 TN, pp. 26–7.
152 See Wollheim 1987, pp. 19–25, p. 359 note 9 on the idea of Ur-painting.

on, for achieving or maintaining what we want to achieve or maintain. An *as if* is a useful fiction. Action Paintings are 'DRAMAS OF AS IF'.[153] 'With traditional esthetic references discarded as irrelevant, what gives the canvas its meaning is not psychological data but role, the way the artist organizes his emotional and intellectual energy *as if* [emphasis added] he were in a living situation'.[154] Though 'The interest lies in the kind of act taking place in the four sided arena [that is the canvas], a dramatic interest',[155] the artist makes or takes those actions *as if* he were intervening in his actual life circumstances, *as if* his actions were actual interventions in the existing social and political order of things.

We are now close to understanding this new painting that Rosenberg regards 'as an act that is inseparable from the biography of the artist', that is 'a "moment" in the adulterated mixture of his life', that is 'of the same metaphysical substance as the artist's existence', and that has 'broken down every distinction between art and life'.[156] But we will not understand it if we see it as Modern Art, if we see it in relation 'to the works of the past, rightness of colour, texture, balance, etc.', or as expressing or representing some aspect of the artist's existence, for example, his 'sexual preferences or debilities'.[157] Taking the hint from the reference to 'the critic who goes on judging',[158] and recalling what he'd written previously in 'Character Change and the Drama' about the way the law defines a person by his overt acts and its judgement being the resolution of those acts, it seems clear that Rosenberg saw an Action Painting as a sequence of lucid and comprehensible actions that enabled a judgement by the painter and the critic, a judgement that is an inseparable part of recognising the painter's identity.[159]

---

153 TN, p. 27.
154 TN, p. 29. The significance of 'Dramas Of As If' the inter-title that Rosenberg gave to this section of 'The American Action Painters', has gone unnoticed. The '*as if*' at this point in the essay is almost certainly derived from Hans Vaihinger's *Philosophie des Als Ob* (1911), which Rosenberg probably knew from reading Vaihinger 1924. In this section of the essay, Rosenberg is pointing to two dramas of *as if*. First (TN, p. 28), there is a negative *as if*, which is that of 'The critic who goes on judging [the new painting] in terms of schools, styles, form – as if the painter were still concerned with producing a certain kind of object (a work of art), instead of living on the canvas – is bound to seem a stranger [to the painter and his act of painting]'. Second (TN, p. 29), there's the positive *as if* that the Action Painter uses for going-on making paintings and realising himself in the act of making a painting.
155 TN, p. 29.
156 TN, pp. 27, 28.
157 TN, p. 29.
158 TN, p. 28.
159 In 'Character Change and the Drama', TN, p. 136 and note, Rosenberg pointed out that 'The Law is not a recognizer of persons; its judgments are applied at the end of a series of acts. ...

> With the American, heir of the pioneer and the immigrant, the foundering of Art and Society was not experienced as a loss. On the contrary, the end of Art marked the beginning of an optimism regarding himself as an artist ... On the one hand, a desperate recognition of moral and intellectual exhaustion; on the other, the exhilaration of an adventure over depths in which he might find the true image of his identity ... Guided by visual and somatic memories of paintings he had seen or made – memories which he did his best to keep intruding into his consciousness – he gesticulated upon the canvas and watched for what each novelty would declare him and his art to be.[160]

Aware that their ideological and material conditions were thoroughly immiserated and freed from – or wanting to be free from – past ideas and beliefs, the Action Painters, their imaginations responding to the pressure of reality, acted according to their historical circumstances and entirely in their own interests. The 'saving moment' came 'when the painter first felt himself released from Value – myth of past self-recognition' and 'attempted to initiate a new moment' in which he would 'realize his total personality – myth of future self-recognition'.[161] It was at that point that the painter's character change became synonymous with revolution. This is Rosenberg on revolutionary action in 'The Pathos of the Proletariat':

> For the worker action is but a possibility, the anguishing possibility of transforming himself into an individual. Hemmed in on the bare, functional stage of industrial production, altogether *there*, without past or vision of paradise, he is, except for this possibility of acting, a mere prop, a thing that personifies. Speaking half-figuratively, to become a human being the proletarian must '*Americanize*' himself, that is, overcome the void of his past by making a new self through his actions.
>
> Yet all the relations of capitalist society forbid the working class to act except as a tool. Hence its free act must be a revolutionary act, one that must subdue 'all existing conditions' and can set itself no limits. The proletarian victim of the modern cannot enter the historical drama as an actor without becoming its hero. In 'the indefinite prodigiousness

---

The judgment is the resolution of these acts'. That's why, for example, 'Razkolnikov ... in *Crime and Punishment* sought judgment so that his act would be completed and he could take on a new existence'.

160   TN, p. 31.
161   Ibid.

of their aims', as Marx described them in *The Eighteenth Brumaire*, the workers signify that with them revolution is a need of the spirit, a means of redemption. Before Marx's internal pioneer opens a frontier without end.[162]

This is what he wrote, or rewrote, in 'The American Action Painters':

> The revolution against the given, in the self and the world, which since Hegel has provided European vanguard art with theories of a New Reality, has re-entered America in the form of personal revolts. Art as action rests on the enormous assumption that the artist accepts as real only that which he is in the process of creating. 'Except the soul has divested itself of the love of created things ...' The artist works in a condition of open possibility, risking, to follow Kierkegaard, the anguish of the esthetic, which accompanies possibility lacking in reality. To maintain the force to refrain from settling anything, he must exercise in himself a constant No.[163]

In other words, the artist must base his work in the practice of the negation of the negative. The 'constant No' here is not merely the mental act of saying 'No', which like many of the so-called practices of negation that characterise 'Modern Art' are but arbitrary and gratuitous signs of caprice. It refers, rather, to the objective ground of such negations and is the vital element of the process of cognition: negation defined as a dialectical moment of objective development, becoming, mediation, and transition. No simple negation of a given negativity can produce a self-sustaining positivity. That's why Rosenberg gave this section of his essay the inter-title: 'It's Not That, It's Not That, It's Not That'.[164]

The Action Painter can only produce effectively if he is in a relation to the dominant culture as a proletarian. Action is the prerequisite of the proletariat's identity. For the proletariat, which is held in an exploited fixed relation to capitalism, the free act, any action made spontaneously and without recourse to myths of the past or the myth of a Utopian future, will be, by definition, revolutionary and will inaugurate the revolution in permanence. Likewise, action is the will-full prerequisite for the vanguard painter's striving to effect his 'identity'. In the crisis period of 1940 and after, an uncertain malignant war-like whole, a world at war and then at Cold War, the painter could either remain a 'personality' or 'personification' and continue putting things together

---

162   AA, pp. 31–2.
163   TN, p. 32.
164   TN, p. 29.

on the canvas by selecting from amongst what remained of Art and Society; or, he could accept that there was nothing, that he had nothing to secure or strengthen, and had to resist or evade the pressure of that no-thing, evade or negate it, and rid himself of all considerations not demanded by the reality of the historical situation and act appropriately and accordingly. And just ... PAINT. He could either carry on producing Modern Art or he could produce an Art of the Modern, make art or – if it were not art – make 'original work demonstrating what art is about to become'.[165]

As I read them, 'The Pathos of the Proletariat' and 'The American Action Painters' were written by a Marxist who refused to succumb to a pessimism that would have been quite alien to the tradition of Marxism. The 'Harold Rosenberg' who wrote 'The Front' at the end of 1934 is still there in these and other essays written in the 1940s and 1950s. So is the proletariat. The proletariat, of course, always has the potential for revolution: '*So long as the category exists, the possibility cannot be excluded that it will recognize itself as a separate human community and revolutionize everything by asserting its needs and its traditionless interests*'.[166] And the American Action Painters provided evidence that there was still a space and some potential for personal revolt and insurrection. For Rosenberg, 'good' Action Painting left 'no doubt concerning its reality as an action and its relation to a transforming process in the artist'.[167] Weak or 'easy' Action Painting lacked 'the dialectical tension of a genuine act, associated with risk and will'.[168] Action Painting was optimistic painting for it enabled the artist to realise an 'identity' that the proletariat, at that moment, could not.

Maybe the Action Painters' action was always, at some level, a failure – unless we think of it as part of a 'revolution' whose outlines were not perceptible in political terms but the potential of which could only be denied at the cost of an entire loss of self.

Rosenberg was able to remain optimistic because his analyses incorporated the dialectic: that 'affirmative recognition of the existing state of things, at the same time also, the recognition of the negation of that state, of its inevitable breaking up'.[169] When it appeared, the dialectical method, which combines the negativity of man's social experience with the need for change, introduced an essential, confident movement into Rosenberg's writing. Remember: the Paris

---

165 TN, p. 24.
166 AA, pp. 56–7.
167 TN, p. 33.
168 TN, p. 34.
169 Marx, *Capital* 1, quoted by Rosenberg in 'The Pathos of the Proletariat', AA, p. 35; Marx in the Postface to the second edition of *Capital* Volume 1, 1873, see Marx 1976, p. 103.

Modern represented 'a dream of living-in-the-present and a dream of world citizenship – resting not upon a real triumph, but upon a willingness to go as far as was necessary into nothingness in order to shake off what was dead in the real. A negation of the negative'. That was how Rosenberg saw the work of the American Action Painters. One could say that Rosenberg's Action Painter, like the proletariat will be when it changes character and becomes one with the drama of history, is someone who is aware that he is nothing and acts to become everything, whose mind, having become free, is externalised as will and acts against the pressure of reality. He tried to let nothing impose upon the act-painting, a purposive productive act that was in its essence critical of Art and Society. Those dramas of *as if* had a kind of revolutionary boldness. When Barnett Newman, in 1948, in response to Rosenberg's question about what *one* of his 'paintings could possibly mean to the world', said that if one 'could read it properly it would mean the end of all state capitalism and totalitarianism', he was surely reminding Rosenberg of *Onement I*. Not that Rosenberg would have needed reminding, of course. His question was thoroughly rhetorical. If the work of the American Action Painters had any meaning, it was about revolutionary political agency arising from the contradictions of capitalism, the reality of which could not be totally excluded if the prospect of radical change was to be kept open … sometime … somewhere … Action Painting was the sign that the possibility of revolution was not totally closed down, that the dynamic of revolution was still there for 'If one is to continue to paint or write as the political trap seems to close upon him he must perhaps have the extremist faith in sheer possibility'.[170]

---

170 Motherwell and Rosenberg, et al. (eds.) 1947, p. 1.

CHAPTER 4

Ideology: Reading Paul de Man Reading Marx and Engels

> Hitherto men have always formed false conceptions about themselves, what they are and what they ought to be.
> KARL MARX and FREDERICK ENGELS, *The German Ideology*

⋮

> Ideology is a process accomplished by the so-called thinker consciously, it is true, but with a false consciousness.
> FREDERICK ENGELS to FRANZ MEHRING, London, 14 July 1893

∴

Over the course of a week at the end of February and beginning of March 1983, a little over eight months before he died of cancer aged sixty-four, Paul de Man gave the Messenger Lectures at Cornell University, where he'd taught from 1960 to 1967.* The lectures, which had been postponed from the autumn 1982

---

* The drift of this essay – but not a draft – met its first public, thanks to an invitation from Martin McQuillan, as a short paper on de Man's interest in Marx that was presented at the annual conference of the International Association for Philosophy and Literature at Le Moyne College and Syracuse University in 2004. Afterwards, it was developed as a teaching aid and way of mapping a programme of ten seminars for graduate students in the School of Fine Art, History of Art and Cultural Studies, University of Leeds, and occupied me until it was abandoned on my retirement from the University in 2006. I thank Neil Cox for taking an interest in it around that time. What you have here has not progressed much beyond what was in place when it was abandoned. That's why it makes no engagement with what's been published since 2006, including the de Man papers, manuscripts and drafts, notes and teaching notebooks that have since been deposited in the Critical Theory Archive at the University of California, Irvine. Nevertheless, what it says about the way that de Man read Marx and Engels still seems fecund, not least because, with two or three exceptions, those scholars, generally but not exclusively academics contracted by universities in the United States of America, who have busied themselves with the de Man corpus, and with keeping its integrity, have shown scant interest in this aspect of his work. No surprise there. It'll probably be of little interest –

because of his illness, were announced under the title 'Rhetoric [and] Aesthetics'. In the order they were given we now know them as: 'Anthropomorphism and Trope in the Lyric' and 'Aesthetic Formalization: Kleist's "*Über das Marionnettentheater*"' (both published in *The Rhetoric of Romanticism*); 'Hegel on the Sublime', 'Phenomenality and Materiality in Kant', 'Kant and Schiller' (all published in *Aesthetic Ideology*); and 'Conclusions: Walter Benjamin's "The Task of the Translator"' (published in *The Resistance to Theory*). De Man had written up the first four lectures by the time he died, the first three perhaps by the time he gave the fourth. The last two were reconstructed from transcripts and audiotapes; these were published together with probably only some of the questions that came from the audience along with de Man's replies. These exchanges are always interesting, but what strikes me as most interesting is that no one seems to have asked him to say anything about the explicit references he'd made to ideology and politics: not only to 'the ideology of the aesthetic'[1] but also, for example, to ideology as 'a norm or a value',[2] to 'pedagogical, historical and

---

and no use – to them. It will be of more interest to those scholars who value Marx and Engels's writing: who are committed to historical materialism; who have not resigned themselves to historical conditions; and are keeping faith with the possibility of changing them. Hopefully, they'll welcome the way it reads de Man's interest in Marx and Engels, especially the way he approached Marx and Engels's writing on 'alienation', 'estrangement', and 'ideology', and find it useful.

Note these abbreviations used throughout the main text and footnotes:

AI   De Man, Paul 1996, *Aesthetic Ideology*, ed. with intro. Andrzej Warminski, Minneapolis and London: University of Minnesota Press.

AR   De Man, Paul 1979, *Allegories of Reading: Figural Language in Rousseau, Nietzsche, Rilke and Proust*, New Haven and London: Yale University Press.

BI   De Man, Paul 1983 [1971], *Blindness & Insight: Essays in the Rhetoric of Contemporary Criticism*, second edition, revised, ed. Wlad Godzich, Minneapolis: University of Minnesota Press, London: Methuen & Co.

CW   De Man, Paul 1989, *Critical Writings 1953–1978*, ed. with intro. Lindsay Waters, Minneapolis: University of Minnesota Press.

RR   De Man, Paul 1984, *The Rhetoric of Romanticism*, New York and Guildford, Surrey: Columbia University Press.

RT   De Man, Paul 1986, *The Resistance to Theory*, ed. with intro. Wlad Godzich, Minneapolis: University of Minnesota Press.

RCC   De Man, Paul 1993, *Romanticism and Contemporary Criticism*, eds. E.S. Burt, Kevin Newmark, and Andrzej Warminski, Baltimore and London: The Johns Hopkins University Press.

And in the footnotes only:

MECW   Karl Marx, Frederick Engels, *Collected Works*, London: Lawrence & Wishart with volume and page(s) referenced thus: *MECW* X, pp. xx–xx.

1 RR, p. 264.
2 RR, p. 242.

political ideologies',³ and to ideology as 'primarily a social and political model or structure', as a 'drive [that] acts upon the reality of history', and as 'a political force'.⁴ Why? Though these were matters that must have been 'getting under people's skin' during the Messenger Lectures, it seems to me that a 'certain reaction', which perhaps was 'bound to occur', ensured that they didn't come up in question time.⁵ Even so, it seems that de Man needed no prompting to talk about them when, immediately after the last lecture, he was interviewed by Stefano Rosso for the Italian National Broadcasting System. Indeed, it seems that he himself brought them into the conversation. Ideology and politics were on de Man's mind – perhaps at the fore – and he wanted to talk about them, though not out of any polemical urging.⁶

At the beginning of the interview, as it's been published, Rosso asks de Man to say something about the science or profession of teaching and his role as a teacher, given his experience as someone who had been educated in Europe and had taught in both Europe and the United States of America. Straightaway de Man points out that, as a teacher, 'in Europe one is of course much closer to ideological and political questions, while, on the contrary, in the United States, one is much closer to professional questions. So the ethics of the profession are very different'.⁷ In Europe, he says, what one teaches is 'separated from the actual professional use that the students, who were mostly destined to teach in secondary school, would make of it. So there was a real discrepancy between what one talked about and what the use value of this could be for the students'.⁸ In the United States, however (and here he's talking about graduate teaching), where 'one teaches future colleagues, one has a direct professional relationship to them'.⁹ There, where teaching can *seem* removed from ideological and political problems in the world outside the University, the ideological and political questions that interest or bother the academic profession can also *seem* somewhat separated from those of the world and society.¹⁰ De Man says that he 'ended up finding the function of teaching in the United States – the

---

3   RR, p. 266.
4   RR, p. 242.
5   The material in scare quotes is taken only a little out of context from de Man himself; see the fifth Messenger Lecture, 'Kant and Schiller', AI, pp. 131–2.
6   RT, p. 121.
7   RT, p. 115.
8   RT, pp. 115–16.
9   RT, p. 116.
10 For an argument that this is (still) the case, see Andrew Delbanco, 'Scandals of Higher Education', *The New York Review of Books*, 29 March 2007, pp. 42–7, and (for resistance see) 'Scandals of Higher Education', *NYRB*, 26 April 2007, p. 66.

function of an academic as distinct from the academic function – much more satisfactory than in Europe, precisely because of the contract one has with the people one teaches'.[11] As far as he was concerned, in the United States one can pursue the activity proper to teaching because, unlike in Europe, the University has no 'predominating cultural function at all ... it is not inscribed in the genuine cultural tensions of the nation'.[12] Perhaps not 'not inscribed'. But not 'removed from', either. For what the 'contract' does, or tries to do, is maintain a false distinction between what, in 'Hypogram and Inscription', published a couple of years before he gave the Messenger Lectures, de Man had referred to as the discourse of the 'monastery' and the 'market place', the 'academy' and the 'public arena'.[13] He may have found the 'ideological situation' in the United States 'slightly more honest' and 'easier to cope with' but he knew well enough that 'the secluded discourse of "pure" speculation and scholarship' was not 'entirely distinct from the public discourse of controversy, less true still that one is unilaterally sound while the other is chaotic, or that the one is free from the ideology that animates and distorts the other. Patterns of obfuscation and lucidity inhabit both and the homologies between these patterns can be organized around shared assumptions, however diversely they may be valorized'.[14] In conversation with Rosso he noted how the academic profession in the United States inhabits and deals with these assumptions and patterns of obfuscation and lucidity – assumptions and patterns that render certain perceptions easily understood and clearly expressed and others obscure and confused – that it shares with the discourse of ideological and political controversy outside the University. It turns them into a problem about 'the relationship of the academic profession to the American political world and society'. In other words, it turns them into a problem of 'the relationship between the "academic" and society at large' as if the former is independent of the latter.[15]

That de Man's audience at Cornell reacted in the way it did – at least in what's been published – and *did not* ask or *could not* ask him to say something more about 'ideology' and 'politics', especially about how the references to ideology and politics in his lectures related to ideology and politics in the world beyond the institution of the University, can be explained, in his terms, by the very professionalism of those who comprised it. The audience was sufficiently 'pro-

---

11 RT, p. 116.
12 RT, p. 117.
13 RT, p. 27. De Man, Paul, 'Hypogram and Inscription: Michael Riffaterre's Poetics of Reading', *Diacritics* 11:4, winter, 1981, pp. 17–35, reprinted as Chapter 3 in RT, pp. 27–53.
14 RT, p. 27.
15 RT, p. 116.

fessional' not to – indeed, it was 'contracted' not to. That's why we should be grateful to Stefano Rosso, a European and relative outsider in this respect, for going on to invite de Man to say something more about the 'frequent recurrence of the terms "ideology" and "politics" [that] we have noticed recently' and about the book with the '"mysterious" chapters on Kierkegaard and Marx' that he seems to have mentioned in his lectures, a book that, six months later, would gain the suggested title *Aesthetics, Rhetoric, Ideology*.[16]

Ideology and politics? 'I don't think I ever was away from these problems', he said, 'they were always uppermost in my mind. I have always maintained that one could approach the problems of ideology and by extension the problems of politics only on the basis of critical-linguistic analysis, which had to be done on its own terms, in the medium of language, and I felt I could approach those problems only after having achieved a certain control over those questions ... I feel now some control of a vocabulary and of a conceptual apparatus that can handle that. It was in working on Rousseau that I felt I was able to progress from purely linguistic analysis to questions which are really already of a political and ideological nature. So that I now feel [able] to do it a little more openly, though in a very different way to what generally passes as "critique of ideology" ... I just feel that one has to face therefore the difficulty of certain explicitly political texts'.[17]

We now know that de Man was planning to work on Kenneth Burke and Roland Barthes on the 'ideology of the body' and on the 'critique of religion and political ideology in Kierkegaard and Marx', (most likely) respectively.[18] Though, as will become clear in due course, de Man claims to have been involved in left politics as a student in the late 1930s, there is little in the essays he wrote in the United States that responds directly to the urgencies of contemporary politics, and certainly nothing that hints that he had anything other than a scholarly interest in the class conflict in capitalist society and the transition to Communism. Be that as it may, it is the case that, in those essays, there is much that evidences that ideology and politics were always on his mind and that, in them, he was moving towards the formulation of an ideology critique of his own. That this was so is somewhat obscured by the fact that de Man was always critical of the ideology critique of others, with the notable exception of that formulated by Marx and Engels. Moreover, heralding matter that will be

---

16   RT, pp. 20–1. Waters, 'Paul de Man: Life and Works', in CW, p. lxx.
17   RT, p. 121.
18   See de Man's letter to Lindsay Waters, 11 August 1983, in Waters, 'Paul de Man', CW, pp. lxix–lxx note 68, which refines the project as it had been articulated in conversation with Stefano Rosso, 4 March 1983, RT, p. 121.

considered at some length later, over a decade before he gave the Messenger Lectures, de Man had pointed to *The German Ideology* as the 'model text for all ideological demystification'. It was surely a reading of *The German Ideology* that would have made up a substantial part of the last chapter and theoretical conclusion of the projected *Aesthetics, Rhetoric, Ideology*.

This essay provides a kind of Guide for Beginners to de Man's interest in the writings of Marx and Engels and the problem of ideology (and politics): one that provides a record of reading undertaken mainly for my own benefit but which, here, might be read as an extended footnote to be added to some already published studies that touch on de Man's interest in what they refer to as 'historical materialism' or 'Marxism'.[19] Intended as exposition rather than critique, it proceeds discursively by peregrination and with some repetition (whereby, in Steinian manner, each repetition carries its own emphasis, in its own context, and points back to the whole from whence it came) and attends to most of the obvious references to Marx and Engels, 'Marxism', 'Marxist criticism' and 'Marxist thought' that can be read in the essays de Man wrote and published as a scholar in the United States. It tends to be generally uncritical with regard to the way that de Man read his chosen philosophical texts (especially those of Heidegger, Rousseau, Kant and Schiller), which has, anyway, already generated an amount of exemplary criticism.[20] Even so, it does occasionally engage with and supplement his reading of Marx, which has not.

De Man was of the opinion that his essays, when read in 'a roughly chronological sequence ... do not evolve in a manner that easily allows for dialectical progression or, ultimately, for historical totalization'.[21] With that observation taken as caution, though this essay takes a roughly chronological approach to reading the corpus of de Man's published writings, it aims neither to demonstrate a dialectical progression nor to formulate a historical totalisation. For that reason it's not interested in puzzling how much de Man might have known about Marx and Marxism during his years as a student and wartime journalist in Belgium before he left for the United States in 1948, at the age of twenty-seven. If it were, it would certainly take into account his writing for *Le Soir* and *Het Vlaamsche Land* and his relation with his uncle Henrik de Man and

---

19   Especially, of course, Warminski, 'Ending Up/Taking Back (with Two Postscripts on Paul de Man's Historical Materialism)' in Caruth and Esch (eds.) 1995, pp. 11–41, and Sprinker, 'Art and Ideology: Althusser and de Man' in Cohen, Tom, Barbara Cohen, J. Hillis Miller, Andrzej Warminski (eds.) 2001, pp. 32–48.
20   See, for example: Gasché, Rodolphe, 'In-Difference to Philosophy: de Man on Kant, Hegel, and Nietzsche' in Waters and Godzich (eds.) 1989, pp. 259–94; Loesberg 1977, pp. 87–108; Redfield 1990, pp. 50–70; and Stoekl 1985, pp. 36–45.
21   RR, p. viii.

Hendrik's politics in relation to the ideas of Marx and Marxism.[22] Nor does it contribute anything to clarify the character of the interest he showed in Marx and Marxism on his arrival in the United States while teaching at Bard College, New York, 1949–50 and the extent of his contacts with the New York Left intelligentsia at that time.[23] Nor does it tease out the implications of the peculiar remark in his letter of 6 June 1955, to Harry Levin, head of the Department of Comparative Literature at Harvard, that his 'interest' in the 'political' and his criticism of 'orthodox Marxism' was the result of 'the long and painful soul-searching' of someone who had 'come from the left and from the happy days of the Front populaire'.[24] Nor does it address directly that tendency in liberal

---

22   For an introduction to Hendrik de Man, see Dodge 1966. See also Dodge 1979. See Derrida 1988, pp. 604–05, on the relationship between Hendrik and Paul de Man.

23   This interest, and de Man's contact with New York's Left intelligentsia – including Dwight MacDonald, Mary McCarthy and Harold Rosenberg – while teaching at Bard College, is documented above in Chapter 4, 'Action, Revolution and Painting (Resumed)', footnote 65.

24   See Waters, 'Paul de Man', in CW, pp. lxv–lxvi at lxv. There is much that is puzzling in this letter, not least this remark. It can't refer to the Comintern directed shift of 1935 from the United Front to the Popular Front as such, which occurred when de Man was only 15 years old, and it is too strong a reference to refer to the Government of National Unity formed in Belgium by Paul van Zeeland also in 1935. Perhaps de Man is referring to the *Front populaire* – an alliance of left-wing political parties, radicals, socialists and communists – that came to government in France, June 1936–June 1937, under the leadership of Léon Blum. Confronted with internal dissensions brought about by the Spanish Civil War, persistent opposition from the French right and the effects of the Great Depression, the *Front populaire* dissolved itself in the autumn of 1938.

In 1937, de Man entered the École Polytechnique at the University of Brussels, where he studied engineering. In 1938, he transferred to the Université Libre de Bruxelles to study chemistry. Whilst studying at the École Polytechnique, he joined *Le Cercle du Libre Examen*, a left-wing student group at the Université Libre de Bruxelles, which was inaugurated in 1928 with the declared position as '*libre-exaministe* [free thinking], democratic, anti-clerical, anti-dogmatic, and anti-fascist'. He wrote for the group's journal, *Jeudi*, and, in 1939, joined the editorial board of its other publication, *Les Cahiers du Libre Examen*. Given that 'Popular Front' was the name of a Communist Party strategy that got attached to a wide variety of initiatives, it may be that de Man regarded the work of *Le Cercle du Libre Examen*, during the time of his association with it, as one of – or as aligned with any number of – those initiatives. With the declaration of the Nazi-Soviet pact of non-aggression and on the outbreak of war, *Le Cercle du Libre Examen* expelled its Soviet-affiliated students. *Les Cahiers du Libre Examen* ceased publication after Germany invaded Belgium in May 1940. In October 1940, de Man changed his degree programme from chemistry to the social sciences to read philosophy. In November 1940, the Gestapo interrogated de Man about his involvement with *Le Cercle du Libre Examen*, but no action was taken against him.

It should be noted that I say nothing in what follows about the complex matter of de Man's journalism for *Het Vlaamsche Land* and *Le Soir* during the Occupation. However,

or supposedly left academic literary criticism that reads the essays that de Man published whilst domiciled in the United States as positing 'the futility, the self-delusion, and the paralysis of political activity, especially oppositional political activity'.[25] Nor for that matter does it address head-on the reading that finds a 'steady, silent anti-Marxist polemic running throughout'[26] those essays or is under the impression that his thinking about Marxism changed 'a great deal in the three decades that separated his earliest from his final essays'.[27] The idea of a 'silent polemic' is difficult to grasp and, as will become clear in what follows, de Man's criticism of Marxism was both explicit and quite loud and forceful. More than that, it was consistent from the 1950s through the 1980s. In the way I read them, in his essays de Man makes and keeps to a distinction between the very general notions 'Marxism', 'Marxist criticism' and 'Marxist thought' and the writing of Marx and Engels specifically. De Man valued the writing of Marx and Engels and, almost certainly for that reason, was a severe critic when it was mutilated or totalized and made definitive as 'Marxism' or 'Marxist criticism' or 'Marxist thought'.

As to the reading that finds de Man's writing, especially the 'early essays', stacked not only 'against Marxism' but also 'against any form of critical thinking that would privilege history as the ultimate ground of interpretive method',[28] though it is the case that he never privileged history – that privilege would be

---

what's presented here, in this essay, with regard to how he read Marx and Engels would suggest that, after the war, that reading constituted a sustained self-critical engagement with the politics and ideology of the Third Reich. Saying this is not to excuse de Man. Rather, I am minded of something Gabriel Josipovici said in his review of Hugo Ott's far from dispassionate *Martin Heidegger: A Political Life*, *The Independent on Sunday*, 8 August 1993, p. 18: 'But my own feeling is that, while we should be pleasantly surprised when people who are clearly apolitical, such as Beckett, find that they are forced to make choices and choose to risk their lives fighting what they see as evil, we should hesitate to condemn those who may have acted reprehensively – for who is to say what we would have done in their place?'

25 Lentricchia 1983, p. 115. As far as Lentricchia is concerned the 'salient target' of de Man's writing, 1973–83, is 'political action and any philosophy (Marxism would be the chief offender) that insists on the potential efficacy of the fully engaged life'.

26 Eagleton, 'Capitalism, Modernism and Post-modernism', in Lodge (ed.) 1992, p. 390. See also: Eagleton 1983, p. 146, Eagleton 1984, pp. 100–4, and his later remarks in Eagleton 1990, espec. p. 10, where he finds in de Man's 'later writings ... a valuable, resourceful politics at work ... *pace* those left-wing critics for whom de Man is merely an unregenerate "formalist". But it is a politics bought at an enormous cost' to the 'potentially positive dimensions of the aesthetic in a way that perpetuates, if now in a wholly new style, his earlier hostility to an emancipatory politics'.

27 Norris 1988, p. 3.

28 Norris 1988, p. 5.

accorded to language, of course – neither did he ever deny 'history' or 'historical reality' as if they were nothing more than 'undecidable text'.[29] Rather, de Man held to a complex notion of 'history', which he derived from Heidegger (arguably his main theoretical resource in the 1950s and early 1960s), that distinguished between *Historie* (from the Greek *historein*, 'to enquire', 'to know'), the systematic study and accounting of past events, the assurance of recorded history, and *Geschichte* (from the German *geschehen*, 'to happen'), events or occurrences that happen and the historicity or historicality [*Geschichtlichkeit*] that pertains to what happens, the way that events happen in the world around us, in real life, to oneself and the people around us, decisive events, perhaps little noticed when they occurred and now unavailable to the backward look, whose effects we might still be living.[30] While there could be no *Historie* without *Geschichte*, *Geschichte* does not necessarily become part of *Historie*. Or, as Guy Debord put it, 'History has always existed, but not always in its historical form'.[31] Heidegger often deploys the term *Historie* disparagingly because, though it should, it doesn't ask about being, about what beings are: since *Dasein* – human existence (being there, the being of human individuals and the entity or person who is a human being-in-the-world) – is 'historical', its questioning about being is also historical: in asking about being we must also enquire into the history of asking about beings as such.[32]

De Man never confused 'history',[33] 'the reality of history',[34] 'the materiality of actual history',[35] or 'an *occurrence*, which has the materiality of something that actually happens, that actually occurs'[36] with the study of past events and the various narratives, interpretations and explanations, summations and totalisations that are made of them. Perhaps the clearest statement of his thinking about history and the insistence on the distinction between *Historie* and *Geschichte* was given during the course of the Messenger Lectures in response to a question as to whether he 'thought of history as a priori in any sense'.[37]

---

29 Eagleton 1983, p. 146.
30 A useful guide to these matters is provided by Inwood 1999, see 'historiology', pp. 90–2, 'history and historicity', 92–5, 'history of being', 95–7.
31 See Debord 2006, Thesis 125.
32 An accessible comprehensive introduction to Heidegger on the question of being can be read in Inwood 1999, see 'being: an introduction', pp. 26–8, *Being and Time*, pp. 28–31, 'being with others and being alongside things', pp. 31–3.
33 CW, p. 65; BI, p. 6.
34 RR, p. 18.
35 RR, p. 262.
36 AI, p. 132.
37 AI, p. 133.

De Man said that he thought of history not 'as a progression or a regression' but 'as an event, as an occurrence ... There is history from the ... moment things *happen*, there is *occurrence*, there is *event*. History is therefore not a temporal notion ... [it is] an emergence which is ... not itself either a dialectical movement or any kind of continuum that would be the case in a Hegelian dialectic, as a negation'.[38]

De Man arrived early at the view that one cannot 'know history in the same way that science knows its object'; such thinking is 'illusory'.[39] And though he thought that history, the 'vocabulary of change and movement as it applies to historical process', was 'mere metaphor', he did not think that it was 'devoid of meaning'. Rather, 'it was but without an objective correlative that can unambiguously be pointed to in empirical reality, as when we speak of a change in the weather or a change in a biological organism'.[40]

'Mere metaphor', then, but one not 'devoid of meaning'. Not only did de Man acknowledge the materiality of history (*Geschichte*) but also seems always to have held to the importance of and, indeed, the necessity of history as the study of past events (*Historie*) – though it 'ended up as a theory of reading', *Allegories of Reading*, his second book, as he himself said, 'started out as a historical study ... a historical reflection on Romanticism'.[41] He was not against history. Nor was he against historicism. As Lindsay Waters has pointed out, de Man 'was himself a historicist', though 'not ... the sort of historicist who thought an age could be reduced to a single quality'.[42] In 'The Inward Generation', published in *The Cambridge Review*, winter 1955, he wrote that he was opposed to that 'kind of nihilism' the essence of which took 'the form of antihistoricism':[43] this was a form of history in which, as Heidegger put it, 'there is nothing to being itself'.[44] In this early essay, 'the conceptualization of history ... together with poetry' is 'the main access kept open to the difficult and

---

38   Ibid. See also de Man's response to Tom Reinart's request to say more about his 'notion of historical events ... occurrences', in the discussion that followed the last Messenger Lecture, 'Conclusions: Walter Benjamin's "Task of the Translator"', RT, pp. 103–4 at 104: 'history as occurrence, as that which occurs, as events that occur ... As such, the occurrence can be textual ... Then there are, in the history of texts, texts which are occurrences'.
39   CW, p. 65.
40   BI, p. 6; RR, pp. viii–ix.
41   AR, p. ix.
42   Waters, 'Paul de Man', in CW, p. xxix.
43   CW, p. 15.
44   De Man's formulation draws on Heidegger's use of Nietzsche, see Inwood 1999, pp. 141–4. In 'The Inward Generation', CW, p. 15, de Man refers to 'nothingness' as 'a desire for serenity which tries to forget and repress the original anxiety' effected by the difference between Being and beings. 'Nothingness' is 'the most insidious and persistent form of nihilism'.

necessary question of being'.⁴⁵ A little earlier in the same year, in 'Tentation de la permanence', published in *Monde Nouveau*,⁴⁶ again following Heidegger, he said that he regarded 'the poetical act (in the general sense that includes all the arts) ... the quintessential historical act ... through which we become conscious of the divided character of our being, and consequently, of the necessity of fulfilling it, of accomplishing it in time, instead of undergoing it in eternity'.⁴⁷ The next year these ideas about history and poetry, the question of being – the ontological difference between Being (*Sein*) (which is not an entity) and (that-which-is an entity) being (*Seinde*) and *that* difference as it characterises the Being *of* being (the ontological difference that's installed or inheres in human existence, which we become aware of as *separation*)⁴⁸ – found their place in a relation of association with his thinking about Marx and Marxism.

All this has been by way of preliminary. We can now begin reading the way in which de Man read Marx ... and Engels.

'The Dead-End of Formalist Criticism' (1956)

In so far as we find it designated *as such* – rather than implied – in the essays published thus far, it seems that de Man's beginning with 'Marxist thought' and, indirectly, with Marx, can be located in the central section of his 1956 essay 'The Dead-End of Formalist Criticism' with its discussion of several passages in William Empson's *Seven Types of Ambiguity* and *Some Versions of Pastoral*.⁴⁹ De Man is especially interested in the latter, which, he observes, drawing on Heidegger, 'is all about separation and alienation, [and] places itself at the outset under the aegis of Marxism; a convergence confirmed by the apparent contradiction of the attraction exerted upon our generation by the problematic poetry and the solution of Marxism'.⁵⁰ Which is to say that, as de Man

---

45   CW, p. 15.
46   De Man, Paul, '*Tentation de la permanence*', *Monde Nouveau* 93, October 1955, pp. 49–61, translated by Don Latimer, 'The Temptation of Permanence', *Southern Humanities Review* 17:3, summer 1983, pp. 209–21, in CW, pp. 30–40.
47   CW, p. 33.
48   Inwood 1999, see 'being: an introduction', 26–8, and 'difference, ontological', pp. 46–9.
49   First published in *Critique*, June 1956, as '*Impasse de la critique formaliste*' and subsequently published in an English translation by Wlad Godzich in BI, 1975, pp. 229–45.
50   BI, p. 240. *The Communist Manifesto*, for example, 'speaks[s] to our heart like a poem ...' and has 'the power of a Beethoven symphony, urging us to become agents of a future that ends unnecessary mass suffering and inspire humanity to realise its potential for authentic freedom' – see Yanis Varoufakis's introduction to Karl Marx and Friedrich Engels, *The Communist Manifesto*, London: Vintage Books, 2018, vii–xxix at vii, viii.

reads it, a good deal of *Some Versions of Pastoral* is concerned with puzzling the lived separation of Being (*das Sein*) from beings (*das Seiendes*), not only in relation to and even as it effects the ways that human beings become alienated or estranged from themselves, from their productive activity and the products produced by it, from nature and from other human beings, but also in relation to Marx and Engels's materialist conception of history as the history of class struggles. A footnote added to the text at this point quotes a remark in Heidegger's 'Letter on Humanism' of 1947 – an essay on Marxism and action, existentialism and humanism, which Heidegger drafted in response to questions from Jean Beaufort about Jean-Paul Sartre – that 'confirms and sheds light on this encounter':

> the world's destiny is heralded in poetry, without yet becoming manifest in the history of Being ... Homelessness [*Heimatlosigkeit*, our lost or abandoned connection to being] is coming to be the destiny of the world. Hence it is necessary to think that destiny in terms of the history of Being. What Marx recognized in an essential and significant sense, though derived from Hegel, as the estrangement of man has its roots in the homelessness of modern man. This homelessness is specifically evoked from the destiny of Being in the form of metaphysics, and through metaphysics is simultaneously entrenched and covered up as such.[51]

---

51   BI, p. 240 note 17. This is taken not from Godzich's translation in BI but from Heidegger, Martin (1947), 'Letter on Humanism', translated by Frank A. Capuzzi and J. Glen Gray, in Heidegger 1993, p. 242, p. 243, which keeps to the distinction between 'homelessness' and 'estrangement' that Godzich loses by translating both as 'alienation'.

By way of glossing this paragraph we should note that destiny (*Geschick*) and history (*Geschichte*) are related. Destiny is the power that sends (*Schicht*) and so makes events or occurrences happen. In other words, destiny (*Geschick*) is the force that effects history (*Geschichte*). See also de Man, 'The Temptation of Permanence', *Critical Writings*, p. 34, where 'destiny' is 'movement' and 'history is the very movement of being, movement whose fundamental ambiguity is the origin of the historicity [*Geschichtlichkeit*] of our being' – which is to say, that destiny [*Geschick*] is the origin of what makes it possible for human beings to study their own history, to take history [*Geschicte*] as an object of history [*Historie*].

See Heidegger 1993, p. 242: 'Homelessness ... consists in the abandonment of Being. Homelessness is the symptom of oblivion of Being. Because of it the truth of Being remains unthought. The oblivion of Beings makes itself known indirectly through the fact that man always observes and handles only beings'.

'Homelessness' and 'alienation' are different but, like 'destiny' and 'history', related. See the passage quoted by de Man where 'alienation' has its roots – it is based in and is nourished by – 'homelessness'.

For Marx on estrangement and alienation (*Entfremdung* or, according to the context

So, de Man's interest in Marx and Marxism, as it begins in published discourse, is informed by his interest in Heidegger's ideas about poetry (*Dichtung*) and history (*Geschichte*) – that is: 'the poetical act ... the quintessential historical act through which we become conscious of the divided character of our being'[52] and Heidegger's own interest in Marx and Marxism, especially the question of being and not-being-at-home, of not feeling 'at home', in relation to alienation or estrangement and modernity. We'll return to this footnote and what it quotes – and doesn't quote – from Heidegger's 'Letter' in a moment. Here, for the purposes of going on, we need only register, in 'The Dead-End of Formalist Criticism', the Heideggerian connotation of 'separation' as an event of Being and the Marxist connotation of 'alienation' as the relationship in which man stands to himself, which is to say alienation as an event of that-which-is-human being separated from the system of production whose product is separation itself.[53]

---

of use, *Entäusserung, Entwirklichung, Versäusserung*) see the *Philosophical Manuscripts of 1844*, First Manuscript, MECW 3, pp. 270–82, and re. Hegel's *Phenomenology* and *Logic*, Third Manuscript, pp. 326–46. Man becomes alienated or estranged from himself when the product of his practical activity appears to him 'as an alien object exercising power over him', and when the 'relation of labour to the *act of production* within the *labour* process' appears not as belonging to him as the objective, given aspect of his subjectivity, but 'as an alien activity not belonging to him'. Since man has a 'species-essence' (*Gattungswessen*) or, as it is also translated, 'species-being', he also alienates or estranges himself from his essence as a human being and from other men, his community.

Man has a species-essence or species-being because unlike 'The animal [which] is immediately one with their life activity' and 'does not distinguish itself from it. It is *its life activity*. Man makes his life activity the object of his will and of his consciousness. He has conscious life activity. It is not a determination with which he directly merges. Conscious life activity distinguishes man immediately from animal life activity. It is just because of this that he is a species-being. Or it is only because he is a species-being that he is a conscious being, i.e., that his own life is an object for him. Only because of that is his activity free activity. Estranged labour reverses this relationship, so that it is just because man is a conscious being that he makes his life activity, his *essential being*, a mere means to *existence*' (MECW 3, p. 276).

In 1845 Marx began to abandon the idea of 'species-essence' or 'species-being' by way of rejecting Feuerbach's idea of '*human* essence' [*menschliche Wesen*]. Thesis 6 of the original *Theses on Feuerbach* asserts that 'the essence of man is no abstraction inherent in each single individual ... an inner, mute, general character which unites the many individuals *in a natural way*' but is 'in its reality ... the ensemble of the social relations' – see Marx, *Theses on Feuerbach*, Thesis 6, in MECW 5, pp. 6–7.

Though Marx continues to develop the notion of alienation from *The German Ideology* (1845–6) through *Capital* 1 (1867), he abandons the idea of 'species-being' or 'species-essence'.

52 CW, p. 33.
53 See Debord 2006, Thesis 27.

De Man begins his discussion of Empson – 'a poet in his own right, and, moreover, a reader of great acuity' – by focussing on the first of the *Seven Types of Ambiguity* and Empson's analysis of the fourth line of Shakespeare's Sonnet 73 in which old age is metaphorised as 'a forest in winter' and likened to 'Bare ruin'd choirs, where late the sweet birds sang'. Empson takes this as an example of the simplest type of ambiguity, 'where one thing is said to be like another and they have several different properties in virtue of which they are alike'; this is an ambiguity which occurs when a word, syntax or grammatical structure, 'while making only one statement, is effective in several ways at once'.[54] After discussing the eight or so experiences that are brought to mind by Shakespeare's forest and ecclesiastical ruins and 'not knowing which of them to hold most clearly in mind', Empson concludes that 'the machinations of ambiguity are among the very roots of poetry ... and almost everything of literary importance'.[55] From this, nudging Empson towards Heidegger's idea that 'The poetic work speaks out of an ambiguous ambiguousness [*zweideutigen Zweideutigkeit*]' that is 'determined by poetry's innermost site',[56] de Man takes the idea that Empson is arguing that 'a fundamental ambiguity is constitutive of all poetry. The correspondence between the initial experience [of the author] and the reader's own [which, because ambiguous ambiguousness renders meaning thoroughly unstable and enables "an infinity of valid readings"] remains forever problematic because poetry sets particular beings in a world yet to be constituted, as a task to fulfill'.[57]

De Man finds confirmation that this is, indeed, what Empson is arguing in chapter seven, the penultimate chapter of *Seven Types of Ambiguity*, and Empson's commentary on George Herbert's 'The Sacrifice', a monologue uttered by Christ on the Cross with the refrain 'Was ever grief like mine?' Here, in Empson's reading of Herbert's poem, Christ is 'scapegoat and tragic hero; loved because hated; hated because godlike; freeing from torture because tortured; torturing his torturers because all-merciful; source of all strength to men because by accepting he exaggerates their weakness; and, because outcast, creating the possibility of society'.[58] Empson concludes that, in 'The Sacrifice', Herbert 'deals ... with the most complicated and deeply-rooted notion of the

---

54   Empson 1947, pp. 2–3.
55   Empson 1947, p. 3.
56   See Heidegger, 'Language in the Poem. A Discussion of Georg Trakl's Poetic Work', first published in *Merkur* 61, 1953, under the title '*Georg Trakl. Eine Erörterung seines Gedichte*', in Heidegger 1959, p. 192.
57   BI, p. 236.
58   Empson 1947, pp. 294–5.

human mind' and uses the poem to illustrate 'the most ambiguous [type of ambiguity] that can be conceived' in which 'the two meanings of the word, the two values of the ambiguity, are the two opposite meanings defined by the context, so that the total effect is to show a fundamental division in the writer's mind'.[59] It's here, as de Man reads him, that Empson, with this seventh type of ambiguity, glimpses that 'true poetic ambiguity proceeds from the deep division of Being itself, and poetry does no more than repeat this division'.[60]

At which juncture, de Man abandons 'The Sacrifice' and Empson's analysis of it to pick up the reference to 'sorrow' in the refrain's source in Lamentations of Jeremiah, 1.12 – reprising something of what he'd said in 'The Temptation of Permanence' with regard to the poetical act – and conclude that the 'fundamental ambiguity' enunciated by poetry is that which 'prevails between the world of the spirit and the world of sentient substance: to ground itself, the spirit must turn itself into sentient substance, but the latter is knowable only in its dissolution into nonbeing. The spirit cannot coincide with its object and this separation is infinitely sorrowful'.[61] In other words, the fundamental ambiguity of which poetry speaks is not only that of Heidegger's ontological difference but also that of Hegel's Unhappy Consciousness in *Phenomenology of Spirit* where 'the consciousness of self' cannot accept that its 'essential nature', rather than being a 'not yet ... unity', is that of a 'dual-natured, merely contradictory being'.[62]

Having associated the ambiguity of poetic or figurative language with the separation of Being from being and situated it in a relation of association with Hegel's Unhappy Consciousness, de Man turns away from Empson's *Seven Types of Ambiguity* back to *Some Versions of Pastoral*, specifically to its central chapter on Marvell's 'The Garden' and to the poem's central strophe, which de Man edits to bring more into line with the Unhappy Consciousness:

> The Mind, that Ocean where each kind
> Does straight its own resemblance find;
> Yet it creates, transcending these,
> Far other worlds, and other Seas,
> Annihilating all that's made
> To a green thought in a green shade.[63]

---

59   Empson 1947, pp. 286–95, p. 244.
60   BI, p. 237.
61   Ibid.
62   Hegel 1977, p. 126: 207.
63   BI, p. 239. De Man omits the volta: 'Meanwhile the mind, from pleasure less, Withdraws into its happiness'.

Perception and creation, conscious and unconscious states, intuitive and intellectual modes of apprehension, the whole material world and nothing material: the point of the poem, says Empson, is 'not that these ... are essentially different but that they must cease to be different if either is to be known'.[64] The passage, says de Man, 'names the very problem' with which *Seven Types of Ambiguity* ended and which defines 'the dialectical armature of ... what Empson calls the pastoral convention': namely, 'the contradictory relations between natural being and the being of consciousness'.[65] In de Man's reading, Empson's *Pastoral* is not so much a genre study as 'an ontology of the poetic ... wrapped ... in ... extraneous matter that may well conceal the essential'.[66]

To round off his discussion of Empson, de Man considers the *Pastoral*'s first chapter, 'Proletarian Literature'. While not making it clear that Empson is 'not trying to say anything about ... politics and economics, only that they do not provide an aesthetic theory',[67] de Man says that this chapter concludes, paradoxically, that Marxist thought is pastoral thought disguised:

> Marxism draws its attractiveness from the reconciliation it promises, in all sincerity to be sure, but with a naive prematurity. 'I do not mean to say', writes Empson, 'that the [Marxist] philosophy [that Man can be made One with Nature, One with the Many, especially in their social aspects] is wrong; for that matter pastoral is worked from the same philosophical ideas as proletarian literature – the difference is that it brings in the absolute less prematurely'.[68]

To which de Man provides the gloss:

> The pastoral problematic, which turns out to be the problematic of Being itself, is lived in our day by Marxist thought, as by any genuine thought. In motivation, if not in its claims, Marxism is, ultimately, a poetic thought that lacks the patience to pursue its own conclusions to their end.[69]

In other words, Marxist thought – 'genuine thought' – is poetic thought because its concern with alienation or estrangement, as the condition of man's lived

---

64 Empson 1935, p. 119.
65 BI, pp. 239, 238.
66 BI, p. 239.
67 Empson 1935, p. 23.
68 BI, p. 240. Empson 1935, pp. 21–2, p. 23.
69 BI, p. 240.

existence, and the way it conceptualises history, registers or is marked by, and so keeps open, the problem of separation or 'the deep division of Being itself'. Yet despite its being 'poetic thought' or of the order of a 'poetic act', Marxist thought is not 'historical' – it's not a 'quintessential historical act' – for, though through it we become conscious of the divided character of being, 'it is bound to the necessity of a reconciliation scheduled to occur at the end of a linear development, and its dialectical movement does not include time [the difference between Being and being and the ontological difference that inheres in the human being as a constant presence] itself as one of its terms. A truly historical poetics would attempt to think the divide in truly temporal dimensions instead of imposing upon it cyclical or eternalist schemata of a spatial nature'.[70]

As far as de Man is concerned, the 'solution of Marxism' depends on holding to a teleological view of history, a mechanics of progress moving towards an inevitable reconciliation of man to his activity and the results or objects produced by it, of man to nature and other human beings, and of man to himself and his possibilities, whereby man will be rescued from his alienation or estrangement in and by the inevitable radical negation of class rule in that 'world yet to be constituted'. Though it allows access to the question of being, of man's being in relation to beings, it takes no account of ontological difference or of the different 'times' that pertain to Being and that-which-is-human being, Being and being-in-the-world – what Heidegger referred to as the *temporality* of the former (which has nothing to do with our everyday experience of past, present and future but is a metaphysical problem, 'the explicit philosophical problem of being, understood in the light of time') and the *timeliness* of the latter (which is our everyday experience of time, 'of (being) on time, in (good) time, at the right time').[71]

Was ever grief like mine? The kind of unspecified Marxist criticism or Marxist thinking that de Man has in mind doesn't recognise, as a 'truly historical poetics' would recognise – and which, according to Heidegger, Marx does recognise – that 'the social forms of separation derive from ontological and metasocial attitudes' and that history is 'but the *sorrowful time of patience*':[72] it doesn't understand that 'the problem of separation inheres in Being'[73] and that alienation as an event of that-which-is-human being proceeds from separation as an event of being. In facing up to this problem, Empson, in his *Pastoral*,

---

70   BI, p. 242.
71   Inwood 1999, see 'time, temporality and timeliness', pp. 220–22, and Polt 1999, p. 111.
72   BI, p. 245.
73   BI, p. 240.

posits a 'warning against certain Marxist illusions',[74] like – the example is de Man's not Empson's – the two 'myths' in Roland Barthes's *Writing Degree Zero*: first, the myth that writing was once, in Classicism/Hellenic Greece, 'a genuinely univocal form';[75] and second, 'the future myth of a "new Adamic world where language would no longer be alienated"' and so would not 'institute a torn condition for the writer'[76] or, as Barthes actually puts it in *Writing Degree Zero*, would not create 'a situation fraught with conflict'.[77] The two myths are related: the first is based in a 'nostalgic envy' or 'naive belief that the Greeks were identical with the image projected by their sculpture'; the second is that, at some time in the future, 'fallen man' will regain the relationship in which he stood to himself in the 'lost Garden of Eden'.[78]

As Barthes explains it, writing at the zero degree is

> writing, freed from all bondage to a pre-ordained state of language ... beyond Literature ... far from living languages and from literary language proper. This transparent form of speech ... a style of absence which is almost an ideal absence of style; writing ... reduced to a sort of negative mood in which the social or mythical characters of a language are abolished in favour of a neutral and inert state of form; thus remains wholly responsible, without being overlaid by a secondary commitment of form to a History not its own ... neutral writing in fact rediscovers the primary condition of classical art: instrumentality. But this time, form as an instru-

---

74 Ibid.
75 BI, p. 241.
76 BI, p. 241.
77 De Man is quoting and then misquoting Barthes 1967, p. 88 and p. 83. The recourse to Barthes's idea of 'myth' is permitted by Empson's use of 'myth' in *Some Versions of Pastoral*, see for example, the discussion in Chapter 1, 'Proletarian Literature', pp. 16–18. It was in *Writing Degree Zero* that Barthes first introduced his extended notion of myth, which he further developed in the essays published in 1957 as *Mythologies*, Paris: Les Lettres nouvelles, and then published in translation in Barthes 1972. See 'Myth Today' in Barthes 1972, p. 134: 'Literature is an undoubted mythical system: there is a signifier, which is this same discourse as form or writing; there is the signified, which is the concept of literature; there is signification, which is the literary discourse. I began to discuss this problem in *Writing Degree Zero*, which was, all told, nothing but a mythology of literary language. There I defined writing as the signifier of the literary myth, that is, as a form which is already filled with meaning and which receives from the concept of literature a new signification'. From here on, Barthes's notion of 'myth' provided de Man with a useful resource for theorising the relation between the referential function of language and ideology. De Man's view of the strengths and weaknesses of both *Writing Degree Zero* and *Mythologies* will be discussed above in due course.
78 See de Man, 'The Literature of Nihilism', in CW, p. 169.

ment is no longer at the service of a triumphant ideology; it is the mode of a new situation of the writer, the way a certain silence has of existing; it deliberately forgoes any elegance or ornament, for these two dimensions would reintroduce Time into writing, and this is a derivative power which sustains History.[79]

In the very last line of *Writing Degree Zero* 'Literature becomes the Utopia of language [*langage*]'.[80] De Man's criticism here is that to posit such a reconciliation of man to his own activity or, strictly speaking, of man to language, as Barthes does, is to fall 'into all the traps of impatient "pastoral" thought: formalism, false historicism, and utopianism'.[81] Language regains or returns to its beginnings by negating style, which is to say by achieving the perfect style of negation. Barthes's Utopianism in *Writing Degree Zero* owes much to his commitment to Marxism, such as it was, and to his (mis)reading of Marx whose thinking offers us no known future ahead of time, and, as we will see in due course, certainly not one of linguistic Utopia. I have to say, then, that if de Man's criticism were directed at Marx's own writing rather than at what Sartre called 'lazy Marxism', 'Marxist criticism' or 'Marxist thought' generally, or such 'Marxist illusions' as de Man finds evidenced in Barthes's *Writing Degree Zero*, one would have to take issue with it, for what is *The German Ideology* if not an extended polemic against formalism, false historicism and Utopianism? That de Man's criticism is not aimed at Marx himself is perhaps suggested by some more remarks in the footnote quoting from Heidegger's 'Letter on Humanism'. Though these could be read as Heidegger eliding the distinction between Marx's conceptualisation of history and how it was appropriated by Marxists, his point is clear enough: It is 'because Marx by experiencing estrangement attains an essential dimension of history [*Geschichte*], that the Marxist view of history [*Geschichte*] is superior to other historical accounts [*Historie*]':[82] superior because it viewed history in terms of alienation and estrangement and kept open the question of Being, even if, to de Man's way of thinking, following Empson, it brings in the 'absolute ... prematurely'.[83]

---

79   Barthes 1967, pp. 77–8.
80   Barthes 1967, p. 88.
81   BI, p. 241. A kind of caveat regarding this criticism can be found in de Man's 'The Resistance to Theory', RT, p. 9, where Barthes 'speaks eloquently of the writer's quest for a perfect coincidence of phonic properties of a word with its signifying function'.
82   BI, p. 240 note 17. This translation is taken from Heidegger 1993, p. 243 – for the original see, Heidegger 1967, p. 170. Godzich's translation in BI elides the crucial distinction between *Geschichte* and *Historie* in Heidegger's German.
83   BI, p. 240.

It is not surprising then, in what follows on from these remarks quoted by de Man, that Heidegger also makes clear how very important he thought it was to engage with Marx's materialist conception of history specifically and Marxism generally: 'But since neither Husserl nor – so far as I have seen till now – Sartre recognizes the essential importance of the historical [*Geschichtlichen*] in Being, neither phenomenology nor existentialism enters that dimension within which a productive dialogue with Marxism first becomes possible. For such a dialogue it is certainly necessary to free oneself from naive notions about materialism, as well as from the cheap refutations that are supposed to counter it. The essence of materialism does not consist in the assertion that everything is simply matter but rather in a metaphysical determination according to which every being appears as the material of labour'.[84]

---

84 Heidegger 1993, p. 243. Though the differences between them are considerable, Marx and Heidegger are similar in as much as the former rejected every supra-historical schema, especially the 'historico-philosophical theory of the general path of development prescribed by fate to all nations' that was often attributed to him (see Marx to the editorial board *Otechestvennye Zapiski*, November 1877, in Marx and Engels 1975, pp. 293–4), and the latter rejected the idea of history as a supra-temporality – 'neither that which has happened just once for all nor something universal that floats above it' (see Heidegger, 1992, *Being and Time*, p. 447) – rather than a way of being, a being towards death, the certainty of death and the uncertainty of when it will occur (see Inwood 1993, pp. 44–6). Neither the historicality of labour, the process of production and class conflict nor Being exists in time. They are both determined by what attaches to time: the temporal properties of, for Marx, production and circulation: labour-time (see Marx 1973, p. 613, and Marx 1976, p. 129, p. 325, p. 435 and Marx 1992, pp. 225–6, 316); production-time (see Marx 1992, p. 124, p. 127, pp. 200–1); and circulation-time (see Marx 1973, p. 538, p. 539, and Marx 1992, p. 204, p. 207, p. 233).

For a brief discussion of the similarities and differences between Marx and Heidegger see Bensaïd 2002, ch. 3, 'A New Appreciation of Time', pp. 81–6.

With regard to Heidegger's 'productive dialogue with Marxism', it is, of course, important to note that Marx and Engels, jointly, do not think about the problem of being with regard to the difference between Being and beings. 'Being' [*Sein*], in as much as they have recourse to it, usually refers to the sum of man's forms of material activity and material intercourse; see, for example, in *The German Ideology*, MECW, 5, p. 36, where they write that 'Consciousness [*das Bewusstsein*] can never be anything else but conscious being [*das bewusste Sein*], and the being [*Sein*] of men is their actual life process'. Nevertheless, there is matter in Marx and Engels that seems to enable that dialogue. For example, *The German Ideology*, The Leipzig Council, III. Saint Max 2, 'Apologetical Commentary', MECW 5, p. 449, in the use of this quotation from Ludwig Feuerbach, *Grundsätze de Philosophie der Zukunft* (*Principles of the Philosophy of the Future*), Zürich and Winterthur: Literarische Comptoir, 1843, p. 49, there is a clear acknowledgement of the problem of being – though, it has to be pointed out, *not* alienation (about which more later) – as a problem of language:

Being [*Das Sein*], based on sheer inexpressibles [*Unsagbarkeiten*], is therefore itself something inexpressible [*Unsagbares*]. Yes, the inexpressible [*Unsagbare*]. Where

Perhaps it was Heidegger's remark that neither phenomenology nor existentialism had entered into 'a productive dialogue with Marxism' that prompted or stimulated de Man's own mature dialogue with Marxism and 'materialism'. That possibility aside, Heidegger's implication is clear enough: Marx's own notion of materialism was anything but 'naive'. Nor, it has to be said, was de Man's, especially as he developed it in the late 1970s and 1980s it comes to encompass not only the 'materiality of actual history' but also 'the literal and material aspects of language',[85] 'the materiality of inscription',[86] 'the material inscription of names',[87] and the 'prosaic materiality of the letter'.[88] There are

> words end, only there does life begin, only there can the secret of being [*das Gaeheimnis des Seins*] be deduced.
> This quotation is used against Max Stirner who, in *Der Einzige und sein Eigenthum* (familiar in the English translation of 1907 as, somewhat misleadingly, *The Ego and Its Own*), Leipzig: Wigand, 1845, thinks that with the word 'Unique' [*Einzige*] 'he has found the transition from the expressible to the inexpressible', a word 'which is simultaneously more and less than a word'. (There will be more on this passage and Marx and Engels's argument with Stirner later in the body of the text above.)
> Moreover, on one occasion, in an always-overlooked passage in Engels 1976 [1878], *Anti-Dühring* (*Herr Eugen Dühring's Revolution in Science*), pp. 51–5, Engels – always of a more philosophical bent than Marx – came close to puzzling the problem of ontological difference. In the first part of *Anti-Dühring*, 'Philosophy', Section 4 'World Schematism', he takes issue with Dühring's tautology that 'All-embracing being [*Sein*] is *one*', that 'being embraces everything', that 'there is nothing outside it', and that being corresponds to the concept of being. Engels observes that 'when we speak of *being* [*Sein*], and *purely* of being, unity can only consist in this, that all the objects to which we are referring – *are*, exist'. Even so, although 'being is common to all ... things', these things are not all the same; they do not exist in an equal manner, 'some being white and the others black, some being animate and the others inanimate, some being perhaps here below and the others perhaps beyond'. Engels then reasons, 'The unity of the world [which "consists in its materiality"] does not consist in its being, although its being is a precondition of its unity, since it must surely first *be* before it can be *one*'. At which point (Engels 1976, p. 54), Engels breaks off and returns to his argument with Dühring. 'Being', he says, 'is an open question beyond the point where our sphere of observation ends'.
> One could hypothesise that Marx, himself, might also have considered the difference between Being and being to be 'an open question'. If he had disagreed with Engels here he would surely have corrected him – Engels *read* the whole of *Anti-Dühring* to Marx before it was published and Marx, himself, contributed the last chapter of Part II on 'Political Economy': see Engels 1976, p. 9.
> As we will see, de Man read Engels's *Anti-Dühring* quite closely, though it is not clear whether he had read it by 1956 when he wrote 'The Dead-End of Formalist Criticism'.

85 'Shelley Disfigured', RR, p. 113.
86 'Hypogram and Inscription', RT, p. 51.
87 'Sign and Symbol in Hegel's *Aesthetics*', AI, p. 102.
88 'Phenomenality and Materiality in Kant', AI, p. 90, and 'Conclusions: Walter Benjamin's "The Task of the Translator"', RT, p. 90.

also materialities that, like the ability to see, are 'purely material'[89] or, like 'the materiality of the mind or of time or the carillon', exist only in the figure of prosopopeia, which is to say in 'the materiality of inscription'.[90]

A moment ago, I said that the references in 'The Dead-End of Formalist Criticism' evidence the beginning of de Man's mature interest in Marx and Marxist thought as it might be identified in the published essays. We need to keep in mind, however, that a beginning is an event or occurrence (*Geschichte*) that has always already happened before it is identified and appropriated by that mode of inquiry, interpretation and explanation that constitutes history (*Historie*);[91] at which point, of course, it becomes, in a sense ahistorical. It's not without interest, then, ahistorically, that more than a quarter-century later, at the moment he was 'facing the difficulty of certain explicitly political texts', and in all probability about to work on Marx and Engels's *The German Ideology*, de Man mentioned to Stefano Rosso that he was 'returning to certain aspects

---

89 'Phenomenality and Materiality in Kant', AI, p. 83.
90 'Hypogram and Inscription', RT, p. 51. I note, for whatever use may be made of it, that, in the 1920s, the Soviet, anti-Stalinist linguistic V.N. Volosinov in his 1929 *Marxism and the Philosophy of Language* – see Volosinov 1986, Part I: chs. 1–2 *passim* – in terms not dissimilar to (but not the same as) those that would become associated with de Man, had puzzled the relations between the 'semiotic material of inner speech', of the 'inner world', the 'inner life ... of consciousness' and the 'material embodiment' or 'material reality of the sign', of the 'material of the word', the 'verbal sign', 'facial expression', the 'movement of the body', etc. – the 'inner sign' ('psyche', 'experience') and the 'outer sign' ('ideology').

Matejka points out in his 'Appendix 1. On the First Russian Prolegomena to Semiotics' to Volosinov 1986, p. 164, that, in summary, Volosinov insists that: 1 'Ideology may not be divorced from the material reality of sign (i.e., by locating it in the "consciousness" or other vague and elusive regions)'; 2 'Sign may not be divorced from the concrete forms of social intercourse'; 3 'Communication and the forms of communication may not be divorced from their material basis'.

Fredric Jameson, in his review of *Marxism and the Philosophy of Language*, *Style*, 8, 3, fall 1974, p. 535, described it as 'the best general introduction to linguistic study as a whole'. Whether he agreed with Jameson or not, de Man was probably also aware of Volosinov's book from its publication in translation in 1973 and that Volosinov may have been the pen name of the literary critic Mikhail Bakhtin whose work is the subject of de Man's 'Dialogue and Dialogism', in RT, pp. 106–14 at p. 109; this essay was first published as 'Reference and Fictionality' in *Poetics Today*, 4, 1, 1983 and contains material that had its first airing at an MLA Forum on 'Fiction and Its Referents' in 1981.

91 For example, de Man's discussion of Empson in 'The Dead-End of Formalist Criticism' is itself a return to, and a development and recasting of, what he had previously said – with reference to Romanticism and 'the present-day state of mind', though not with reference to Marx and Marxism – about ambiguity, political and aesthetic beliefs, Hegel's Unhappy Consciousness, the separation between man's inner consciousness and the totality of what he is not, the difficult and necessary question of Being, Heidegger and history, in his essay 'The Inward Generation', CW, pp. 14–16.

of Heidegger' and recalled how much the 'Letter on Humanism' had been discussed, not least, presumably, in his own intellectual circle in Belgium, when it was first published in 1947, a year before he quit Europe for the United States of America.[92]

'Georg Lukács's "Theory of the Novel"' (1966)

Ten years later, in a conference paper that was subsequently published as 'Georg Lukács's "Theory of the Novel"', de Man resumed his thinking about alienation. This time he approached the concept by way of the two 'myths' he'd identified at work in Barthes's *Writing Degree Zero*: that, in some mythic Edenic future, the human being will come to repossess a truly univocal form of language and so overcome the lost unity between itself and its world.[93]

Contrary to what he took as the then conventional wisdom which, especially in the United States, found a lack of continuity between Lukács's early pre-Marxist work and his Marxist work, de Man finds there an important continuity, a consistency that links the pre-Marxist 'The Theory of the Novel' (1914–15) and the Marxist *History and Class Consciousness* (1923). Lukács's concern with alienation provides that consistency and continuity. However, though it may be 'reassuring' for many American academics (subject, like the American public generally, to manufactured consent to the belief that Marxism means or equates to Soviet Communism) to assume it, de Man says, not everything that is '*evil* [emphasis added] in the later Lukács came in as the result of his Marxist conversion'.[94] The concern with 'alienation' is also there in the early 'The Theory of the Novel'. And as we encounter the concept in the later *History and Class Consciousness*, as de Man realises and Lukács came to realise, its meaning is, even then, somewhat removed from the meaning it had for Marx.[95]

De Man quotes this passage from Lukács's 'The Theory of the Novel':

> The epic individual, the hero of the novel, originates in the alienation from the outside world. As long as the world is inwardly one, no real qual-

---

92   RT, pp. 119, 121.
93   BI, pp. 51, 54, 55.
94   BI, p. 51.
95   Lukács's self-acknowledged confusion in *History and Class Consciousness* with regard to Marx's notion of 'alienation' and the impact that, in 1930, his reading of Marx's then newly deciphered but not yet published *Economic and Philosophical Manuscripts* had on his thinking, can be read in Lukács 1971, p. xxxi.

itative distinctions occur among its inhabitants; they may well be heroes and scoundrels, worthy men and criminals, but the greatest hero only rises by a head's length above his fellow-men, and the noble words of the wise can be understood even by the fools. The autonomy of inwardness becomes possible and necessary only when the differences between men have grown to be an unbreachable gap; when the gods have grown silent and no sacrifice or prayer is capable of loosening their tongues; when the world of action loses contact with that of the self, leaving man empty and powerless, unable to grasp the real meaning of his deeds ...: when inwardness and adventure are forever distinct.[96]

Since alienated man cannot fulfil himself in actual unity with the world, he craves, instead, to transcend it in consciousness, in retrieving an experience of harmonious unity that he associates with the Greek ideal and 'the blessed times ... when the fire that burns in our souls is of the same substance as the fire of the stars'.[97]

The pre-Marxist Lukács might well be theorising the novel with regard to alienation, but, in as much as alienation is one of the 'evils' that characterises Marxism generally and the Marxist Lukács specifically, the evil, in this instance, as de Man observes, is that Lukács is 'much closer ... to Schiller than to Marx'.[98] In other words, Lukács's thinking in the 'Theory of the Novel' is much closer to Schiller's thinking in 'Letters on the Aesthetic Education of Man' (1794–95) and 'On Naive and Sentimental Poetry' (1795–76) – where 'aesthetic education' is the most productive response to alienation – than to the youthful Marx's in the *Economic and Philosophic Manuscripts* and *The German Ideology* – where alienation becomes 'an "unendurable" power, i.e., a power against which men make a revolution'.[99]

Before we leave 'Georg Lukács's "Theory of the Novel"', it's worth noting another difference between Lukács and Marx, one that de Man might not have been aware or, if aware, chose not to make explicit. De Man draws attention to the way that Lukács uses the 'idealized fiction' of man's 'unity with the world' in a mythical ancient Greece 'to state a theory of consciousness that has the struc-

---

96   BI, p. 54.
97   BI, p. 54.
98   Ibid. Redfield 1990, pp. 50–70, provides an interesting critical engagement with de Man's reading of Schiller.
99   See Marx, *Economic and Philosophical Manuscripts of 1844*, MECW 3, pp. 296–97, and Marx and Engels, *The German Ideology*, in MECW 5, p. 48.

ture of an intentional movement', one that 'implies a presupposition about the nature of historical time'.[100] Lukács, says de Man, holds to a 'linear conception of time' or a 'reified idea of temporality' and so narrates 'the development of the novel as a continuous event, as the fallen form of the archetypal Greek epic'.[101] The point I add here is that, in 'The Theory of the Novel', Lukács's notion of historical time and the novel's relation to the art of Hellenic Greece are quite unlike Marx's notion of historical time and the way he historicised the relation of the nineteenth-century novel to the Greek *epos* and the Greek *epos* to the nineteenth century. Marx, as de Man knew, held to a nonlinear conception of time and narrates the historical process as constituted by different moments of production and circulation, cycles and turnovers, moments of interruption and rupture. However, de Man may not have known or chose not to mention that, in the *Grundrisse*, Marx discusses the ways that 'the Greek arts and epic are bound up with certain forms of social development' and concludes that the Greek *epos* 'can no longer be produced in their world epoch-making, classical stature' because they presuppose an undeveloped stage of society, a particular division of labour and certain social conditions, certain forms of social development and imagination, and so on, which have vanished and can never return.[102] Marx thought it relatively easy to grasp how 'the Greek arts and epic are bound up with certain forms of social development'.[103] The difficulty that they presented to understanding was that 'they still afford us artistic pleasure and that in *a certain respect* [emphasis added: he doesn't tell us in what respect] they count as a norm and as an unattainable model'.[104] It should be pointed out, however, that the pre-Marxist Lukács, when he penned 'The Theory of the Novel', would not have known of the *Grundrisse*, which remained unpublished until it was issued in German and in two volumes, in 1939 and 1941 respectively, under the editorship of the Marx-Engels-Lenin Institute, Moscow.[105]

---

100 BI, pp. 54–5.
101 BI, pp. 58–9.
102 Marx 1973, pp. 110–11.
103 Marx 1973, p. 111.
104 Marx 1973, p. 111.
105 Dietz Verlag, Berlin, published a second German edition in one volume, minus illustrations and facsimiles, in 1953.

'The Contemporary Criticism of Romanticism' (1967)

In the spring of 1967 de Man gave the Christian Gauss Seminar at Princeton University under the general title 'Romanticism and Contemporary Criticism', six lectures that all, in one way or another, dealt with Romanticism as a 'truly historical consciousness'.[106]

The first lecture, 'The Contemporary Criticism of Romanticism',[107] focuses on the 'antiromantic overtones' implied in 'certain recent developments in French criticism', especially in the work of those critics 'that have been most strongly attracted to structuralism', namely Roland Barthes and René Girard.[108] It's in this lecture that de Man, who previously had thought about Marx in relation to Heidegger and alienation in relation to the separation between Being and beings, begins to engage directly and openly with the question of ideology in terms suggestive of Marx and Engels. Though Barthes, whose essay 'Myth Today' will be an always present resource in de Man's thinking about ideology and to whose work on ideology he was planning to return in *Aesthetics, Rhetoric, Ideology*,[109] is very much an active presence here, de Man takes Girard's *Mensonge romantique et vérité romanesque* of 1961 as evidencing most clearly the then most recent antiromantic trend in writing about Romanticism.[110]

Mensonge romantique et vérité romanesque is a study of desire as it is represented in the novels of Cervantes, Flaubert, Stendhal, Proust and Dostoevsky. This desire is neither spontaneous nor direct but mediated by an Other. Girard uses the terms 'romantic' and 'romanesque' to signify 'an essential, yet elusive, difference' between novels that 'passively reflect the presence of a mediator without ever revealing it' and novels that 'actively reveal' the mediator.[111] Since

---

106 RCC, pp. vii, 97.
107 Originally titled 'Romanticism and Demystification', this lecture was retitled 'The Contemporary Criticism of Romanticism' when, along with the other Gauss Seminar lectures, it was published in RCC, pp. 3–24.
108 RCC, pp. 4,5.
109 See Waters, 'Paul de Man: Life and Works', in CW, p. lxx.
110 René Girard's *Mensonge romantique et vérité romanesque*, Paris: Grasset, 1961, became available in an English translation by Yvonne Freccero, published by Johns Hopkins University Press in 1965 under the title *Deceit, Desire, and the Novel*. Girard, as Chair of Romance Languages at Johns Hopkins University, organised with Richard Macksey and Eugenio Donato the international conference on 'The Languages of Criticism and the Sciences of Man', October 1966, that introduced structuralism to the United Sates, see also footnotes 126 and 127 below. In 1968, de Man and Girard became colleagues at Johns Hopkins University when de Man moved there from Harvard University to take up the post of Professor of Humanities.
111 Girard 1965, pp. 1–17, p. 16 note 2.

the term '*romanesque*' is somewhat ambiguous in that it denotes, for example, both chivalric romances and *Don Quixote*, and so can be both 'synonymous with the romantic and ... indicate the destruction of romantic pretensions'.[112] Girard tends to use the term 'novelistic' in its place. He cites Proust's *Jean Santeuil* as a 'romantic' novel, while *A la recherche du temps perdu* provides him with an example of a 'novelistic' novel.[113] De Man, however, despite his interest in this distinction is just as interested in the way that Girard uses the word 'romantic' to name both 'a historical period at the beginning of the nineteenth century' and 'a recurrent aberration that plagues the mind of Western man at least since the Renaissance' – 'the illusory autonomy of the self', etc.[114]

'Aberration': Since matters of vocabulary are important, it should be noted that though Girard uses the word 'aberration' with reference to the 'romantic' and to 'Romanticism', he does not use it in the way de Man uses it here. Not quite. Girard uses 'aberration' according to its primary meaning or conventional usage. So, for example, when, in his discussion of Stendhal's *Le Rouge et le Noir*, Girard refers to Julien Sorel's love for Mathilde as an 'aberration', the aberration in question is a momentary lapse or deviation from the Stendhalian hero's normal, usual or typical sensibility.[115] Sorel's love for Mathilde is aberrant. The meaning of de Man's 'aberration' is somewhat different, for his 'aberration' has been a more or less omnipresent aspect of man's sensibility and consciousness since the Renaissance and, as such, might best be regarded not as an aberrant condition but as the norm.

'Aberration': It's a term that de Man had used several times in the 1950s that became key in his writing from the late 1960s through the 1980s. It warrants a long excursus, one it will receive later. All that needs to be pointed out at this juncture is that in 'The Contemporary Criticism of Romanticism' 'aberration' functions in a relation of association with '*illusion*', a term that also occurs in Girard's *Mensonge romantique et vérité romanesque*, always, as in this example, according to conventional usage:

> The romantic *vaniteux* always wants to convince himself that his desire is written into the nature of things,[116] or, which amounts to the same thing, that it is the emanation of serene subjectivity, the creation *ex nihilo* of a

---

112 Girard 1965, pp. 16–7.
113 Girard 1965, p. 27.
114 RCC, p. 6.
115 Girard 1965, p. 91.
116 Girard 1965, p. 7, 'A *vaniteux* will desire any object so long as he is convinced that it is already desired by another person whom he admires'.

> quasi-divine ego. Desire is no longer rooted in the object perhaps, but is rooted in the subject; it is certainly not rooted in the Other. The objective and subjective fallacies are one and the same; both originate in the image we all have of our own desires. Subjectivisms and objectivisms, romanticisms and realisms, individualisms and scientisms, idealisms and positivisms appear to be in opposition but are secretly in agreement to conceal the presence of the mediator. All these dogmas are the aesthetic or philosophical translation of worldviews peculiar to internal mediation. They all depend directly or indirectly on the *mensonge* [deceit or self-deception] that is spontaneous desire. They all defend the same illusion of autonomy to which modern man is passionately devoted.[117]

With this in mind, we can say that de Man's use of the word 'aberration' holds within it or connects a false perception or false impression of reality with an assertion that *that* impression is true to reality. An aberration turns or tropes a delusion – in this instance, the *mensonge romantique* or self-deception that the individual is possessed of an almost divine, autonomous subjectivity – into a statement of fact.[118] This 'aberration' operates on two levels: one general; and one specific. Generally, it asserts the illusion 'as a philosophical truth about the nature of human existence, a descriptive statement about our way of being in the world'.[119] And, specifically, in terms of aesthetic theory, it asserts that a work of art is 'a self-generated world of the subject's own making'.[120] Bringing the general and the specific together, the subject is taken as the ontologically prior place of origin and constitutive focus of the world: it is the necessary condition for the existence of all relationships; and its relation to all parts of the world is quite different from the relations that pertain between those parts.[121] Following Girard's way of reading it, de Man finds that, in the romantic novel, the situation is otherwise. Though the main character or subject is the centre of the novel, that centre is ontologically weak, for the main character or subject is utterly dependent on an Other 'who acts as mediator and governs in fact all the decisions it proudly claims as its own'.[122] Deceiving ourselves that we are thoroughly self-possessive, self-centred and autonomous subjects, we think that our desires originate spontaneously from within ourselves; whereas we actu-

---

117   Girard 1965, pp. 15–6, trans. slightly amended (see Girard 1961, p. 24).
118   RCC, pp. 6,7,8.
119   RCC, p. 6.
120   Ibid.
121   Ibid.
122   Ibid.

ally derive them from others. Desire in the romantic novel is never spontaneous or autonomous. It is always copied or imitated from Others. The desire for an object is always prompted by the desire of another person – the 'mediator' – for that same object. Which means that the relationship between subject and object is never direct but always a non-gestalt triangulation between subject *and* mediator *and* object. Though the subject seems to desire the object, he or she actually desires what an Other – the mediator – desires. The subject or main character, writes de Man reading Girard:

> may be a perfectly sensible and rational person, but in anything involving the mediator he is totally lacking in self-insight, radically blind to the actual state of his consciousness. This self-delusion is what leads him to call himself autonomous at the moment when he is in fact the unconscious slave of another's decisions. The mystified claim at autonomy characterizes for Girard the romantic false consciousness.[123]

This is the *mensonge romantique* that, as Girard demonstrates, the author of the nineteenth-century novelistic novel, in the work of the novel and only in the novel, reacts against and, effecting the *vérité romanesque*, 'slowly and painfully ... overcomes in himself the romantic he used to be and who refuses to die'.[124] The nineteenth-century novelistic novel understands, as Girard puts it, that 'the myth of autonomy' is 'exactly the reverse of what it pretends to be':[125] it clarifies the contradiction and disposes of its mystery – in de Man's terms, it narrates the 'demystification' of 'romantic false consciousness'.

'False Consciousness': As far as I can make out, Girard makes no mention of it in *Mensonge romantique et vérité romanesque*. De Man had used it in October 1966, perhaps while he was working on, or preparing to draft, the Gauss Seminar, when he responded from the floor to Barthes's presentation to the conference at Johns Hopkins University on 'The Languages of Criticism and the Sciences of Man'.[126] Without mentioning it by name, but with Girard's *Mensonge romantique et vérité romanesque* in mind, it was clear to him that, 'with regard to the question of the narrator or the "double ego"', Barthes had a 'false

---

123 RCC, p. 7.
124 RCC, p. 8.
125 Girard 1961, pp. 108, 106; Girard 1965, pp. 113, 111.
126 The papers from this conference were published as Macksey, Richard and Eugenio Donato (eds.) 1970. Along with Barthes, those who delivered papers at the conference included Jacques Derrida, Lucien Goldman, Jean Hyppolite, Jacques Lacan, Georges Poulet, Tsvetan Todorov, and Jean-Pierre Vernant. Barthes's presentation was published as 'To Write: An Intransitive Verb?' pp. 134–45, and for de Man's response see p. 150.

consciousness of classicism, romanticism, Mallarmé and the novels of contemporary writers such as Robbe-Grillet and Philippe Sollers'. Why? Because with regard to the 'narrator' or 'double ego', he turned the complication of the ego or the grammatical I, the first person singular pronoun, into an object of theoretical observation and then, regarding it as a thing, substance or person, made 'consciousness undergo a reification'. False consciousness is reifying consciousness.[127]

'False consciousness': Marx and Engels theorised ideology as made of 'false conceptions' that we 'have always formed' about ourselves, about what we are and what we ought to be, of the nature of man or 'man's own being'.[128] But these conceptions are not thoroughly false for they are effected by and refer to actual material relations.[129] Rather, they are idealised conceptions arrived at consciously but with a false consciousness.[130] That the 'false consciousness' that's theorised in 'The Contemporary Criticism of Romanticism' already connoted, for de Man, the 'false consciousness' of Marx and Engels's 'ideology' is confirmed a moment later when he points out that anti-romantic formulations similar to Girard's can be read not only in the novels that Girard studies and in the contemporary criticism of Romanticism but also in the writing of Nietzsche, and the 'Hegel-oriented early Marx'.[131] These formulations, says de Man – not citing Girard's *Mensonge romantique et vérité romanesque* but with Lévi-Strauss's *Mythologiques: Le cru et le cuit* in mind,[132] and also, no doubt, as will become clear directly, Barthes's own *Mythologies* – are 'perhaps best classified under the general heading of demythification'.[133] De Man would also apply the term 'demythification' to 'such diverse aspects of contemporary thought

---

127 Ibid. As far as de Man was concerned, Barthes's presentation was also flawed insofar as it was based on an optimistic myth of progress in the history of consciousness in which phenomenology – 'the last active form of philosophy' – was replaced by psychoanalysis, linguistics and the linguistic exploration of literary texts: a progress that was not borne out by the achievements of Barthes's own so-called *semio-critical* analyses, which showed no marked advance over the achievements of the Russian and American formalists. Moreover, Barthes was 'simply wrong' when he referred to the facts of literary history, 'things that are false within a typically French myth'.
128 Marx, Karl and Frederick Engels 1976 'Preface', p. 23. See also Engels, Letter to Conrad Schmidt, 27 October 1890, in Marx and Engels 1991, p. 657.
129 Marx and Engels, *The German Ideology*, MECW 5, p. 59.
130 Frederick Engels, Letter to Franz Mehring, London, 14 July 1893, in Marx and Engels 1991, p. 659.
131 RCC, p. 9.
132 RCC, pp. 11–12.
133 RCC, p. 8.

as neo-Marxism, neo-Freudianism, phenomenological analysis[134] both theological and secular, and even certain forms of linguistic analysis'.[135] This antiromantic tendency, he continues, is most conspicuous in the field of literary criticism. In the formalist tradition, for example, it's there in Edward Everett Bostetter's *Romantic Ventriloquists* (1963). And it's there in more ethically oriented criticism, where it 'takes on ideological forms:'[136] on the left, in Lukács's 'later writing on realism and on irrationalism;' and on the right, in the New Criticism associated with Irving Babbitt, T.E. Hulme and T.S. Eliot.[137] Nevertheless, in its affinity with structuralism Girard's criticism goes further:

> It transcends categories such as form and morality toward their common ground in the self. By stating the problem in terms of a dialectical relationship between an authentic and a false consciousness, it is the degree of transparence of a consciousness to its own light that comes under investigation. The myth is that of the possibility of consciousness; hence the shift from the general understanding of a mythical theme (or demythification) to that of the particular myths by which the self deliberately conceals its own being (or de*myst*ification). By calling this movement of self-concealment ... a myth, we imply by the same token that the main entity by means of which and within which this dialectic of concealment and revelation takes place is language. The particular myth under scrutiny then becomes that of a privileged language that would belong to a truly autonomous subject, a myth that is historically defined as the central myth of romantic literature.[138]

As an extrapolation gifted to Girard, 'false consciousness' seems perfectly compatible with his idea of the '*mensonge romantique*' and puts nothing into his text that is not permitted by its occasional references to Marx and Marxism, which, though often critical, usually in terms compatible with those already developed by de Man of the latter, are by no means thoroughly negative and always suggestive. Also, 'false consciousness' seems a not unreasonable inference to draw from that moment in the preliminaries to the fifth chapter of *Men-*

---

134   See RCC, p. 196 note 4, added by the editors, which tells us that here the Heideggerian 'of Dasein' is crossed out in the original manuscript.
135   RCC, p. 8.
136   This usage is, of course, conventional: these forms of literary criticism evidence thinking characteristic of an individual, group, or culture.
137   RCC, p. 9.
138   Ibid.

songe romantique et vérité romanesque where Girard tropes the 'false intuition' [*intuition menteuse*] or the seemingly unmediated understanding effected by metaphysical desire – the desire *to be* – as the 'illusion' from which 'reality springs' and for which 'reality provides a misleading guarantee'.[139]

The problem of Romanticism is, then, that of a recurrent aberration, which is here understood as a historically and culturally specific way of thinking with a false consciousness. The *mensonge romantique* is not *per se* false for it holds within it a *vérité romanesque*. It is, rather, the effect of an active back-and-forth between an authentic consciousness (of material relations) and an ideal, inauthentic consciousness (of material relations), self-revelation and self-concealment, and the amount, range or scope to which a consciousness can become available to scrutiny by a reified consciousness. Since this is a problem *of* language, it is a problem best attended to in relation to language.

Mensonge romantique and *vérité romanesque*; inauthentic consciousness and authentic consciousness; self-concealment and self-revelation; reified consciousness and consciousness. We are now in a position to recognise how much the turn to rhetoric and the change in the 'tone' and 'substance' of de Man's approach to literary criticism, which occurs at the end of the 1960s, was connected to his interest in the relation between false consciousness and consciousness, which is to say to his interest in 'ideology'. De Man points to 'The Rhetoric of Temporality', 'with its deliberate emphasis on rhetorical terminology', as auguring the change.[140] 'The Rhetoric of Temporality' was written and published in 1969, around the time that de Man was readying his first book of collected essays for press under the, in retrospect, unsurprising title: *Blindness & Insight: Essays in the Rhetoric of Contemporary Criticism*.[141]

'Roland Barthes and the Limits of Structuralism' (1972)

De Man had been familiar with the work of Roland Barthes probably since the publication of *Writing Degree Zero* in 1953. As we've seen, he referred to it in his 1956 essay 'The Dead-End of Formalist Criticism'. And, as we've also seen, he'd engaged with Barthes directly ten years later at the Johns Hopkins conference on 'The Languages of Criticism and the Science of Man'. Sometime in the

---

139   Girard 1965, p. 101 [Girard 1961, p. 106].
140   BI, p. xii. See also Waters, 'Paul de Man', in CW, pp. lii–lix.
141   Paul de Man, 'The Rhetoric of Temporality', first published in Charles Singleton, *Interpretation: Theory and Practice*, Baltimore: Johns Hopkins University Press, 1969. It was reprinted as Chapter 10 in Paul de Man, BI, pp. 187–228.

early 1970s, probably in 1972 on the occasion of the publication, in that year, of Annette Lavers' translation of *Mythologies*[142] – a collection of essays that, for the most part, were written between 1954 and 1956, which were first published in 1957 – *The New York Review of Books* commissioned him to write an essay on Barthes. However, on receipt, the editors thought that what he'd submitted provided a 'too negative review' and decided not to publish it.[143] Whence the original typescript remained unpublished until, nearly twenty years later, it was transcribed and edited by Thomas Pepper for publication under the title 'Roland Barthes and the Limits of Structuralism' for inclusion in *Yale French Studies*.[144] The commission gave de Man the opportunity to review the different moments in the theoretical development of someone he considered 'one of the most agile minds in the field of linguistic studies'[145] and to resume his own thinking about the nature of 'idealised fictions' and '*mensonges romantiques*', self-deception and 'aberration', 'myth' and 'false consciousness' and the always-formed false conceptions produced by it – in a word, ideology. It also gave him the chance to develop the criticism he'd made at the Johns Hopkins conference in 1966 by demonstrating how Barthes's approach relies on the very idea of 'myth' that he himself criticises in 'Myth Today', the theoretical-polemical essay in which Barthes tried to demonstrate the efficacy of integrating his mode of analysis with ideology critique.

De Man's criticism pertains to a theory of language and the way it's used. Barthes applies the vocabulary of structuralist linguistics to the analysis not only of linguistic texts but also, in *Mythologies*, to a range of diverse social and cultural 'myths' such as a professional wrestling contest, advertisements for soap powder and detergent, and striptease. Most important is the myth that featured on the front cover of *Paris Match*, 25 June–2 July 1955, which is the analytical object or main focus of the longest essay, 'Myth Today'. The cover of this issue of *Paris Match*, published just seven months after the beginning of the Algerian War of Independence, in November 1954 – and only two months before French troops and *pied-noir* vigilantes murdered between 1,200 and 12,000 Muslims, in response to the murder of more than 120 people in Philippeville by a Front Liberation Nationale-incited mob – features a full-page,

---

142 Barthes 1972.
143 See de Man, 'Roland Barthes and the Limits of Structuralism', RCC, pp. 164–77. On the circumstances of the commissioned essay's subsequent rejection see Waters 1995, pp. 39–40 note 15.
144 De Man, Paul, 'Roland Barthes and the Limits of Structuralism', *Yale French Studies* 77, *Reading the Archive: On Texts and Institutions*, 1990, pp. 177–90.
145 RCC, p. 175.

full-colour photograph of 'a young negro soldier, dressed in a French uniform, making the military salute, eyes raised, undoubtedly fixed on a fold in the tricolour'.[146] 'Myth Today' is a still vivid piece of political writing that analyses how myth turns French imperiality and the military, cultural and economic violence that characterises colonialism into an incontrovertible natural state of affairs: Look at this good black soldier saluting the tricolour just like one of our own white boys.

'Myth', says Barthes, is 'a type of speech' or, as de Man puts it, using the word he'd employed in his 1966 essay on Lukács to characterise the Greek ideal, a 'fiction'.[147] Though one knows that an event or an occurrence narrated in a fictional narrative – or an event or occurrence conceived as a form of literature – is not reality, in reading it, consuming it, one acquiesces to the 'deceit' that it is.[148] De Man, following what Barthes says about myth, explains that 'it is the nature of fictions to be more persuasive than facts and especially persuasive in seeming more real than nature itself'.[149] Fictions are the 'most marketable *commodity* [emphasis added] manufactured by man'[150] and when they're 'enlisted in the service of collective patterns of interest, including interests of the highest moral or metaphysical order, fictions become ideologies'.[151] As Barthes points out, there is myth on the Left and myth and on the Right but 'statistically, myth is on the Right'.[152]

Ideology depends on the illusionary adequation of sign and meaning.[153] Structuralist linguistic analysis, which focuses on the functions and interrelation of signifiers independent of meaning, liberates the objective properties or material aspect of the signifier from its semantic function, puts the illusion in doubt by problematising the identity between sign and meaning. Barthes refers to his mode of analysis, which he considers to be a general science alongside linguistics, as *semiology* (a term first used by the Swiss linguist Ferdinand de Saussure in his posthumously published *Course in General Linguistics* of 1916). Semiology studies signs independently of meanings; semantics concentrates on meaning. Barthes's analyses of non-linguistic social and cultural texts or myths are subversive because they bring out the structure of myth and the

---

146 Barthes 1972, p. 116, trans. amended.
147 RCC, pp. 169–70.
148 RCC, p. 168.
149 RCC, p. 169.
150 RCC, p. 170.
151 Ibid.
152 Barthes 1972, with regard to 'Myth Today' see 'Myth on the Left', pp. 145–48, 'Myth on the Right', pp. 148–56.
153 RCC, p. 170.

way it is utilised by various interests[154] – the photograph of the black soldier on the cover of *Paris Match* being an excellent case in point. At which point, appropriating something de Man had said in 'The Contemporary Criticism of Romanticism', on a political level, the question of who is exploiting whom and to what effect has to be considered.[155] Because of this, Barthes's analyses must always be subversive of ideology, even when limited to linguistic texts.

So, de Man acknowledges the 'political implications' of the demystifying power of Barthes's semiocritical semiology, the way his method disposes of the mystery of a specific myth. However, he thinks that Barthes's achievements and the method used to achieve them are so admirable that the latter brings about its own mystification, especially with regard to the claims Barthes makes regarding its scientificity.[156] While not denying the demystifying power of Barthes's analyses, de Man questions whether their methodological basis in structural linguistics is epistemologically sufficiently strong to be regarded as scientific.

A science of literature should be able to account for the illusionary referentiality of literature without itself being deceived by that illusion.[157] The standard way of dealing with this problem is by avoiding it 'as when Roman Jakobson rightfully asserts that language is autotelic, i.e., "focused on the message for its own sake", rather than on its meaning'. This gets 'rid of all the mess and muddle of signification', enables 'a scientific discourse covering the entire field of literary syntax', but leaves the 'privileged adequation of sign and meaning that governs the world of literary fictions' in place 'as the ideal model towards which all semantic systems tend'.[158] The referential function of language 'is dismissed as contingency or ideology and not taken seriously as a semantic interference within the semiological system'.[159] In other words, it is treated summarily – if at all – as the result of some unexpected event or occurrence or solely as a result of being appropriated and manipulated by political or moral interests and not seen as an effect of language itself.[160]

De Man points out that though Barthes knows that literature 'can never be reduced to a specific meaning or set of meanings, yet is always reductively interpreted as if it were a statement or message', he actually denies, in for example

---

154   Ibid.
155   RCC, p. 11.
156   RCC, pp. 170–1.
157   RCC, p. 171.
158   RCC, pp. 171–2.
159   RCC, p. 172.
160   Ibid.

'Myth Today', that 'literary science' has to explain this 'pattern of error'. Barthes sees that as

> the task of historians, thus implying that the reasons for the *recurrent aberration* [emphasis added] are not linguistic but ideological. The further implication is that the negative labour of ideological demystification will eventually be able to prevent the distortion that superimposes upon literature a positive assertive meaning foreign to its actual possibilities. Barthes has never renounced this hope; in a recent interview, despite many nuances and reservations, he still speaks of 'the ultimate transparency of social relations' as the goal of the critical enterprise. Yet, in the meantime, his methodological postulates have begun to erode under the impact of the question that he hoped to delegate to other, more pragmatic disciplines.[161]

De Man's judgment, and he was not alone in making it, is that Barthes's semiocritical semiology can't be considered a science because it can't interpret and explain itself according to its own semiological model.[162] Jorge Larrain, for example, in his book *The Concept of Ideology*, and of course unaware of de Man's unpublished essay, made much the same criticism a few years later.[163] Larrain made the point, with reference to Barthes's *Système de la mode* (1967), that although Barthes's practical analyses are stimulating the analogy with structural linguistics on which they depend demands a 'superior methodological precision' than Barthes provides. 'The discourse itself, beyond its content', writes Larrain, 'should provide some clues for determining the mythical level' – the level at which the interference within the linguistic system keeps on recurring and causing myth as 'a type of speech'. In this respect, 'Barthes does not seem very successful, despite the fact that he accepts that such an analysis depends upon a linguistic analysis'.[164] Since Barthes's semio-critical semiological analysis of ideology can't demystify what it sets out to demystify, it falls back into the error of that very mystification: adherence to the myth of an unmediated connection between sign and referent. Though history, to which Barthes abjures in 'Myth Today', and somewhat later in *Critique et vérité*, might be able to explain why a particular meaning came to be accepted as *the*

161　RCC, pp. 173–4.
162　RCC, p. 174.
163　See Larrain 1979, ch. 5, 'Ideology and Structural Analysis', 'Semiology 1: Barthes and Greimas', pp. 132–40.
164　See Larrain 1979, pp. 134–5.

meaning, it cannot explain how and why that meaning was effected in the first place so as to become available for appropriation by those 'collective patterns of interest, including interests of the highest moral or metaphysical order'.[165] Ideology depends on an illusory correspondence or coincidence between sign and referent. It's an effect of language that needs explaining, and can only be explained, not by recourse to history ... or politics ... or ethics ... or metaphysics but by and in terms of the analytic study language.

It's here, in 'Roland Barthes and the Limits of Structuralism', that de Man – in this context, almost certainly following Barthes's directions – points to Marx and Engels's *The German Ideology* as 'the model text for all ideological demystifications',[166] which is to say, to the paradigmatic example of how to analyse and understand ideology not as 'false consciousness' *as such* but, as Engels put it, 'a process accomplished by the so-called thinker consciously ... but with a false consciousness'.[167] In due course it will become clear that Marx and Engels regard this process as linguistic, a process that brings consciousness to practical consciousness by and in language.

The following year, in 'Semiology and Rhetoric', published in *Diacritics* in the autumn of 1973,[168] de Man reiterated something of what he had said about the demystifying power of semiology, again with reference to Marx. Semiology, he wrote:

> demonstrated that the perception of the literary dimensions of language is largely obscure if one submits uncritically to the authority of reference. It also revealed how tenaciously this authority continues to assert itself in a variety of disguises, ranging from the crudest ideology to the most refined forms of aesthetic and ethical judgment. It especially explodes the myth of semantic correspondence between sign and referent, the wishful hope of having it both ways, of being, to paraphrase Marx in *The German Ideology*, a formalist critic in the morning and a communal moralist in the afternoon, serving both the technique of form and the substance of meaning.[169]

---

165 RCC, p. 170.
166 RCC, p. 169.
167 There are several obvious references to *The German Ideology* in Barthes 1972, re 'Myth Today' see for example *Mythologies*, p. 141, p. 144, and p. 151.
168 De Man, Paul, 'Semiology and Rhetoric', *Diacritics*, 3, 3, fall 1973, pp. 27–33; reprinted in Josué V. Harai, ed., *Textual Strategies: Perspectives in Post-Structuralist Criticism*, Ithica: Cornell University Press, 1979, pp. 121–40. Subsequently included as ch. 1 in AR, pp. 3–19.
169 AR, pp. 5–6.

That last sentence is hardly a 'paraphrase'. It is, rather, one of those 'aphoristic formulations' that de Man often made that might strike one as 'deliberately provocative' in its 'all-or-nothing generality and ... slightly defiant irony'.[170] Here de Man is telling us, in other and fewer words, that in *The German Ideology* Marx and Engels recognise and deal with the way that ideology effects, and is itself effected by, the illusion of a direct connection between language and reality. However, at this point, there's probably more in de Man's mind than that. His remark about 'the wishful hope ... of being ... a formalist critic in the morning and a communal moralist in the afternoon' resonates with what he'd said some six years before in the first Gauss Seminar lecture, 'The Contemporary Criticism of Romanticism', about the way that Girard's approach to the self-mystification characteristic of Romanticism went beyond the anti-romantic tendency in formalist criticism (with its almost exclusive focus on the language, technique and style of a text) and more ethically oriented criticism (with its attention to meaning and moral judgment). As de Man put it, Girard 'transcended' both formalist and ethical criticism by emphasising that formal and ethical concerns had their mutual domain in the self and by restating the problem of Romanticism not in terms of self-concealment and self-mystification but in terms of a 'dialectic of concealment and revelation' that is brought about mainly by means of 'a language that would belong to a truly autonomous subject'. It's easy to miss that here, as will become clear later, de Man is citing Marx and Engels's thinking in *The German Ideology* not only as an authoritative example of how to transcend or mediate the separation between sign and referent but also, in other terms, form and morality. In effect, as we'll see, he is, in part, heralding what he would say some ten years later in the third Messenger Lecture, 'Hegel on the Sublime', that, with regard to puzzling ideology, Marx and Engels's *The German Ideology* was 'aesthetic thinking' along the lines of Kant's *Third Critique*.

'Metaphor (*Second Discourse*)' (1973)

Before we look at what Marx and Engels have to say about ideology – and its relation to language – in *The German Ideology* we need to direct our attention to how de Man moved away from doing 'purely linguistic' analyses of his chosen texts to considering 'questions that were already of a political and ideo-

---

170 See Hillis Miller, J., '"Reading" Part of a Paragraph in *Allegories of Reading*', in Waters & Godzich (eds.) 1989, p. 155.

logical nature'. This move occurred, as de Man pointed out in his conversation with Rosso, when he began to produce the series of essays on works by Jean-Jacques Rousseau that make up the second part of *Allegories of Reading*. It seems likely that he was working on the first of these, 'Theory of Metaphor in Rousseau's Second Discourse', which was published in the spring 1973 issue of *Studies in Romanticism* and six years later in *Allegories of Reading* as 'Metaphor (*Second Discourse*)', when he drafted his essay on Barthes for *The New York Review of Books*. In that essay he had likened structuralism as an 'intellectual movement' and as 'a methodological blueprint for scientific research' to the 'state of nature' that Rousseau had narrated in *A Discourse on the Origin of Inequality*, the *Second Discourse*. Rousseau's idea of man in a state of nature (*homme sauvage*), de Man said, quoting Rousseau himself, is something that '"no longer exists, has perhaps never existed and will probably never come into being", but which we nevertheless cannot do without'.[171] The '*homme sauvage*', which Rousseau sets out by 'laying all the facts aside',[172] is, says de Man, a 'fiction', a 'radical fiction' or 'a pure fiction'.[173] What is the significance of this fiction to the real world? Rousseau needed it 'in order to form a proper judgment of our present state',[174] and to that effect it's probably best to think of it – like structuralism taken as a method of scientific research – as a kind of Vaihinger-like 'practical fiction', a fiction that is useful to deploy *as if* it were true so as 'to provide us with an instrument for finding our way about more easily in the world'.[175] However, de Man argues that this fiction or practical fiction has persistently been taken not as Rousseau intended but as fact – a fact that was then appropriated as 'a literal model' of 'a theory of history and society ... that could be transposed *tel quel* from the text to the political or social situation that it represents or prefigures'.[176] Thus appropriated, Rousseau's practical fiction has its life as a 'reductive ideology that results from a repression of the political faculty [the political aspect of Rousseau's thinking] ... carried out by literary language'.[177] This appropriation goes as far back as Schiller.[178] De Man cites Louis Althusser's 1970 essay 'Sur le Contrat Social (Les déclages)' by way of giving a contemporary example of it.[179] While de Man acknowledges that this

---

171 RCC, p. 171. Rousseau 1993, see 'A Discourse on the Origin of Inequality', 'Preface', p. 44.
172 Rousseau 1993, 'A Discourse on the Origin of Inequality', p. 50.
173 AR, pp. 136, 137.
174 Rousseau 1993, 'A Discourse on the Origin of Inequality', p. 44.
175 See Vaihinger 1924, p. 15.
176 AR, p. 136.
177 AR, 137–8.
178 AR, p. 137.
179 See Althusser 1970, pp. 5–42, and 'Metaphor (*Second Discourse*)', in AR, pp. 137–38. See also the reference to Althusser's criticism in 'Allegory of Reading (*Profession de Foi*)', AR, p. 224.

criticism is not unfounded, as he reads the *Second Discourse*, Rousseau's 'state of nature' retains its meaning as a practical fiction and not – as it's usually read – as a kind of Barthesian myth that effects a relation of literal correspondence or coincidence with its referent. What, then, is its significance with regard to the actual world? What connects the practical fiction of man in a state of nature to the lived material and mental actuality of man in civil society, propertyless and alienated from his own activity and its objects, from himself and from other human beings? Why has it proved such an indispensable tool for understanding man's present condition?[180] How do the fictional and practical aspects of the *Second Discourse* – the 'pure fiction' of the '*homme sauvage*' in the first part and the 'narrative involving such concrete political realities as private property, contractual law, and modes of government' in the second part – come together into a coherent whole that would reveal the foundations of human society?[181] In answering these questions, much depends on the way de Man reads a 'polemical digression' on the origin of language in the middle of the first part of the *Second Discourse*, which, he says, has no obvious, direct association with Rousseau's main argument.[182] So what's it doing there?

De Man begins his reading with some remarks on Rousseau's notion of freedom – 'the power to will or, rather, the power to choose, as well as the feeling of this power'[183] – which, he says, is almost indistinguishable from '"will power", since the power to choose is precisely the power to transgress in nature whatever would entail the end of human power'.[184] Unlike animals, which make their decisions by instinct, man makes his decisions by the exercise of free will.[185] Rousseau, somewhat misleadingly, as de Man points out, calls this power 'perfectibility'. Misleadingly because the effects of perfectibility are as regressive as they are progressive. As Rousseau puts it in a passage not cited by de Man, 'It would be melancholy, were we forced to admit that this distinctive and almost unlimited faculty is the source of all human misfortunes; that it is this which, in time, draws man out of his original state, in which he would have spent his days insensibly and in innocence; that it is this faculty, which, successfully producing in different ages his discoveries and errors, his vices and virtues, makes him at length a tyrant both over himself and nature'.[186]

---

180   AR, p. 137.
181   Ibid.
182   AR, p. 135.
183   AR, p. 140.
184   Ibid.
185   Rousseau 1993, 'A Discourse on the Origin of Inequality', p. 59.
186   Rousseau 1993, 'A Discourse on the Origin of Inequality', p. 60.

De Man provides a list of some of perfectibility's progressive and retrogressive effects.

> The potential transgression that occurs whenever the concepts of nature and of man are associated – in the *Essay on the Origin of Language* all examples destined to illustrate the 'natural' language of man are acts of violence – transforms all human attributes from definite, self-enclosed, and self-totalizing actions into open structures: perception becomes imagination, natural needs [*besoins*] become unfulfillable passions, sensations become an endless quest for knowledge all of which deprive man forever of a central identity ('the more one meditates ... the greater the distance becomes between our pure sensations and the simplest forms of knowledge').[187]

What turned man in his original state, at one with himself and nature, into man alienated from himself and nature, perception into imagination, and the satisfaction of basic needs into desires? How did man develop the ability to make fire, work metals and become an agriculturalist and manufacturer? Man could not have done these things by his 'own powers alone'.[188] The state of nature necessitated that he 'invent' language,[189] for 'It is impossible indeed to conceive how a man ... without the aid of communication and the spur of necessity, could have bridged so greater gap' as the 'distance between sensation and knowledge'.[190]

Perfectibility is derived from the primal categories of freedom and will, and it evolves, as language evolves, moving from particular denomination to general ideas.[191] 'Moreover [Rousseau writes] general ideas can only enter the mind by means of words and our understanding can seize upon them only by means of propositions. This is one of the reasons why animals could never acquire such ideas, nor the perfectibility that depends on it (*C'est une des raisons pourquoi les animaux ne sauraient se former de telles idées, ni jamais acquérir la perfectibilité qui en dépend*)'.[192] De Man's attention is drawn to this passage, which, he says, is 'avoided rather than stressed in most readings of the *Second Discourse*', perhaps because it contains a problem of translation and interpret-

---

187 AR, p. 140.
188 Rousseau 1993, 'A Discourse on the Origin of Inequality', p. 62.
189 Rousseau 1993, 'A Discourse on the Origin of Inequality', p. 64.
190 Rousseau 1993, 'A Discourse on the Origin of Inequality', p. 62.
191 AR, p. 142.
192 AR, p. 142.

ation. 'Since the French language does not distinguish between "which" and "that", it is impossible to decide by grammatical means alone whether the sentence should read: "animals could never acquire perfectibility, since perfectibility depends on language" or ... "animals could never acquire the kind of perfectibility that depends on language".[193] De Man is 'wary of accepting uncritically the common sense and admirable prudence' present in the latter reading, preferring, instead, the former where language is the decisive determining factor for all human self-advancement, development and progress. He finds nothing in Rousseau's work to suggest that Rousseau thought that 'linguistic perfectibility' is separate from 'historical perfectibility in general'.[194] Hence the detour on the origin of language in the *Second Discourse* that illustrates the 'impossibility of passing from nature to culture by natural means' and, in doing so, facilitates the transition *from* the pure, radical or practical fiction of man in a state of nature and the discussion of the powers of freedom, will and perfectibility in the first part of the *Discourse* to the analysis of the actual structures of political economy – private property, government and law in civil society – in its second part.[195]

Man has history, says de Man paraphrasing Rousseau, because, unlike animals, he can 'perform the specifically linguistic act of conceptualization', a process of 'substituting one verbal utterance (at the simplest level, a common noun) for another on the basis of a resemblance [between it and other entities] that hides differences which permitted the existence of entities in the first place' (AR, 144–45). Rousseau thinks that, at first, man gave each and every object its own 'particular name without regard to genus or species' for, as it were, he saw everything as what it was and not another thing.[196] As he began to see certain similarities among these different particularly named objects so he was able to bring them together 'under common and generic denominations' ... such as 'tree'.[197] But seeing different entities as similar 'is not, in itself, a conceptualization' for animals as well as men must be able to see things as similar.[198] Perception, sensation, memory and imagination may be involved but animals cannot form general ideas and abstractions, which can only be conceived and comprehended by means of language. Rousseau says that 'It is necessary to state propositions and to speak in order to have general ideas; for as soon as

---

193 AR, p. 143. De Man is here citing Jean Starobinski's note in Rousseau 1964, p. 1327 note 8.
194 AR, p. 144.
195 AR, p. 141.
196 Rousseau 1993, 'A Discourse on the Origin of Inequality', p. 67.
197 Rousseau 1993, 'A Discourse on the Origin of Inequality', p. 68.
198 AR, p. 145.

the imagination stops, the mind can only proceed by means of discourse',[199] by moving from sensory cognition to conceptual cognition, from *perceiving* things and *perceiving* things *as* similar to forming general ideas about perceptions in and by way of language.[200]

De Man finds Rousseau's example of the way that man came up with the proper name 'tree' puzzling. Although Rousseau asserts – in de Man's translation – that 'the first nouns could only have been proper nouns',[201] he distinguishes between each and every object receiving its particular name and the process of conceptualization that brings about a generic proper name such as 'tree'.[202] In de Man's reading of it, Rousseau's account of how each group of similar entities received its generic proper name indicates that those names were not literal denominations but metaphors.[203] In which case, the transition *from* man in a state of nature *to* man in society originated in a kind of linguistic category mistake that mistook figural language and connotation for literal denomination. Which would render Rousseau's narrative of perfectibility incoherent.[204]

Did Rousseau, de Man asks, 'separate figural from literal language and does he privilege one type of discourse over the other?'[205] De Man, as it were, gives Rousseau time to think this through, and so avoid or rectify the incoherence and contradiction he seems to write in the *Second Discourse*, by redirecting our attention to the analogous discussion in the third section of the later *Essay on the Origin of Language* where Rousseau asserts that 'man's first language had to be figurative' and that 'figural language predates literal meaning'.[206] This passage is especially vivid in relation to the *Second Discourse* because it tells the story of the origin of the word 'man', of how man came to name himself, and, in linguistic terms, of the origin of inequality.

> A primitive man [*un homme sauvage*], on meeting other men, will first have experienced fright. His fear will make him see these men as larger and stronger than himself; he will give them the name *giants*. After many experiences, he will discover that the supposed giants are neither larger nor stronger than himself, and that their stature did not correspond to

---

199 Ibid.
200 Ibid.
201 AR, p. 147.
202 AR, pp. 145–6.
203 AR, p. 146.
204 AR, p. 147.
205 Ibid.
206 AR, pp. 147–8.

the idea he had originally linked to the word giant. He will then invent another name that he has in common with them, such as, for example, the word *man*, and will retain the word giant for the false object that impressed him while he was being deluded.[207]

In this story, the *homme sauvage*'s state of alarm at coming upon some other *hommes sauvages* and naming them 'giants' is not based on any objective perception for it will become apparent to him that the others are neither larger nor stronger than he is. The word 'giants' doesn't actually name the objective properties of the others: it names a subjective property, the strong barely controlled emotion – the fear – felt by the *homme sauvage*. The seemingly literal denomination 'giants' is already metaphor, and 'man' is a metaphor substituted for that metaphor. Though the first metaphor is in error because the *homme sauvage* is equal to the other *hommes sauvages* in size and strength, it is not wrong in as much as it expresses his state of alarm correctly. 'Metaphor', says de Man 'is error because it believes or feigns to believe in its own referential meaning'. But 'this belief is legitimate only within the limits of a given text … As soon as one leaves the text it becomes aberrant'.[208] 'Metaphor', de Man continues, 'overlooks the fictional, textual element in the nature of the entity it connotes. It assumes a world in which intra- and extra-textual events, literal and figural forms of language can be distinguished, a world in which the literal and the figural are properties that can be isolated and, consequently, exchanged and substituted for each other. This is an error, although it can be said that no language would be possible without this error'.[209] If one reads Rousseau's assertion, in the *Second Discourse*, that 'the first substantives could be nothing more than proper names'[210] in the light of his own demonstration, in the *Essay on the Origin of Language*, that 'the first language had to be figural', then, says de Man, Rousseau must have thought of denomination as 'a hidden, blinded figure'.[211]

Conceptualisation, it turns out, is a 'double process' made of two 'levels' or moments, each effecting an 'aberration' or 'distortion'.[212] As we've seen, six years before, in 'The Contemporary Criticism of Romanticism', 'aberration' referred to a process similarly made of two levels or moments whereby a false impression of reality is turned into an assertion of truth to reality. Here, in

---

207   AR, p. 149.
208   AR, p. 151.
209   AR, pp. 151–3.
210   Rousseau 1993, 'A Discourse on the Origin of Inequality', p. 69.
211   AR, p. 153.
212   AR, pp. 153–4.

'Metaphor (*Second Discourse*)', the first moment is the more or less unintentional invention – because it originates in the instinctual state of alarm felt by the *homme sauvage* – of the word 'giants', which is taken as the literal denomination of the others whereas it is, in fact, a metaphor of the *homme savage*'s fear of them. This distortion, says de Man, is unintentional and 'results exclusively from a formal, rhetorical potential of language' – it is caused by the structure of language, which generates the word 'giants'.[213] The second moment *is* intentional but, nonetheless, it also effects a distortion. After having gained more knowledge and skill from observing various events or occurrences, the *homme sauvage* measures himself against the 'giants' and discovers that he is their equal in size and strength and invents the word 'man' to name both them and himself. This moment, says de Man, makes deliberate use of the category of number in order for the *homme sauvage* to reach the reassuring conclusion that he need not fear the others. But number is not a literal property of things. The bridge between perception and reason, it's an arithmetical value representing a particular quantity of something expressed, in this case, by a word; it's 'just one more conceptual metaphor devoid of objective validity and subject to the distortions that constitute all metaphors'.[214] In this reading of Rousseau's *Essay on the Origin of Language*, 'man' is invented in two moments of distortion or misrepresentation: one in an unintentional moment of sensory cognition, which spontaneously produces a 'wild metaphor'; and one in a moment of conceptual cognition that produces another metaphor, a considered metaphor that 'equates with the literary, deliberate and rhetorical use of the spontaneous figure'.[215] The consequences of this are, as de Man makes clear, far reaching:

> the invention of the word man makes it possible for 'men' to exist by establishing the equality within inequality, the sameness within difference of civil society, in which the suspended, potential truth of the original fear is domesticated by the illusion of identity. The concept interprets the metaphor of numerical sameness as if it were a statement of literal fact. Without this literalization, there could be no society. The reader of Rousseau must remember that this literalism is the deceitful misrepresentation of an original blindness. Conceptual language, the foundation of civil society, is also, it appears, a lie superimposed upon an error. We can therefore hardly expect the epistemology of the sciences of man to be straightforward.[216]

---

213   AR, p. 154.
214   Ibid.
215   AR, pp. 154–5.
216   AR, p. 155.

The transition from conceptualisation to society suggested in the story of the origin of the word 'man' is plainly stated in the opening paragraphs of the second part of the *Discourse on the Origin of Inequality*, which sets the trajectory for what follows in a 'coherent movement that extends from freedom to perfectibility, from perfectibility to language, from language to man, and from man to political society'.[217] In these paragraphs, society begins not with the ways that the development of human labour (the development of the forces of production) created and transformed relationships between human beings (the division of labour) but in the way that those developments and changes brought about the 'quantitative comparison of conceptual relationships'.[218] Here is the key passage as quoted by de Man:

> The repeated contacts between man and various entities, and between the entities themselves, must necessarily engender in the mind of man the perception of relationships. These relationships, which we express by words such as large, small, strong, weak, fast, slow, fearful, bold, and other similar ideas, when compared to man's needs, produced, almost without his being aware of it, some kind of reflection, or rather, some form of mechanical prudence that taught him to take the precautions he needed for his safety. ... The resemblances that time allowed him to observe [between his fellow men], the human female and himself, made him infer [*juger de*] those which he could not perceive. Noticing that all of them behaved in the same way that he himself would have behaved in similar circumstances, he concluded that their way of thinking and feeling was entirely in conformity with his own.[219]

And, not quoted but alluded to by de Man, here is Rousseau's conclusion:

> This important truth, once deeply impressed on his mind, must have induced him, from an intuitive feeling more certain and much more rapid than any kind of reasoning, to pursue the rules of conduct, which he had best observe towards them, for his own security and advantage.[220]

The terms of this description are those used in the story of the origin of man in the *Essay on the Origin of Language*: 'passion (fear), measurement and meta-

---

217 Ibid.
218 Ibid.
219 AR, pp. 155–6.
220 Rousseau 1993, 'A Discourse on the Origin of Inequality', p. 86.

phor (inferring invisible properties by analogy with visible ones)'.[221] But what of 'this important truth' that prevailed on man to engage in, follow, and submit to a system of government? 'We should now realize', says de Man, 'that what Rousseau calls "truth" designates, neither the adequation of language to reality, nor the essence of things shining through the opacity of words, but rather the suspicion that human specificity may be rooted in linguistic deceit'.[222] In other words, we shouldn't confuse the word 'truth' with any referent that might be attached to it, but, rather, that what we take to be 'man' – 'men', 'society', 'civil society' – may be a Girard-like *mensonge romantique*, a self-deceit or self-delusion effected by language.

The origins of language and society are interconnected and reciprocal. The historical course of the development of society and politics is 'structured like and derived from a linguistic model' that 'exists independently of nature and independently of the subject'.[223] The beginnings of society – political society and civil society – coincided with the 'blind metaphorization' of the fear that the *homme sauvage* felt when he came across some others of his kind. As far as de Man is concerned, 'all forms of human language' are 'political', they relate to and are imbued with 'politicality' – society, public affairs and government.[224] And 'if society and government derive from a tension between man and language' then, just as perfectibility contains an antagonism or possibility of retrogression, the political derives from and contains 'the possibility of contingent error':[225] of, for example, mistaking a name for the reality to which it refers or with regard to making decisions about power and the organised control over a group of human beings. Because of this, the antagonism between man and language, between emotional qualities and ideas and the demands or implications put on them by language, 'becomes a *burden* [emphasis added] for man rather than an opportunity'.[226] The relations between man and language are always strained. As we saw a moment ago, de Man would make much the same point in some of the same words ten years later in the third Messenger Lecture, 'Hegel on the Sublime', where, with regard to Kant's Third Critique, he argued that aesthetic theory is 'the critique of critiques' because 'it critically examines the possibility and the modalities of political discourse, and the inescapable *burden* [emphasis added] of any linkage between discourse and action'.[227]

---

221 AR, p. 156.
222 Ibid.
223 Ibid.
224 Ibid.
225 AR, p. 156.
226 AR, pp. 156–7.
227 AI, p. 106.

De Man takes two 'directives' from this reading of the *Discourse on the Origin of Inequality* and the *Essay on the Origins of Language*. The first with regard to the structure of the *First Discourse* and the transition *from* the literary language that narrates the practical or pure fiction[228] of man in a state of nature *to* the language that narrates non-fictional man in the reality of civil society. The second with regard to the way the *Second Discourse* moves from 'qualitative concepts such as needs, passions, man, power, etc., to quantitative concepts involving numbers such as rich, poor, etc.', *from* a very general understanding of equality *to* a specific understanding based on the unequal ownership of property.[229] The very first sentence of the second part of the *Second Discourse* states: 'The first man, who after having fenced in a plot of land went on to say "*this belongs to me*" and found other men naïve enough to believe him [*assez simples pour le croire*], was the true founder of civil society'.[230] De Man reads this sentence in the same way that he read the story of the origin of 'man'. It moves *from* passion (greed) though measurement *to* metaphor, *from* everyone having access to sufficient land to satisfy his basic needs *to* someone with an excessive desire for land staking a claim to a bit of it as his private property. Thus effecting a degree of propertylessness in and inequality in relations with others. Rousseau's thinking about politics is, then, not based in ethical considerations but in economics. But this economics, writes de Man, is 'the correlative of linguistic conceptualization and is therefore neither materialistic, nor idealistic, nor merely dialectical since language is deprived of its representational as well as of transcendental authority. The complex relation between Rousseau's and Marx's economic determinism could and should be approached from this point of view'.[231]

It is unfortunate that this perceptive analysis and directive to further study, which a footnote acknowledges is informed by Engels's *Anti-Dürhring*,[232] should be marred by recourse to such a problematic concept for serious students of Marx as 'economic determinism'. 'Economic determinism' suggests that given what happens in some total of relations of production (the economic structure or real foundation of society) nothing else could have happened in the forms of consciousness (the ideological superstructure) *as if* the connection accords to the law of conservation of energy and momentum.[233] However,

---

228 AR, p. 158.
229 AR, p. 157.
230 Ibid.
231 AR, p. 158.
232 Ibid., note 35.
233 Two useful brief philosophical expositions of whether Marx and Engel's 'historical mater-

despite de Man's recourse to the term, there is nothing in the analysis that immediately preceded it or in what he took from or found confirmed by Engels's *Anti-Dühring* – which cites Marx's *Capital* alongside Rousseau's *Discourse on the Origin of Inequality* – to suggest that he thought that Marx was a determinist of any kind. Indeed, only months before, in the essay that would be reprinted in *Allegories of Reading* as 'Genesis and Genealogy (Nietzsche)',[234] he had made clear how Marx's notion of history had participated in the rejection of exactly that kind of teleology which held that future occurrences or events were inevitable, predictable and bound to happen regardless of whatever men and women do, which narrated events or occurrences as 'moving towards an end and ordered in the prospective temporality of a genetic movement'.[235] As a 'critical "deconstruction" of the organic model' of history, the materialist conception of history 'creates radical discontinuities and disrupts the linearity of the temporal process to such an extent that no sequence of actual events or no particular subject could ever acquire, by itself, full historical meaning. They all become part of a process that they neither contain nor reflect, but of which they are a moment. They can never be the source or the end of the movement, but since the movement consists of their totalisation, they can still be said to share in the experience of this moment'.[236] As it's used in 'Metaphor (*Second Discourse*)', then, de Man's use of the term 'economic determinism' with reference to Rousseau's and Marx's approach to theorising political economy is to say the least clumsy, blind to his own insight that ideas are no more wholly a product of their political economic context than they are wholly independent of it.[237]

---

ialism' is a kind of determinism can be read in Bottomore et al. 1983, see the entry on 'determinism' by Roy Bhaskar, pp. 117–19, and Wood 2004, see ch. 8, 'Materialism, Agency and Consciousness', espec. pp. 112–18.

234 De Man, Paul, 'Genesis and Genealogy in Nietzsche's Birth of Tragedy', *Diacritics* 2:4, winter 1972, pp. 44–53, reprinted as 'Genesis and Genealogy (Nietzsche)', AR, ch. 4, pp. 79–102.
235 AR, pp. 79–80.
236 AR, p. 81.
237 Before moving away from this discussion, it's worth noting the following from de Man's '*Le devenir, la poésie*', which was published in *Monde Nouveau* 105, November 1956, with its criticism of crude economic determinism, see the translation, 'Process and Poetry', CW, pp. 64–75 at p. 65: 'Such [thinking that believes it can know history in the same way that science knows its object], in fact, is the origin of the oversimplifications history is subject to when it is characterised as a *labour* governed solely by the principle of utility, and on the basis of which it becomes possible to remove in a radical way both art and poetry from the sphere of its action'. A cursory reading of the *Economic and Philosophical Manuscripts* and *The German Ideology* would be sufficient to demonstrate that this could not have been directed at Marx and Engels. '*Le devenir, la poésie*' was published just four or five months after 'The Dead-End of Formalist Criticism', also in *Monde Nouveau* – see the discussion

Since de Man, in his footnote directing us to it, does not quote the passage from Engels's *Anti-Dürhring* that he has in mind, it is worth giving it almost in full. It illustrates better than would a paraphrase the correspondence between Rousseau and Marx that attracted his attention:

> In the state of nature and savagery men were equal; and as Rousseau regards even language as a perversion of the state of nature, he is fully justified in extending the equality of animals within the limits of a *single* species also to the animal-men recently classified by Haeckel hypothetically as *Alali*, speechless.[238] But these equal animal-men had one quality which gave them an advantage over the other animals, perfectibility, the capacity to develop further; and this became the cause of inequality. So Rousseau sees progress in the birth of inequality. But this progress contained an antagonism, it was at the same time retrogression.
>
> All subsequent advances (beyond the state of nature) meant so many steps seemingly towards the *perfection of the individual*, but in reality towards the *decay of the species*. ...
>
> Each new advance in civilisation is at the same time a new advance in inequality. All institutions set up by the society which has arisen with civilisation turn into the opposite of their original purpose.
>
> It is an incontestable fact, and the basic maxim of all constitutional law, that the peoples gave themselves chiefs to safeguard their liberty and not to enslave them.
>
> Nevertheless, the chiefs necessarily become the oppressors of the peoples and intensify their oppression to the point at which inequality, carried to the utmost extreme, is again turned into its opposite and becomes the cause of equality: before the despot all are equal – equally ciphers.

---

above. That De Man's comments were directed against the idea of 'economic determinism' becomes clear when they are placed alongside these remarks in Empson 1935, p. 19, from whence they may have been appropriated: 'Literature is a social process, and also an attempt to reconcile the conflicts of an individual in whom those of society will be mirrored. (The belief that man's ideas are wholly the product of his economic setting is of course as fatuous as the belief that they are wholly independent of it.)'

238 Ernst Heinrich Philipp August Haeckel (1834–1919), a German biologist and philosopher who popularized Charles Darwin's work in Germany. The *Alali*, 'speechless ape-men' or 'speechless primitive men', are hypothesized in his *The Evolution of Man*, II, 1874.

Those persons who might be interested in how Engels theorised the origin of language are directed to his 1876 essay 'The Part Played by Labour in the Transition from Ape to Man', in Marx and Engels 1991, pp. 339–49, see pp. 341–42.

> Here we have the final measure of inequality, *the last point which completes the circle and meets the point from which we set out*: here all private individuals become equal once more, just because they are nothing, and the subjects have no other law than their master's will. But the despot is only master so long as he possesses force, and therefore he cannot complain of the use of force as soon as he is driven out. ... Force alone maintained him, force overthrows him, and thus everything takes its natural course.
>
> So inequality once more turns into equality, though not into the former natural equality of speechless primitive men, but into the higher equality of the social contract. The oppressors are oppressed. It is the negation of the negation.[239]

Though Marx's notion of the dialectic was not as universal as Engels's – with regard to the negation of the negation, for example, it was specific to Capitalism – and neither presupposed nor entailed a dialectics of nature,[240] Engels finds in Rousseau's *Discourse on the Origin of Inequality* 'not only a line of thought which corresponds exactly to the one developed in Marx's *Capital*, but in detail, too, a whole series of the same dialectical turns of speech as Marx used: processes which in their nature are antagonistic, contain an internal contradiction; transformation of one extreme into its opposite; and finally as the kernel of the whole thing, the negation of the negation'.[241]

Since there is nothing in Engels's commentary to suggest otherwise, it seems likely that both he and Marx considered that once returned from his condition of inequality and propertylessness, man will continue to alienate himself in language[242] – language being the material in which man realises himself by losing himself, where he becomes Other in order to become himself.

Despite revealing an interest in Marx and Engels's critique of political economy in his essay on Rousseau's *Second Discourse*, it is perhaps not surprising, given the interest he'd shown in it previously, that, when facing up to the difficulties presented by other political texts, de Man directed himself not to Engels's *Anti-Dühring* or Marx's *Capital* but to Marx and Engels's *The German*

---

239 Engels 1976, pp. 177–8. See Rousseau 1993, 'A Discourse on the Origin of Inequality', pp. 91–2, p. 102, p. 114.
240 See, for example, Engels 1955, and Engels 1976, 'Preface' II, pp. 11–16, Introduction, pp. 28–31, p. 33.
241 Engels 1976, pp. 178–9.
242 See note 84 above regarding Marx's knowledge of and contribution to Engels's *Anti-Dühring*.

Ideology (especially the way it drafted a materialist conception of history and a critique of ideology). What he found there can be read in 'The Resistance to Theory', one of de Man's most obviously particular and intentionally political essays.

'The Resistance to Theory' (1982)

'The Resistance to Theory', published as the lead essay in the 1986 collection of the same name, was drafted some years before in response to a request from the Modern Languages Association – de Man's own scholarly and professional association – to write the section on literary theory in its planned *Introduction to Scholarship in Modern Languages and Literatures*. The commission required that he 'provide the reader with a select but comprehensive list of the main trends and publications in the field ... synthesize and classify the main problematic areas and ... lay out a critical and programmatic projection of the solutions which can be expected in the foreseeable future'.[243] What de Man provided, much against the grain, was an explanation of 'why the main theoretical interest of literary theory consists of the impossibility of its definition'.[244] Not surprisingly, de Man's essay wasn't used and another essay was commissioned that would be 'closer to the professional questions' that the MLA thought needed addressing. The MLA's reaction to de Man's essay was not only understandable but also symptomatic of the extent to which, in the United States, the academic profession considered 'theory as an obstacle to scholarship and, consequently, to teaching'.[245] One could say that, as far as the MLA was concerned, de Man's essay did not accord well to the ideologies and politics of the profession.

In the course of his essay, de Man gives several explicit formulations of what constitutes the resistance to literary theory: 'The resistance to theory is a resistance to the use of language about language', specifically the reflexive use of language;[246] 'The resistance to theory is in fact a resistance to reading', that is to every instance of language-use, literary and non-literary discourse, and even spoken language;[247] 'The resistance to theory is a resistance to the rhetor-

---

243 RT, p. 3.
244 Ibid.
245 RT, p. 4.
246 RT, p. 12.
247 RT, pp. 15; 17–18.

ical or tropological dimension of language';[248] and 'Nothing can overcome the resistance to theory since theory *is* itself this resistance'.[249] The rhetorical structure of language never ceases to occasion interpretation and always withholds or denies a single, stable meaning; and, since literary theory is inevitably and unavoidably made of rhetorical language effecting multiple, unstable meanings, it cannot overpower or best the resistance opposed to it. Even though literary theory's interpretations of the resistance to theory will be technically correct and irrefutable, they will 'still avoid and resist the reading they advocate'.[250]

By way of giving an example of the resistance to theory de Man points to those critics who have claimed that he pays attention only to words and denies any reality beyond those words. De Man's response to this is that, to the contrary, 'the referential function of language is not being denied – far from it: what is in question is its authority as a model for phenomenal cognition'.[251]

> Literature is fiction not because it somehow refuses to acknowledge 'reality' but because it is not *a priori* certain that language functions according to principles which are those, or which are *like* those, of the phenomenal world.
>
> It is therefore not *a priori* certain that literature is a reliable source of information about anything but its own language. It would be unfortunate, for example, to confuse the materiality of the signifier with the materiality of what it signifies. This may seem obvious enough on the level of light and sound, but it is less so with regard to the more general phenomenality of space, time or especially of the self; no one in his right mind will try to grow grapes by the luminosity of the word 'day', but it is very difficult not to conceive the pattern of one's past and future existence as in accordance with temporal and spatial schemes that belong to fictional narratives and not to the world. This does not mean that fictional narratives are not part of the world and of reality; their impact on the world may be all too strong for comfort ...[252]

De Man, reiterating what he had said elsewhere, and for some time, makes the point that any text, discourse or utterance, any instance of literary and non-literary language, is a form of fiction. It's fiction not because language makes no

---

248 RT, p. 17.
249 RT, p. 19.
250 RT, p. 19.
251 RT, pp. 10–11.
252 RT, p. 11.

reference to reality (for what meaning would it have if it did not?) but because the laws that are the basis of the way we perceive the material world seem not to govern the way we communicate our perceptions of it. The seemingly direct connection between the materiality of a word – de Man's example is the word 'day' – and the materiality of the thing it refers to – 'luminosity' or the period of radiated light between sunrise and sunset – is misleading.[253] The natural, direct link that pertains in sense perception – the immediate contact that one has with the external world through the senses – is not present in language. There is a difference between the physical processes of *seeing* (light emitted from the sun is reflected off objects in the external world into the eye; it enters the eye through the cornea, which bends it and passes it through the pupil; it then hits the lens, which focuses light rays onto the retina as an inverted image; the optic nerve then carries that image as electrical impulses – signals of light, dark and colours – to the brain where they are assembled into another image, this one the right-way up) and *seeing* those retinal sensations *as* something (having what is seen coalesce in the context of prior knowledge about what is seen and language so as to be able to name it 'day'). In language, the relationship between the phonic or scopic substantiality of the sign ('day') and its referent ('luminosity' or the period of radiated light between sunrise and sunset) is based not on the immediate sensory or phenomenal experience of *seeing* but is effected by cognition, by orienting oneself in relation to the process of linguistic conceptualisation ... by *seeing ... as*.[254]

Though 'a language entirely freed of referential constraints is properly inconceivable',[255] the rhetorical structure of language gives it such great freedom from referentiality[256] that the meaning of any text, discourse or utterance cannot be properly thought of as caused or brought about by 'considerations of truth and falsehood, good and evil, beauty and ugliness, or pleasure or pain'.[257] It is the 'absence of any ["necessary"] link between utterance and a referent' that makes language a form of fiction[258] and an unreliable means of communicating knowledge about the world. Despite that, these fictions tell us about our lives, about how we have lived, live, and might live. They represent our feelings and thoughts about our surroundings, patterns of ideas and beliefs about

---

253 RT, p. 11.
254 My use of 'seeing' and 'seeing ... as' – which seems to me to do little violence to reading this passage – is taken from Wittgenstein 1968, 193e–204e, *passim*, and Hanson 1972, pp. 5–30, *passim*.
255 RT, p. 49.
256 RT, p. 10.
257 RT, p. 10.
258 AR, p. 292.

the here and now, past and future, about Being and beings. And, as de Man pointed out in 'Roland Barthes and the Limits of Structuralism', when these fictions are 'enlisted in the service of collective patterns of interest' – most especially, of course, the interests of particular classes in conflict with each other – and become 'ideologies', their effects can be overpoweringly uncomfortable.

> What we call ideology is precisely the confusion of linguistic with natural reality, of reference with phenomenalism. It follows that, more than any other mode of inquiry, including economics, the linguistics of literariness is a powerful and indispensable tool in the unmasking of *ideological aberrations* [emphasis added] as well as a determining factor in accounting for their occurrence. Those who reproach literary theory for being oblivious to social and historical (that is to say ideological) reality are merely stating their fear at having their own ideological mystifications exposed by the tool they are trying to discredit. They are, in short, very poor readers of Marx's *German Ideology*.[259]

Ideology: Ideological aberrations: Aberration: We began to consider the peculiarities of aberration when we first encountered it in de Man's reading of Girard's *Mensonge romantique et vérité romanesque* and thereafter in 'Roland Barthes and the Limits of Structuralism' and 'Metaphor (*Second Discourse*)'. Before we progress with 'The Resistance to Theory', we should take that previously announced excursus into what de Man meant by 'aberration:' the aberration that is anything but aberrant; that is always-present; that makes the aberrant true and turns the truth of the aberration into a lie; and that when, because belief is legitimate only within the limits of the (con)text, this error is pointed out, denies it turns the truth back into a lie.[260] In this respect, as we'll see, aberration and ideology are almost synonymous: both make the unbearable bearable, the thinkable more or less unthinkable, the aberrant normal, and – remember Rousseau's example of the first man to fence in some land and say 'this belongs to me' – give a quality of inevitably to what is in fact a specific and disputable relation to the relations of production.[261]

---

259   RT, p. 11.
260   AR, p. 151.
261   AR, p. 157.

Excursus: Aberration[262]

Is it [the unity of a consciousness and its objects] not rather a play of language, an illusion as arbitrary as the shape of the constellations which share a common plane only as the result of an optical appearance?

DE MAN, 'Tropes (Rilke)'

⋯

A consciousness of the fallacy of our senses is one of the most important consequences of the study of nature. This study teaches that no object is seen by us in its true place, owing to aberration; that

---

262   Geoffrey Bennington, 'Aberrations: de Man (and) the Machine', in Waters and Godzich (eds.) 1989, pp. 209–22. Bennington counts – but, unfortunately, doesn't identify – at least fifty uses of aberration and its cognates in *Allegories of Reading*. To give just three or four examples of my own: in 'Semiology and Rhetoric' there are 'the vertiginous potentialities of referential aberration' (AR, p. 10) and 'the aberrations of the poets' (AR, p. 17); in 'Rhetoric of Tropes (Nietzsche)' (AR, p. 109) 'philosophical models such as the phenomenology of consciousness' are 'aberrations'; and in 'Allegory of Reading (*Profession de Foi*)' there are 'the aberrations of figural language' (AR, p. 245).

Bennington offers an interesting and useful discussion of what he thinks de Man meant by 'aberration' in relation to de Man's idea of the 'text-as-machine', the machine that is 'like the grammar of the text when it is isolated from rhetoric, the merely formal element without which no text can be generated' and which, from 'a certain perspective … may be concealed by aesthetic, formalistic delusions' – see 'Excuses (*Confessions*)', AR, pp. 294–9 at p. 294.

Bennington points to two kinds of aberration: one (AR, 216) that 'depends on a principle of great generality that could no doubt be formalized whenever one of a series of elements is also used transcendentally with respect to that series in order to totalize, dominate, or explain it … This type of aberration comes from bogus reasoning and self-confirming claims'; and another (AR, p. 217, p. 216) that implies that the element that's taken as transcendent with regard to the series is, in fact, neither 'simple' nor 'secure' and 'leads us to de Man's own sense of "aberration" or the "impossibility of reading"'. See also, utilising Bennington, McQuillan 2001, pp. 122–3.

Warminski, 'Ending Up/taking Back', in Caruth and Esch (eds.) 1995, pp. 24–5, provides another reading of De Man's use of 'aberration', one that to some extent reduces 'aberration' to something 'aberrant'.

I've taken note of Warminski, McQuillan and Bennington but, as the epigraphs suggest, what follows takes a different approach, one that is more sympathetic to the way that 'aberration' (from the Latin *aberrare*, meaning to wander or go astray) is deployed in optics where it refers to the action of straying or to an individual instance or effect of that straying.

the colours of substances are solely the effects of the action of matter upon light; and that light itself, as well as heat and sound, are not real beings, but modes of action communicated to our perceptions by the nerves.

MARY SOMERVILLE, *The Connection of the Physical Sciences* (1834)

∴

To suppose that the eye with all its inimitable contrivances for adjusting the focus to different distances, for admitting different amounts of light, and for the correction of spherical and chromatic aberration, could have been formed by natural selection ... should not be considered as subversive of the theory.

CHARLES DARWIN, *The Origin of Species* (1859)

∴

When we read 'Metaphor (*Second Discourse*)', we noted that de Man explained 'aberration' as made of two levels or, better still, two moments of conceptualisation – one spontaneous or unintentional, the other intentional – that effect the word 'man'.[263] Though one cannot say for certain that 'discourse about man is referential or not',[264] any narrative, any cognitive discourse, says de Man in 'Self (*Pygmalion*)', with reference to the *Second Discourse*, is always the story of 'a man [speaking] of man ... to men'[265] for a 'narrative that endlessly tells the story of its own denominational aberration ... can only repeat this aberration at various levels of rhetorical complexity'.[266] The process of conceptualisation that de Man reads in the *Second Discourse* whereby 'The unwarranted substitution of knowledge for mere sensation becomes paradigmatic for a wide set of aberrations all linked to the propositional power of language in general' and permits 'the radical possibility that all being, as the ground for entities, may be linguistically "gesetzt" [posited], a correlative of speech acts' ('Rhetoric of Persuasion (Nietzsche)').[267] In other words, aberration is a 'linguistic event ...

---

263   AR, pp. 153–4.
264   AR, p. 161.
265   AR, p. 160.
266   AR, p. 162.
267   AR, p. 162.

within which the entire process of substitution and reversal' takes place and inside is swapped for outside, effect for cause, subject for object, 'tongue' for language, and figures of speech for truth ('Rhetoric of Tropes (Nietzsche)').[268] To rephrase something that was said a moment ago: This process not only turns a falsehood into truth but can also turn that falsehood towards truth. For example, though Rilke's *Elegies* and the *Sonnets* 'have been the main source of evidence in trying to prove the adequacy of Rilke's rhetoric to the truth of his affirmations, yet his notion of figural language eliminates all truth claims from his discourse'. Rilke's poetry 'gains a maximum convincing power' in the way it simultaneously effects truthfulness and rejects it ('Tropes (Rilke)').[269] Or, as de Man puts it in his reading of a passage in Proust's *A la recherche du temps perdu*, 'If one of the readings is declared true, it will always be possible to undo it by means of the other; if it is decreed false, it will always be possible to demonstrate that it states the truth of its aberration' ('Reading (Proust)').[270] If truth is a moment of falsehood then there is in every falsehood a moment of truth. Though it is difficult to know whether this simultaneity leaves the text 'in negative certainty' or 'suspended in ignorance of its own truth or falsehood' ('Semiology and Rhetoric'),[271] it 'may well turn out to be an exemplary model in trying to understand the aberrant [mistaken] interpretation of Romanticism that shapes the genealogy of our present-day historical consciousness' ('Genesis and Genealogy (Nietzsche)').[272] In as much as an 'aberrant interpretation' of Romanticism mistakes the aberration of truth for the truth of the aberration it does not diverge from the *normal* interpretation of Romanticism, from the accepted, standard interpretation of that 'truly historical consciousness' that is grounded in the substitution of knowledge for sensation, and so on and so forth.

De Man's essays of the 1970s reprise the observation he'd made in 'The Contemporary Criticism of Romanticism', the first Gauss Seminar lecture of 1967: 'Aberration', whose 'systematic recurrence extends throughout the entirety of classical metaphysics' ('Rhetoric of Tropes (Nietzsche)'),[273] is such a regular, typical, usual, unavoidable, necessary and 'not necessarily intentional' ('Rhetoric of Persuasion (Nietzsche)')[274] action and effect of the 'formal, rhetorical

---

268   AR, pp. 108; 110–11.
269   AR, pp. 50–1.
270   AR, p. 76.
271   AR, p. 17.
272   AR, p. 102.
273   AR, p. 109.
274   AR, p. 123.

potential of ... language' ('Metaphor (*Second Discourse*)')²⁷⁵ that one can hardly describe it as being in any way aberrant. Indeed, 'no human self could come into being' without what might be regarded as the fundamental aberration of 'self-autonomy ... asserted as a philosophical truth about the nature of human existence' ('Rhetoric of Tropes (Nietzsche)').²⁷⁶

So why does de Man name the consequence of this process of substitution and reversal 'aberration'? We might move closer to understanding what he's getting at if we think about what it names in the study of optics, the scientific study of sight and the behaviour of light. There are good reasons for doing this not least because de Man himself, increasingly from the late 1960s through the 1980s, was preoccupied with 'the fundamental epistemological metaphor of understanding as seeing',²⁷⁷ which depends on 'the necessary link between the existence and the knowledge of entities, on the unbreakable strength of the tie that unites the sun (as entity) with the eye (as the knowledge of the entity)'.²⁷⁸ In the narrated world of Proust's *A la recherche du temps perdu* this metaphor, which begins, as it were, in an actual light and dark, an actual outside and inside, sets up a system of relays that allows the properties to enter into substitutions, exchanges, and crossings, turns 'natural light' into 'the light of art'.²⁷⁹ 'If the sounds of nature are akin to those of speech', de Man wrote in 'Anthropomorphism and Trope in the Lyric', 'then nature also speaks by ways of light, the light of the senses as well as of the mind ... the reconciliation of knowledge with phenomenal, aesthetic experience, is summarized in the figure of speaking'.²⁸⁰ As one commentator put it, de Man wanted to '*visualize language* – that is, to identify the fully reciprocal relations between the light *in* the world, what gives the world to us in vision, and the light we throw *on* the world in speech'.²⁸¹ He wanted to *visualise* the linguistic act of conceptualisation and

---

275   AR, pp. 154–6.
276   AR, p. 111.
277   See 'Reading (Proust)', AR, p. 60 note 5.
278   'Reading (Proust)', AR, pp. 60–1 note 5 at p. 61.
279   AR, pp. 60–1 note 5.
280   RR, p. 258.
281   See Whitney Davis, 'Opticality and Rhetoricity in Paul de Man's "Historical Materialism"', in Davis 1996, pp. 232–53 at p. 233. Davis's essay proceeds chiefly from the same passages in de Man's 'Phenomenality and Materiality in Kant' that will concern us directly but from a different tack. Davis regards de Man as a 'linguistic idealist' who 'wanted to think himself ... to be engaged in a material history – that is to say a *non*theological one – [of the word]'. Davis's 'material history' is emphatically not Marx and Engels's materialist conception of history or the historical and material preconditions of its formulation.

For more on the reciprocal relations of light *in* the world and *on* the world in de Man

did so by reference to optics, wherein 'aberration' refers to a performance of the optical system and the kinds of image produced by it.

De Man's interest in optics as it comes into place in the 1960s is evidenced, for example, in 'Criticism and Crisis', which was published in the spring 1967 around the time of the first Gauss Seminar lecture.[282] Here, while discussing the interpretation of myth in *Tristes tropiques* and *Le Cru et le cuit*, he commented on the use that Lévi-Strauss made of seeing as a metaphor for cognition.

> The relative unity of traditional myths always depends on the existence of a privileged point of view to which the method itself denies any status of authenticity. 'Contrary to philosophical reflection, which claims to return to the source', writes Claude Lévi-Strauss in *Le Cru et le cuit*, 'the reflective activities involved in the structural study of myths deal with light rays that issue from a virtual focal point. ...' The method aims at preventing this virtual focus from being made into a *real* source of light. The analogy with optics is perhaps misleading, for in literature everything hinges on the existential status of the focal point; and the problem is more complex when it involves the disappearance of the self as a constitutive subject.
>
> These remarks have made the transition from anthropology to the field of language and, finally, of literature. In the act of anthropological intersubjective interpretation, a fundamental discrepancy always prevents the observer from coinciding fully with the consciousness he is observing. The same discrepancy exists in everyday language, in the impossibility of making the actual expression coincide with what has to be expressed, of making the actual sign coincide with what it signifies.[283]

De Man returns to the quotation from Lévi-Strauss at the end of his essay. Lévi-Strauss, he says,

> had to give up the notion of [the individual, 'romantic'] subject to safeguard reason. The subject, he said, in fact, is a 'foyer virtuel' [virtual focal point], a mere hypothesis posited by scientists to give consistency to the behaviour of entities. The metaphor in his statement that 'the reflective activities [of the structuralists] deal with light that issues from a virtual

---

      see, for example, 'Anthropomorphism and Trope in the Lyric', *The Rhetoric of Romanticism*, p. 258.
282 De Man, Paul, 'The Crisis of Contemporary Criticism', *Arion* 6:1, spring 1967, pp. 38–57, reprinted, revised as 'Criticism and Crisis', Chapter 1, *Blindness & Insight*, pp. 3–19.
283 BI, pp. 10–11.

focal point' stems from the elementary laws of optical refraction. The image is all the more striking since it plays on the confusion between the imaginary loci of the physicist and the *fictional* entities that occur in literary language. The virtual focus is a quasi-objective structure posited to give rational integrity to a process that exists independently of the self. The subject merely fills in, with the dotted line of geometrical construction, what natural reason had not bothered to make explicit; it has a passive and unproblematic role. The 'virtual focus' is, strictly speaking, a nothing, but its nothingness concerns us very little, since a mere act of reason suffices to give it a mode of being that leaves the rational order unchallenged.[284]

Another example of de Man's interest in optical systems – specifically, the way an image is produced by the image-forming optical system of the human eye – can be read much later, towards the end of his life, in his fourth Messenger Lecture, 'Phenomenality and Materiality in Kant', an essay that has provoked several rigorous critical engagements with his particular way of reading Kant but which, here, in the sprit of explication, as it were, is taken more or less on trust.[285]

In 'Phenomenality and Materiality in Kant' de Man puzzles a 'materialism' – a concern only with matter and its movements and modifications – in Kant's writing about the aesthetic that 'posterity has not yet begun to face up to'.[286] This he does by reading the sections on the sublime in the second book of *The Critique of Judgement* where Kant tries to establish a difference between the mathematical sublime and the dynamic sublime, between the teleological sublimity effected by the Great Pyramids and the interior of St Peter's, Rome (which were made to overwhelm the beholder), and the sublimity effected by 'objects of nature' (which must provoke a purposefully purposeless, non-teleological judgment). Kant's examples from nature are 'the sight of the starry heaven' and 'the sight of the ocean':

> If, then, we call the sight of the starry heaven *sublime*, we must not place at the foundation of judgment concepts of worlds inhabited by rational beings and regard the bright points, with which we see the space above us filled, as their suns moving in circles purposefully fixed with refer-

---

[284] BI, pp. 18–19.
[285] See especially Gasché, 'In-Difference to Philosophy: de Man on Kant, Hegel, and Nietzsche', in Waters and Godzich (eds.) 1989, pp. 259–94.
[286] AI, p. 89.

ence to them; but we must regard it, just as we see it [*wie man ihn sieht*], as a distant all-embracing vault [*ein weites Gewölbe*]. Only under such a representation can we range that sublimity that a pure aesthetic judgment ascribes to this object. And in the same way, if we are to call the sight of the ocean sublime, we must not think of it as we ordinarily do, as implying all kinds of knowledge (that are not contained in immediate intuition). For example, we sometimes think of the ocean as a vast kingdom of aquatic creatures, or as the great source of those vapors that fill the air with clouds for the benefit of the land, or again as an element that, though dividing continents from each other, yet promotes the greatest communication between them; all these produce merely teleological judgments. To find the ocean nevertheless sublime we must regard it as poets do [*wie die Dichter es tun*], merely by what the eye reveals [*was der Augenschein zeigt*] – if it is at rest, as a clear mirror of water onlybounded by the heavens; if it is stormy, as an abyss threatening to overwhelm everything.[287]

De Man finds it difficult to accept these examples. Though he acknowledges that what Kant says is remarkable in that it anticipates passages in Romantic poetry, he knows of no poets who 'perceive the world in an architectonic rather than a teleological way', that is to say as an 'apriori previous to any understanding'.[288] And 'how can the architectonic then be said to be opposed to the teleological? How are we to understand the term *Augenschein* in relation to other allusions to sensory appearance that abound in the attempts to define or describe the sublime?'[289] Much depends on the way that de Man reads *Augenschein*, a 'redundant word ... in which the eye, tautologically, is named twice, as eye itself and as what appears to the eye'.[290]

De Man notices an example in the Kantian corpus that seems to match the poet who regards the starry heaven and the ocean 'merely by what the eye reveals', 'merely by what appears to the eye' or 'merely by what strikes the

---

287 AI, p. 80. See Kant in *Werkausgabe, 10*, p. 196. De Man's translation is taken, slightly amended, from Kant 1951, pp. 110–11. His change to the text is significant and somewhat puzzling. Bernard translates '*bloß ... nach dem, was der Augenschein zeigt*' as 'merely by what *strikes* the eye' (emphasis added), which de Man changes to 'merely by what the eye *reveals*' (emphasis added). I find this odd insofar as Bernard's 'strikes' seems to suit de Man's reading of the passage better than does 'reveals', for light does indeed strike the eye, whereas the eye doesn't reveal anything.
288 AI, p. 82.
289 AI, p. 81.
290 AI, p. 82.

eye' – 'bloß ... nach dem, was der Augenschein zeigt' – in 'a lesser known passage' in the *Jäche Logik*. This passage attends to the *twofold* relation that cognition has

> first ... to the *object*, second ... to the *subject*. In the former respect it is related to *representation*, in the latter to *consciousness*, the universal condition of all cognition in general. (Consciousness is really a representation that another representation is in me.) In every cognition we must distinguish *matter*, i.e. the object, and form, i.e. *the way in which* we cognize the object.²⁹¹

In de Man's translation, what follows on from this narrates the story of

> a wild man [*ein Wilder*] who, from a distance, sees a house of which he does not know the use. He certainly observes the same object as does another, who knows it to be definitely built and arranged to serve as a dwelling for human beings. Yet in formal terms this knowledge of the selfsame object differs in both cases. For the first it is mere intuition [*bloße Anschauung*], for the other it is both intuition and concept.²⁹²

Reading this translation, we could say that Kant's 'wild man' cannot *see* the object *as* a house. He is conscious that a representation is in him but cannot bring it to consciousness as form and then attach a concept to it. The material of sensibility or sensation is presented to the mind but unlike Rousseau's *homme sauvage*, who is able to spontaneously generate a 'wild metaphor' to name the fear caused by what he sees, Kant's *Wilder* is thoroughly nonplussed by what strikes his eye. De Man, however, nudging the word 'mere' away from what Kant meant by it in the *Third Critique* (where the 'merely by what the eye reveals'/'by what strikes the eye' – 'bloß ... nach dem, was der Augenschein zeigt' – is in opposition to the purposiveness of determinate judgments) and here in the *Logic* (where the 'mere intuition' – 'bloße Anschauung' – must at least carry the spatial-temporal categories of perception and a gestalt, i.e. a distinct 'object'), says that the wild man 'merely sees'.²⁹³

---

291 Translation taken from Kant, *Lectures on Logic*, trans. and ed. by J. Michael Young, Cambridge, Cambridge University Press, 1992, *The Jäche Logic*, p. 544.
292 AI, p. 81.
293 AI, p. 81. Another take on de Man's reading of Kant in 'Phenomenality and Materiality in Kant' is provided by Andrzej Warminski, '"As the Poets Do It": On the Material Sublime', in Cohen, Hillis Miller, Warminski (eds.), *Material Events*, pp. 3–31.

As far as de Man is concerned, the poet in the *Third Critique* 'who sees the vault of the heavens is clearly like the savage' in the *Logic*.[294] 'The link', he says, 'between seeing and dwelling, *sohen* and *wohnen*, is teleological and therefore absent in pure aesthetic judgment'.[295] In which case, asks de Man (appropriating a term from ophthalmology and neurology to rename 'mere seeing' and the tautological *bloß ... nach dem, was der Augenschein zeigt*): how can mind effect a 'pure aesthetic judgment' of '*pure ocular vision*' if 'pure ocular vision' cannot be brought to consciousness as a 'concrete representation of ideas (*Darstellung von Ideen*)'?[296] And, since 'the sublime does not reside in the natural object but in the mind of man ... the burden of the argument, much rather than emphasizing the purely inward nature of the sublime, becomes the need to account for the fact that it nevertheless occurs as an outward, phenomenal manifestation' as the way in which an actual material object becomes accessible to the ocular sense.[297] It is here – in a way that seems permitted by something Kant says a little later in the same section of the *Logic* where, when considering the difference between distinct and indistinct representations in terms of the *sensible* and *the intellectual*, he makes reference to the sight of the starry heaven, in particular to the Milky Way[298] – that de Man identifies the 'radical materiality of sublime vision', the material of 'mere seeing', of seeing what and 'merely ... by what the eye reveals/by what strikes the eye': *Augenschein*. Not material objects as such but *light* reflected off the extensions of material objects into the eye. *Light*. 'Not the sudden discovery of a true world as an unveiling, as the a-letheia of Heidegger's *Lichtung*'[299] but the immaterial materiality of the movements and modifications of light – *light* as itself the material of pure ocular vision: a 'phenomenality ... that ... is not material'.[300] As Mary Somerville put it, light

---

294   AI, p. 81.
295   AI, p. 83.
296   Ibid.
297   Ibid.
298   See Kant in *Werkausgabe*, 6, pp. 459–60.
299   AI, p. 82.
300   See de Man's remarks in response to Christopher Fynsk following the fifth Messenger Lecture, 'Kant and Schiller', AI, p. 161, about Heidegger 'on the word *Schein* [shine, emit or reflect light, appearance], and the phenomemalism of the word *Schein* ... [who] in talking of *Lichtung* ... understands phenomenality in a way which would not have been accessible to Husserl ...' de Man says, 'There is an extension of the notion of phenomenality, an ontologization of the notion of phenomenality which is highly suggestive, and which has held me enthralled for many years ... But I think that it is not material'.
 I realize that I may be taken to task if I don't mention Cohen, Cohen, Hillis Miller, Warminski (eds.) 2001. The title of the editors' introduction to *Material Events*, 'A Materiality without Matter', is taken from Derrida's essay, 'Typewriter Ribbon: Limited Ink (2)

isn't a 'being' but a kind of action or process communicated to our perception by the nerves. In which case, how can one connect this event or occurrence with understanding and language? How can one conceptualise mere seeing or pure ocular vision? As far as de Man is concerned, it can 'hardly be called literal, which would imply its possible figuralization or symbolization by an act of judgment. The only word that comes to mind is that of a *material* vision, but how this materiality is then to be understood in linguistic terms is not, as yet, clearly intelligible ... In the same way and to the same extent that this vision is purely material, devoid of any reflexive or intellectual complication, it is also purely formal, devoid of any semantic depth and reducible to the formal mathematization and geometrization of pure optics'.[301] *Light* as 'matter', as an object of perception, can only be brought to consciousness – formalised, mapped or diagrammatised – according to the mathematical and geometrical laws and procedures of optics as lines and points, planes and surfaces, heights, slopes and angles of incidence. Or, as de Man put it in 'Criticism and Crisis', around the time of the first Gauss Seminar lecture, and similarly drawing on Lévi-Strauss's thinking on the reflective activity of light rays, with the subject filling in, with the dotted lines of geometrical construction, what reason fails to make explicit.[302] Thus, says de Man, Kant's *Critique of Judgement*

> ends up ... in a formal materialism that runs counter to all values and characteristics associated with aesthetic experience, including the aesthetic experience of the beautiful and of the sublime as described by Kant and Hegel themselves. The tradition of their interpretation, as it appears from near contemporaries such as Schiller on, has seen only this one, figural, and if you will, 'romantic' aspect of their theories of the imagination, and has entirely overlooked what we call the material aspect. Neither has it understood the place and the function of formalization in this intricate process.[303]

So, given that, according to Sections 24 through 29 of the *Third Critique*, the sublime depends on the articulation of imagination with reason (by way of either

("within such limits")', pp. 277–360, wherein Derrida, 'apropos of de Man' and mentioning 'Phenomenality and Materiality in Kant' (and the earlier 'Kant's Materialism'), but focusing on texts other than those read here, puzzles his own idea of 'what might be a thinking of mechanistic materiality without materialism and perhaps even without matter' (see p. 281).

301 AI, pp. 82; 83.
302 BI, p. 19.
303 AI, p. 83.

the faculty of cognition or desire), how does imagination, as a tool of reason, translate the abstractions of reason back into the phenomenal world of appearances and images if what has to be brought to consciousness as the 'concrete representation of ideas' (*Darstellung von Ideen*) is effected not by the material world as such but by a 'phenomenality ... that ... is not material', 'mere seeing', 'pure ocular vision' (*Augenschein*)?[304] How does the imagination fit with or adjust to reason and how does the aesthetic mediate between the perceptual and the conceptual, theoretical reason and practical reason, metaphysical philosophy and transcendental philosophy and so unify critical philosophy? In answering this question, de Man notices how Kant relies not on 'tight analytic argument' but on 'a story, a dramatized scene of a mind in action'[305] and the leverage provided by the apposition of near phonemes, on 'the play of the letter and syllable, the way of saying ... as opposed to what is being said ...',[306] to turn *Verwunderung*, the 'astonishment that borders on terror' that is the initial effect of the sublime (imagination's failure to grasp magnitude), *into Berwunderung*, 'tranquil admiration' (imagination's success as an agent of reason).[307] The imagination 'becomes adequate (*angemessen*) to reason on the basis of its inadequacy (*Unangemessenheit*) to this same reason in its relation to nature'.[308] At the end of 'Phenomenality and Materiality in Kant', in the very last sentence, it all comes down to language, linguistic conceptualisation and especially to 'the prosaic materiality of the letter', which 'no degree of obfuscation or ideology can transform ... into the phenomenal cognition of aesthetic judgment'.[309] This is the *truth* that's revealed in and by Kant's *Critique of Judgement* that has been overlooked and carried forward by Kant's legatees: the reconciliation of consciousness with representation, knowledge with phenomenal experience that's given in and by an aesthetic judgment is but another self-deceit or self-delusion effected by the process of linguistic conceptualisation. It's another *mensonge romantique*, another bit of ideology – aesthetic ideology.

Before we quit 'Phenomenality and Materiality in Kant' we should keep in mind, however, that the 'prosaic materiality' is not quite the commonplace fact or appearance of the letters printed on the page or the sound of spoken syllables prior to and opposed to their signifying function. It is, rather, the way that the visual or aural sensory affect of the fact or appearance of the 'prosaic

---

304 Ibid.
305 AI, p. 86.
306 AI, p. 89.
307 AI, p. 84.
308 AI, p. 86.
309 AI, p. 90.

materiality of the letter' (phonemes and graphemes), 'inscription' or language, speaking or writing properly understood as an material event or occurrence effects a direct connection with what it refers to, either a material event or object in nature or an act or object of mind. And not only speaking and writing but also, as Barthes demonstrated in the essays in *Mythologies*, all meaningful social practices, material events and occurrences. It requires no great effort to situate this 'obfuscation or ideology', and the reference to the 'formal mathematization or geometrization' of light that takes place in 'pure optics', in a close relation of association with de Man's reference to 'ideological aberrations' in the passage we're reading from 'The Resistance to Theory' – a passage that directs the reader to *The German Ideology*.

∴

> Once into his library, however, and having fixed his one eyeglass in the corner of his eye, in order to take your intellectual breadth and depth ...
> 'Speaking with Karl Marx', *Chicago Tribune*, 5 January, 1879

We now need to bring 'aberration' into clearer focus. The human eye is subject to several defects each of which can produce an optical aberration.[310] These occur when light from one focal point of an object, after transmission through the optical system, does not converge at (or does not diverge from) a single point. An optical aberration is a distortion in the image formed by a defective optical apparatus, especially, in natural optics, as it is caused by a defect in the cornea or lens of the eye. An ideal eye with no focusing imperfections will ensure that all rays of light focus to a single point on the retina but, in actuality, all eyes have some degree of imperfection. To give one example: astigmatism, a very common optical aberration amongst humans – it is a defect usually present at birth and affects most people to some degree – occurs when the front surface of the cornea is slightly irregular in shape (a bit like a rugby ball) and so has different focal lengths for rays of different orientation. Astigmatism causes the rays of light to focus unequally so that they never form a single spot. Some rays may focus on the retina, while others may focus in front of the retina. Some areas of vision may be clear, while others may be distorted.

---

310   What follows is taken from:
      www.astrosurf.com/luxorion/report-aberrations.htm; www.olympusmicro.com/primer/anatomy/aberrationhome.html; www.scienceworld.wolfram.com/physics/OpticalAberrations.html; www.telescope-optics.net/eye_aberrations.htm; www.eyeway.org/inform/Astigmatism.htm; www.sinopt.com/software1/usrguide54/evaluate/paraxopt.htm.

The brain can correct some common optical aberrations, such as chromatic aberration. Others, such as astigmatism, it cannot.

The illusion and delusion that leads one to take linguistic reality for natural reality, reference for phenomenalism, is, so to speak, the result of an unavoidable and inescapable imperfection inherent in the structure and process of linguistic conceptualisation. De man *visualises* this in terms of the way a defect in the lens of a human eye or a placement of optical elements within the system causes an aberration and a blurred or distorted image to be sent to the brain, which taking that image as the subjective form of the object outside the eye makes sense of it as best it can. In terms of the way that de Man theorises it, there's a fundamental defect or misplacement of elements – especially with regard to fictionality, figurality, superimposed ordering and rhetoricity – in the process of linguistic conceptualisation that prevents what has to be expressed from coinciding with its actual expression. However, once expressed, and externalised in the immediate materiality of language, that mistaken expression, which is made of a distortion or 'lie' superimposed on a defect or 'error', is taken for the truth of what had to be expressed. Even so – simply to remind us – no human self could come into being were it not for this unavoidable linguistic aberration.[311]

Aberration: With that much now in place, but before returning to 'The Resistance to Theory', it is worth taking note of what seems to be the earliest use of the term in the essays that de Man produced after he'd moved to the United States. This can be found in 'Montaigne and Transcendence', an essay that began as a paper de Man presented whilst a graduate student in comparative literature at Harvard University, 1952–5, which was then published by Georges Bataille's journal *Critique* in 1955.[312] As we'll see directly, its context of use is explicitly with reference to politics and ideology; and as we've seen, de Man by this time had some kind of presence within the New York Left – which is to say Marxist – intelligentsia.[313]

'Montaigne and Transcendence' can be taken as establishing – and perhaps was even intended to establish – de Man's beginning in the institution of the university in his adopted country. That it provides the transatlantic entry to

---

311 AR, p. 111. Outside optics, one might also theorise de Man's use of 'aberration' in a relation to Kenneth Burke's use of 'deflection' or Freud's 'displacement' (as Jacques Lacan brought it into a mutual relation with rhetorical procedures), see de Man, 'Semiology and Rhetoric', AI, p. 8.
312 Waters, 'Paul de Man', CW, pp. xxxi–xxxii – see Paul de Man, *'Montaigne et la transcendence'*, *Monde Nouveau* 93, October 1955, pp. 41–7.
313 See above, Chapter 3, 'Action, Revolution and Painting (Resumed)', p. 63, note 65.

his concern with 'selfhood' and the 'structure of self-understanding and self-representation', which comes to the fore in the essays written in the 1970s, is not in doubt – though not thus far by way of the self's figural and epistemologically unreliable structure: rhetorical categories had not yet been substituted for existential ones.[314]

As de Man reads them, the *Essays* show that Montaigne is not 'the subjectivist, the chronicler of pure immanence' that he has been taken to be.[315] In other words, they are not 'the reflection of an absolute subjectivity'.[316] Montaigne's thought is not structured around the outright 'rejection of transcendence' but is best understood as dialectical – 'every *contra* has a *pro*, and the more vigorous the *contra*, the more powerful the *pro*' – and moves not towards 'static equilibrium' but 'infinite reflections'.[317] Indeed, as far as de Man is concerned, the *Essays* afford us 'one of the fullest and profoundest descriptions of the difficult problem of transcendence, the problem of our ambiguous relations with our own being', the dominant quality of which is 'an impatience with our own limits' manifested 'by the exercise of reason, the attraction of an absolute morality, and finally, by the creation of form' – by epistemology, ethics, and, 'in a diffuse fashion', aesthetics.[318]

Montaigne recognises that subjectivity interposes an impassable or impenetrable screen between mind and matter, that the former can never know the latter, that knowledge is never absolute, that absolute truth is an impossibility, and that any attempt to give objective form to the subjective is bound to fail. Despite that, as de Man reads him, Montaigne refuses to let mind fall into 'the despair of its ignorance' and returns again and again to reflect on its failure *to know*. This is not an easy attitude to adopt since 'The man who has admitted once and for all the impossibility of an abstractly formulable truth deprives himself of all the false security we find in the illusion of governing matter and ourselves'.[319]

Montaigne argues that the 'rational faculties do not act passively under the sway of some superhuman power'.[320] They are driven not by 'truth' but by the 'desire to know', which gives man the pleasure of constructing truth. 'The complication begins once we realize that this desire seeks to destroy itself by dis-

---

314 Waters, 'Paul de Man', CW, p. lxi.
315 CW, p. 3.
316 Ibid.
317 CW, p. 4.
318 Ibid.
319 CW, p. 8.
320 CW, p. 5.

solving in a world of fixed laws in which subjectivity is ultimately suspended'.[321] Montaigne refuses to let the desire *to know* be destroyed in this state of suspended subjectivity. Mind thinks because thought gives it 'human satisfaction' and thought 'cannot tolerate for a moment the notion of its own destruction'.[322] It persists in its repeated attempts *to know* itself and, despite the failures, does not despair of its impotence but in becoming aware of that impotence gains a suppleness and elasticity of perception and understanding. Yet just as mind is not destroyed in the realization that it cannot transcend itself, and that 'the negation of an absolute knowledge implies the negation of a knowable good', so it does not abandon the attraction of an absolute morality or, at least, the attraction of a moral orthodoxy.[323] It gets to grips with the ritualistic conservatism of this orthodoxy and with the 'wretched myths' (not yet the myths of Barthes and Lévi-Strauss but widely held false notions about actual natural and social phenomena, just the same) and the 'sclerotic bureaucracies' (rigid systems of government) into which they degenerate and which are nothing more nor less than 'the dangerous structures [that] men have produced in hopes of achieving some sort of rule' (the ideological and repressive state apparatuses that the ruling class would control in order to maintain their power and ensure the reproduction of the relations of production).[324] De Man – no doubt not only drawing on his own response to Nazism and the German occupation of Belgium but also making the point that, in the 1950s, the world of learning in the United States was not at all removed from the discourse of the public arena – gives 'nation' and 'race' (myths that concerned Barthes two years later in 'Myth Today') as two vivid examples of the 'most factitious loyalties' to which the 'wretched myths' appeal.[325] Though it cannot transcend the attraction of

---

321 CW, p. 6.
322 CW, pp. 5; 6.
323 CW, p. 8.
324 CW, p. 10.
325 CW, p. 10. De Graef 1993, ch. 3, 'The Temptation of Irony', pp. 29–35, see espec. p. 30 and p. 35, reads 'Montaigne and Transcendence' as a 'response to the crisis adumbrated in de Man's war time journalism and to the blueprint for the preservation of European civilisation surrounding that crisis'. While not denying that 'Montaigne and Transcendence' might well be made of such a response, it should also be read in relation to the then contemporary situation in the USA. We should not forget that it was written and published at precisely the moment when the 'sclerotic' McCarthyist phase of the Cold War was disseminating and asserting its own morally wretched versions of what constituted absolute truth and absolute morality with reference to nation and race, Americanness and un-Americanness – a moment of American tragedy that is presently being restaged in Trump's neo-Fascist farce (and providing proof, if proof were needed, that choreographed confusion and absurdity can be more terrifying than the suffering invoked by tragedy, for

moral orthodoxy, mind can, at least, identify and describe the structures and loyalties of the myths it engenders. This process of identification and description – as it would seem to be thirty years later in his reading of Kant's *Critique of Judgement* – is, 'in a diffuse fashion', that of 'a formal and aesthetic order' in which is acknowledged 'the failure of the aesthetic' or the impossibility of mind's attempts to give 'the serene stability of objects' to 'the fluidity of subjective consciousness'.[326]

De Man is here situating Montaigne's 'epistemological transcendence' in relation to Husserl's phenomenology,[327] which distinguishes between how objects are perceived and how they depend on the cognitive activities of seeing, hearing, touching, and so on, between the object given and the subjective activity that we must perform to let it be given. Just the same, though mind and matter are correlative, they can never be reconciled. The most one can do is engage in the precise phenomenological description of the object and the corresponding mental activity, also described phenomenologically. In his *Essays*, Montaigne warns us that 'he does nothing but *describe*' – he is never normative.[328] 'Since Husserl', de Man says, 'we have learned to find in this fundamental humility of the mind, which cannot claim to legislate but only to describe, the best source of resistance to the *aberrations* [emphasis added] of our time'.[329]

Though Husserl is de Man's acknowledged resource, his reading of Montaigne's *Essays* is also informed, unacknowledged, by Merleau-Ponty's philosophy of ambiguity and Heidegger's *Being and Time*:[330] 'the problem of the ambiguity of our relations with our own being'.[331] This might well be the moment – another kind of beginning in published discourse – when de Man became for a while, as he would later remark, 'uncomfortably stuck in ontologism'.[332] In 'Montaigne and Transcendence', he insists on the absolute irreconcilability of mind and matter, subject and object, which, in the publications that immediately follow, he will relate to the 'ontological crisis', the 'awareness

---

it offers no cathartic pleasure what so ever). 'Montaigne and Transcendence' provides us with a good example of how the discourse of the 'academy' is never distinct from the discourse of the 'public arena' and also, in this instance, of how de Man did not try to keep the one free from the other.

326 CW, pp. 10–11.
327 CW, p. 8.
328 CW, p. 4.
329 CW, p. 8.
330 De Graef 1993, p. 182 notes 2, 3.
331 CW, p. 4.
332 Waters, 'Paul de Man', CW, p. lxxii note 92 quoting a letter from de Man to Wlad Godzich, 10 March 1982.

of a deep separation between man's inner consciousness and the totality of what is not himself' that becomes predominant around 1800 and characterises the 'romantic experience', Hegel's 'Unhappy Consciousness', Heidegger's 'separation', and 'the alienation experienced by all the century's great minds'.³³³ Not least, of course, by Marx and Engels.

Explicated thus, and no matter to what extent it inaugurates his post-war thinking about epistemology, morality and aesthetics, and so on and so forth, 'Montaigne and Transcendence' can be taken as marking the beginnings of de Man's future concern with alienation, the structure of self-understanding and self-representation, 'illusion' and *aberration* – 'the illusion of governing matter' and 'the aberrations of our time' – which, of course, are notions integral to his thinking about politics and ideology.

'The Resistance to Theory' (Continued)

We should now return to where we left off with 'The Resistance to Theory':

> ... What we call ideology is precisely the confusion of linguistic with natural reality, of reference with phenomenalism. It follows that, more than any other mode of inquiry, including economics, the linguistics of literariness is a powerful and indispensable tool in the unmasking of *ideological aberrations* [emphasis added] as well as a determining factor in accounting for their occurrence. Those who reproach literary theory for being oblivious to social and historical (that is to say ideological) reality are merely stating their fear at having their own ideological mystifications exposed by the tool they are trying to discredit. They are, in short, very poor readers of Marx's *German Ideology*.³³⁴

In part, de Man is here only reiterating with reference to *The German Ideology* what he'd said in his 1973 essay on Rousseau's *Second Discourse*: that the economic of Rousseau's political economic theory is 'a correlative of linguistic conceptualization' and that both Rousseau's and Marx's economics 'should only be approached from this point of view'.³³⁵ Ideology begins in a process

---

333 See de Man, 'The Inward Generation', CW, p. 14, p. 15, and 'Poetic Nothingness: On a Hermetic Sonnet by Mallarmé', CW, p. 28, first published as '*Le néant poétique (commentaire d'un sonnet hermétique de Mallarmé)*', Monde Nouveau 88, April 1955, pp. 63–75.
334 RT, p. 11.
335 AR, p. 158.

of linguistic conceptualization, of forming general ideas about things by way of and in language, of connecting sensation with knowledge, it follows that a knowledge of the parts and purposes of language or the 'linguistics of literariness'[336] – the way a text is structured by 'fictionality' (the possible absence of an empirical referent), 'figurality' (the presence of representational or nonrepresentational tropes) and 'superimposed ordering' (the way the choice of words is determined by nonsemantic reasons), and, especially with regard to its 'rhetoricity', effects 'the persistent threat of misreading' – has to be considered a necessary, indispensable resource for exposing the true character of ideological aberrations. Economics, and for example, history, can 'demystify' the content or meaning of particular historically and culturally specific ideological aberrations, Barthesian 'myths' or 'fictions', but that is as much as it can do. It cannot account for how and why they occur or for how and why they occur so regularly as to be the unavoidable norm. It can't explain 'aberration' or 'myth' as a type of speech that's always and inevitably present there to be stolen by any paralysing bureaucracy or menacingly repressive structure of the Right or the Left to validate its particular order of things, to naturalise and make real its specific place in history.[337]

At the end, the whole weight of the second paragraph of the passage we've been reading is directed at those scholars of language and literature who resist literary theory, faulting and censuring de Man for having forgotten or for being ignorant of 'social and historical (that is to say ideological) reality'.[338] De Man sees in this resistance evidence that these adversary readers are afraid of having their own ideological aberrations, self-delusions or self-mystifications, myths, fictions or *mensonges romatiques*, exposed by the very theory they're resisting. It's clear to him that they haven't read *The German Ideology* as attentively as one would have expected – though, surely, not many members of the MLA would have read it anyway.

---

336   RT, p. 11. De Man appropriated the term 'linguistics of literariness' and the three characteristics or functions of 'literariness' from Henryk Markiewicz, 'The Limits of Literature', *New Literary History* 4, 1972, pp. 5–14, at pp. 13–14, to which he responded in 'Literature and Language: A Commentary', *New Literary History* 4 (1972), pp. 181–92, at pp. 186–88, subsequently republished in BI as Appendix B, pp. 277–89 at pp. 283–5.

337   In mind here were some remarks of T.J. Clark in his discussion paper 'Preliminary Arguments: Work of Art and Ideology', presented at the informal session organised by O.K. Werckmeister on the theme of Marxism and art history, College Art Association Annual Conference, Chicago, IL, 1976 – this paper constitutes a vivid engagement with art historians and specifically Marxist social historians of art who are resistant to theory; it's not without interest that it pre-dates de Man's engagement with his own professional association by some six years.

338   RT, p. 11.

The implication couldn't be clearer. As far as de Man is concerned, in *The German Ideology*, the extensive first draft of their materialist conception of history and 'the model text for all ideological demystification', Marx and Engels attend to social and historical reality and the problem of ideology, the process accomplished by the so-called thinker and the always-formed false conceptions formed by it, in the same way, or in much the same way, as he does. However, it's difficult to tell from what we've read how much of de Man's initial thinking about ideology was appropriated from *The German Ideology* or received its confirmation therein at a later date. De Man was nothing if not a close reader, though one who read the texts that interested him in a particular way. He may well have found in *The German Ideology* insights from which he had benefited and upon which he had been relying for some time. That's having it both ways and leaving the matter undecidable. We need now to look at what de Man took from and/or read confirmed in Marx and Engels's text.

There can be no doubt that the passage quoted below, which he could have been directed to by Barthes who used it in 'Myth Today', is one that de Man must have had in mind whenever he referred to *The German Ideology*.[339] It can be found in *The German Ideology*'s first chapter – the chapter on Feuerbach and the opposition of materialist and idealist ways of seeing – and is generally accepted as the *locus classicus* for puzzling ideology. It comes early in the fourth section of the chapter. After Marx and Engels have rehearsed what they regard as the 'essence' of their 'materialist conception of history' (that human beings 'are productively active in a definite way' and enter into 'social and political relations' that are determined by that 'definite way'), they go on to consider the relations that pertain between 'social being and consciousness'. It's here that we read:

> The production of ideas, of conceptions, of consciousness, is at first directly interwoven with the material activity and the material intercourse of men – the language of real life. Conceiving, thinking, the mental intercourse of men at this stage still appear as the direct efflux of their material labour. The same applies to mental production as expressed in the language of the politics, laws, morality, religion, metaphysics of a people. Men are the producers of their conceptions, ideas, etc., that is, real, active men, as they are conditioned by a definite development of their productive forces and of the intercourse corresponding to these, up to its furthest forms. Consciousness [*das Bewusstsein*] can never be anything else than

---

339   See Barthes 1973, p. 141.

conscious being [*das bewusste Sein*], and the being of men is their actual life-process. If in all ideology men and their relations appear upside-down, as in a *camera obscura*, this phenomenon arises just as much from their historical life-process as the inversion of objects on the retina does from their physical life-process.[340]

This paragraph is dense. Compressed. Compact. And makes its points with reference to two optical systems. It moves *from* Rousseauesque thinking about the beginnings of human society, consciousness and language (first labour, then, after it and with it, speech), language as the existence of a communal way of life expressing itself/a communal way of life expressing itself into existence as a community *to* the place of language in bourgeois society – the then 'fullest form' of society – and the relation that pertains between consciousness and material actuality therein. Marx and Engels conceive of language at its beginning as 'the language of real life' because it was integral to and even coincident with the way that human beings engaged in productive activities and interacted with others in those activities. Marx and Engels assume – though they seem not to have the slightest doubt – that, at this stage, consciousness was a direct effluence (the metaphor is of water, air, or *light*) of the ways in which human beings were productively active. Likewise the consciousness that human beings go on to develop, which is represented in and by 'the language of politics, morality, religion, metaphysics, etc.', is also determined by their produced means of production (their tools and utensils, machinery, storehouses, infrastructure),

---

[340] Marx and Engels, *The German Ideology*, MECW 5, p. 36. It is important to note that Marx, himself, seems never have had recourse to the camera obscura as a simile or metaphor for the process accomplished by ideology after using it in *The German Ideology* preferring, instead, to turn to natural optics – see, for example, this passage in *Capital* 1, pp. 164–5:

The mysterious character of the commodity-form consists therefore simply in the fact that the commodity reflects the social characteristics of the products of labour themselves, as the socio-natural properties of these things. Hence it also reflects the social relation of the producers to the sum total of labour as a social relation between objects, a relation that exists apart from and outside the producers. Through this substitution, the products of labour become commodities, sensuous things that are at the same time suprasensible or social. In the same way, the impression made by a thing on the optic nerve is perceived not as a subjective excitation of that nerve but as the objective form of a thing outside the eye. In the act of seeing, of course, light is really transmitted from one thing, the external object, to another thing, the eye. It is a physical relation between physical things. As against this, the commodity-form, and the value relation of the products of labour within which it appears, has absolutely no connection with the physical nature of the commodity and the material [*dinglich*] relations arising from this. It is nothing but the definite social relation between men themselves that assumes here, for them, the fantastic form of a relation between things.

labour power and the social organisation of production. However, as they will make clear, this consciousness – the consciousness that's represented in the language of politics, morality, etc. – is '*abstracted*' from those produced means of production, etc., from the actuality of man's physical, material existence. Man's awareness of himself and his circumstances can never be anything but a conscious awareness of his material life and the way he interacts with others. However, if Marx and Engels have got it right – and that '*if*' in all ideology' is surely rhetorical – the ideas that man develops about his actual circumstances as they're represented in the language of politics, etc., misrepresent those circumstances, contradict them and, as it were, invert them, turn them upside-down. Whereupon Marx and Engels invoke two similes by way of explanation. First, ideology like the *camera obscura* is a man-made instrument of man's ingenuity, which immaterialises actual material (makes light of it) and produces an inverted picture of material reality, of man's actual productive activity and social relations. (In their Preface to *The German Ideology* Marx and Engels write similarly that the self-satisfied philosophy of the Young Hegelians 'only *mirrors* [emphasis added] the wretchedness of the real conditions in Germany'.)[341] But, secondly and more to the point perhaps, unlike the *camera obscura*, which makes a show of the system and how its mechanicals work, ideology inverts its objects *seemingly* naturally (and as unconsciously and as unavoidably) in much the same way that the human eye processes light energy ... and the mind brings what is reflected therein to consciousness.

In the next paragraph Marx and Engels try out other metaphors in place of these optical inversions of material activity and material intercourse, as it were sampling 'reflexes and echoes' (automatic responses to stimuli and reflected sounds), 'phantoms' (illusions) and 'sublimates' (solid substances changed into vapours) of 'material life'.[342]

Fifty years later in a letter to Franz Mehring, Engels was to provide that useful gloss on his and Marx's thinking in this section of *The German Ideology*, viz., 'Ideology is a process accomplished by the so-called thinker consciously ... but with a false consciousness'. Why? Because 'the real motive forces impelling him remain unknown to him'.[343] He had said much the same thing a few years earlier in a letter to Conrad Schmidt where he also made the point that the inversion 'that presents the image the wrong way up ... does so without the beholder being aware of it ... And ... in as much as it is not recognised, con-

---

341   Marx and Engels, *The German Ideology*, MECW 5, p. 23.
342   Marx and Engels, *The German Ideology*, MECW 5, p. 36.
343   Engels, Letter to Franz Mehring, London, 14 July 1893, *Marx, Engels, Selected Works in One Volume*, p. 659.

stitutes what we call an *ideological view*'.³⁴⁴ One might say that it constitutes an 'ideological aberration'. However, since 'in all ideology men and their relations appear upside-down, as in a *camera obscura*' then, as we've seen, in every moment of ideological falsehood that's taken for truth there's a seemingly aberrant truth to be glimpsed that will contradict it. Or to reprise what de Man said in 'Reading (Proust)', it will always be possible to demonstrate that an ideological aberration states the truth of its aberration.

At which juncture in *The German Ideology* Marx and Engels *seem* to abandon their thinking about the relations between social being and consciousness. After reiterating that 'real living individuals', 'developing their material production and their material intercourse, alter, along with their real existence', 'their thinking and the products of their thinking', they go on to present their 'method of approach'. This is based on and enabled by several premises. They give four of these, each one representing an aspect of what they regard as 'primary historical relations'. First, for human beings to exist and 'make history' they must, by their own material labour, satisfy their basic needs: they must eat, drink, find shelter, and so on.³⁴⁵ Second, The satisfaction of those basic needs leads to new needs and this 'creation of new needs is the first historical act'.³⁴⁶ Third, human beings produce new life by procreation and thus form families; at this stage the family is the only social relation but with 'increased needs' comes the need for 'new social relations'.³⁴⁷ Fourth, the satisfaction of basic needs and the production of new life by procreation have a double relation: it is both a natural relation of the individual to him/herself and a social relation between several human beings. The way that human beings produce their objects, the forces of production available to them and the relations within which they produce those obects, determines the form and condition that their society takes. It is necessarily dynamic and 'ever taking on new forms'. Hence 'the history of humanity'.³⁴⁸ This 'history' happens regardless of 'any political or religious nonsense' or 'ideology' – the previously mentioned politics, laws, morality, religion, metaphysics, etc., of a people – that seems to hold them together.³⁴⁹ At which point in their discourse, in another passage that *must* have caught de Man's attention, if only because (to pre-empt a little what follows) we know that he

---

344 Engels, Letter to Conrad Schmidt, 27 October 1890, *Marx, Engels, Selected Works in One Volume*, p. 656.
345 Marx and Engels, *The German Ideology*, MECW 5, pp. 41–2.
346 Marx and Engels, *The German Ideology*, MECW 5, p. 42.
347 Marx and Engels, *The German Ideology*, MECW 5, pp. 42–3.
348 Marx and Engels, *The German Ideology*, MECW 5, p. 43.
349 Marx and Engels, *The German Ideology*, MECW 5, p. 43, p. 36.

read it as rhyming with or following the structure of Rousseau's *Second Discourse* and Kant's *Third Critique*, Marx and Engels regain or return to thinking about the relation between social being and consciousness.

> Only now, after having considered four moments, four aspects of primary historical relations, do we find that man also possesses 'consciousness'. But even from the outset this is not 'pure' consciousness. The 'mind' [*Geist*] is from the outset afflicted with the curse [*Fluch*] of being 'burdened' [*behaftet*] with matter, which here makes its appearance in the form of agitated layers of air, sounds, in short, language. Language is as old as consciousness, language *is* practical, real consciousness that exists for other men as well, and only therefore does it also exist for me.[350]

If Marx and Engels seem to De Man to abandon their discussion of social being and consciousness, they do so because it becomes necessary, as it did with Rousseau when he penned the *Discourse on the Origin of Inequality*, to draft a theory of language.

In Marx and Engels's materialist conception of history consciousness is 'a social product'.[351] In the first place, man's consciousness is 'merely consciousness concerning the immediate *sensuous* environment' and 'the limited connection that an individual has with other persons and things outside the individual who is growing self-conscious'.[352] In other words, it's a kind of 'purely animal consciousness of nature', a nature that, as yet, has not been forced and altered or much changed.[353] And yet it's more than this because man is 'conscious of the necessity of associating with the other individuals around him'; he has 'the beginning of a consciousness that he is living in society'.[354] But man in a state of nature could not become man in society by natural means. He had to externalise his *need* to associate productively with other human beings in and by way of language in order to develop social relations, to make the transition *from* (man in a state of) nature *to* (man in) society. Language facilitates and mediates between the natural relation of the individual to itself and the social relation between itself and other human beings, between nature and society. Human beings *needed* to develop language. And language has 'matter': first as sounds; and then, Marx and Engels imply, as visual signs. And this matter proves

---

350   Marx and Engels, *The German Ideology*, MECW 5, pp. 43–4.
351   Marx and Engels, *The German Ideology*, MECW 5, p. 44.
352   Ibid.
353   Ibid.
354   Ibid.

to be not only a 'burden' but also a 'curse' on man's social being and his consciousness of himself or 'mind'.

As man's productive activity and the relations determined by it develop and increase, along with the production and satisfaction of new needs, human beings increase their numbers – there's an 'increase of population'.[355] With these increases, the division of labour, 'which was originally nothing but the division of labour in the sexual act, then the division of labour which develops spontaneously or "naturally" by virtue of natural predisposition (e.g. physical strength)', develops also into the division between material and mental labour.[356] Indeed, the 'division of labour only becomes truly such from the moment when a division of material and mental labour appears'.[357] From which moment, say Marx and Engels, 'consciousness *can* really flatter itself that it is something other than consciousness of existing practice ... from now on consciousness is in a position to emancipate itself from the world and proceed to the formation of pure theory, theology, philosophy, morality, etc.'[358] With the development of the division between material and mental labour, language – 'the material in which the thinker is active'[359] – not only mediates *between* man's immediate sense of material actuality *and* actual materiality but also, so vivid is its own immediate sensuous material actuality that its mediating function is obscured, *it* is taken for *that* sensuous materiality. This, it seems, is the 'curse' – or part of the curse – that language suffers by 'being burdened with matter'.

We came across this idea of language in some way being a 'burden' – though not quite being burdened with matter – in two of de Man's essays: 'Rousseau (Second Discourse)' and 'Hegel on the Sublime'. The coincidence between de Man and Marx and Engels with regard to the use of 'burden' in these contexts may well be coincidental. Though probably not. Assuming that the coincidence is deliberate, then de Man's use of 'burden' would be an unacknowledged appropriation, a kind of hinge that moves the knowing reader back and forth between de Man's thinking about language and the passage on language in Marx and Engels's in *The German Ideology*. However, with regard to Marx and Engels's 'pure theory, theology, philosophy, morality, etc.' and the 'politics, laws,

---

355 Ibid.
356 Ibid.
357 Marx and Engels, *The German Ideology*, MECW 5, p. 45 – there's a marginal note by Marx here: 'The first form of ideologists, *priests*, is coincident'.
358 Ibid.
359 See Marx, *Economic and Philosophical Manuscripts*, MECW 3, p. 298, and Marx 1975, trans. Benton, p. 350, where Marx is already thinking of language as having a materiality.

morality, religion, metaphysics of a people', de Man adds, apropos of Rousseau's *Essay on the Origins of Language* and *Discourse on the Origin of Inequality* and the way in which 'society and government derive from a tension between man and language', that politics and politicality and 'all forms of language', because language is subject to contingent error, is a 'burden for man rather than an opportunity'.[360]

Though Marx and Engels were committed to doing theoretical work, they not interested in theoretically probing politics understood as the activities of government or the art or science of government. They were concerned with theorising the total complex of relations between people living in society and, specifically, the essential characteristics of the state, class, class struggle and revolution, colonisation, and so on. And two things were clear to them: that the political ideas of any classed society are mystified; and that the real conflicts of material interests are presented as conflicts of and about ideas. These matters, which are there developed in *The German Ideology*, it seems to me, are what de Man, coming out of his readings of Rousseau, means by 'politicality'. The burden of all forms of language, politics and politicality – all manner of linguistic and non-linguistic signs like those that occupied Barthes in *Mythologies*[361] – is not only that society is a correlative of linguistic conceptualisation but also that in and by way of language broadly conceived real material conflicts are turned into abstractions: as Marx and Engels put it, they are turned upside-down and given an immaterial materiality as reflexes and echoes, phantoms and sublimates that are taken to '*really* represent something without representing something *real*'.[362]

De Man, Marx and Engels: They all understand social being and consciousness, language and society as interconnected and theorise ideology not only in terms of the dialectical relation between an authentic consciousness and an inauthentic consciousness but also as a linguistic event or occurrence, a process of linguistic conceptualisation – metaphorised with reference to science of optics – that is affected by some kind of unavoidable *aberration* that causes an imperfect image of what it's trying to focus on and refer to. That imperfect image, when conceptualised and externalised in and by language, is then burdened with and cursed by a phenomenal materiality so immediate and vivid that it and what it communicates seems more natural and real than the actu-

---

360 AI, pp. 156,157.
361 For a good example of Marx thinking in terms of language broadly conceived – specifically with regard to names and battle cries, costumes, drapes and masks – see the second paragraph of *The Eighteenth Brumaire of Louis Napoleon*.
362 Marx and Engels, *The German Ideology*, MECW 5, p. 45.

ality to which it seems to refer. Unaware of the real motive forces determining our material and mental activity and intercourse, radically blind to our genuine consciousness because of the way it's reified and made inauthentic in and by language saturated with the possibility of contingent error, we mistake what's represented in thought's 'immediate actuality' for our 'actual world',[363] for our material activity and intercourse, our very human being and Being's relation with beings. In de Man's terms, glossing Marx and Engels, in all ideology we mistake reference for phenomenalism: which reference is more often than not the 'ideal expression of the dominant material relations, the dominant material relations grasped as ideas; hence of the relations which make one class the ruling one, therefore, the ideas of its dominance'.[364]

And what's a mistake if not a take? And, as Hank Williams knew to his cost, 'It don't take but one mistake and you can lose every take'.

In *Capital* Volume One, published in 1867, Marx provides this specific example of how the prosaic materiality of bourgeois practical, real consciousness or ideology – in this case, following de Man's example in 'The Rhetoric of Temporality', the materiality of a signifier, a word – perverts the actual material relations that characterise the market exchange between worker and capitalist.

> The sphere of circulation or commodity exchange, within whose boundaries the sale and purchase of labour-power goes on, is in fact a very Eden of the innate rights of man. There alone rule Freedom, Equality, Property and [Jeremy] Bentham. Freedom, because both buyer and seller of a commodity, let us say labour-power, are determined only by their free will. They contract as free persons, who are equal before the law. Their contract is the final result in which their joint will finds a common legal expression. Equality, because each enters into relation with the other, as with a simple owner of commodities, and they exchange equivalent for equivalent. Property, because each disposes only of what is his own. And Bentham, because each looks only to his own advantage. The only force bringing them together, and putting them into relation with each other, is the selfishness, the gain and the private interest of each. Each pays heed to himself only, and no one worries about the others. And precisely for that reason, either in accordance with the pre-established harmony of things, or under the auspices of an omniscient providence, they all work together to their mutual advantage, for the common weal, and in the common interest.

---

363   Marx and Engels, *The German Ideology*, MECW 5, p. 41.
364   Marx and Engels, *The German Ideology*, MECW 5, p. 59.

When we leave this sphere of simple circulation or the exchange of commodities, which provides the 'free-trader *vulgaris*' with his views, his concepts and the standard by which he judges the society of capital and wage-labour, a certain change takes place, or so it appears, in the physiognomy of our *dramatis personae*. He who was previously the money-owner now strides out in front as a capitalist; the possessor of labour-power follows as his worker. The one smirks self-importantly and is intent on business; the other is timid and holds back, like someone who has brought his own hide to market and now has nothing else to expect but – a tanning.[365]

'Freedom'. 'Equality'. 'Property'. 'Bentham'. Some twelve years before the publication of *Capital*, Marx and Engels, in *The German Ideology*, had pointed out that these concepts – 'Bentham' being Marx's metonym for the idea of exchange as a hedonistic self-sufficient relation – are specific to civil society, that they are 'dominant' and that the each one is taken at its word as universally valid.[366] You could say that these words seem full of sense. But as it is, nothing is like or equal on earth, except in name. And naming is not reality.[367] De Man would have said that they are mere metaphors but not ones devoid of meaning. It's not that they have no meaning but that bourgeois ideology has distorted and inverted the sense of what they mean. Between perception and the 'word' there's a gap in which our sense of the material world is turned upside-down ... and a lie comes to be. One must go to the place of the lie to find the truth. For the material actuality to which the words refer is a place of unfreedom, inequality, propertylessness, egoistic calculation and the continued separation of the human world and human relationships and conditions from the historical specificity of human nature itself.[368]

---

365 Marx 1976, p. 280.
366 *Marx and Engels, The German Ideology*, MECW 5, p. 60, p. 62.
367 Adapted from the exchange between Polynices, the Chorus and Eteocles in Euripedes's *Phoenician Women*, in Euripedes 2011, pp. 89–90.
368 'Democracy' is another word that the bourgeoisie takes as naming something real, something that sense should tell us *is* the case. Yet it, too, is a 'contradiction ... an untruth, nothing but hypocrisy (theology ...), at the bottom' for it refers not to 'people power' (from the Greek *demos* and *kratos*), the 'power of the people,' or 'rule by the people' but to a system of government whereby, every few years, the oppressed are given permission to decide which 'member of the ruling class' will 'misrepresent them in Parliament' so as to better maintain their oppression for another few years. See Marx, 'Progress of Social Reform on the Continent', *The New Moral World* no. 17, 4 November 1843, Marx, Engels, CW 3, p. 393; and Marx, *The Civil War in France*, 1871, in Marx, Karl and Frederick Engels 1991 [1968], *Karl Marx & Frederick Engels, Selected Works in One Volume*, p. 275.

In the section of *The German Ideology* that's devoted to an almost line-by-line critique of Max Stirner's *The Ego and Its Own* (1844) there's an analysis of the language of the bourgeoisie that proceeds by way of what de Man would have recognised as 'the linguistics of literariness'. At one point Marx and Engels attend to several words favoured by the bourgeoisie, including and starting with 'property': *'propriété*–property [*Eigentum*] and characteristic feature [*Eigenschaft*]; property-possession [*Eigentum*] and peculiarity [*Eigentümlichkeit*]; "*eigen*" ["*one's own*"] – in the commercial and in the individual sense; *valeur*, value, *Wert*; commerce, *Verkehr*; *échange*, exchange, *Autausch*, etc. ...' These specific words, which seem to coincide with 'economic facts', they conclude, lie wholly in 'the sphere of synonymy'. They then go on to demonstrate how one idea is transformed into another and how the identity of two quite different things is proven to be the same by the use of apposition.[369] Marx and Engels are critiquing just the kind of moves that de Man had identified in Kant's discussion of the sublime.

By way of concluding or of coming to a provisional conclusion, it's worth quoting one more passage from *The German Ideology*, one that occurs towards the end of Marx and Engels's discussion of Stirner's *The Ego and Its Own* and relates to the belief that naming might yet coincide with reality.

> One of the most difficult tasks confronting philosophers is to descend from the world of thought to the actual world. *Language* is the immediate actuality of thought. Just as philosophers have given thought an independent existence, so they were bound to make language into an independent realm. This is the secret of philosophical language, in which thoughts in the form of words have their own content. The problem of descending from the world of thoughts to the actual world is turned into the problem of descending from language to life.
>
> We have shown that thoughts and ideas acquire an independent existence in consequence of the personal circumstances and relations of individuals acquiring independent existence. We have shown that exclusive, systematic occupation with these thoughts on the part of ideologists and philosophers, and hence the systematisation of these thoughts, is a consequence of the division of labour, and that, in particular, German philosophy is a consequence of German petty-bourgeois conditions. The philosophers have only to dissolve their language [the language of morality, religion, metaphysics and so on] into the ordinary language [the language

---

369   See Marx and Engels, *The German Ideology*, MECW 5, pp. 231–2, and 274–7.

of real life, which is directly interwoven with the material activity and the material intercourse of men] from which it is abstracted, in order to recognise that it is a *distorted* language [emphasis added] of the actual world, and to realise that neither thoughts nor language in themselves form a realm of their own, that they are only *manifestations* of actual life.[370]

Sancho [Max Stirner], who follows the philosophers through thick and thin, must inevitably seek the *philosopher's stone*, the squaring of the circle and elixir of life, or a '*word*' which as such would possess the miraculous power of leading from the realm of language and thought to actual life. Sancho has been so infected by his long years of association with Don Quixote [Franz Zychlin von Zychlinski] that he fails to notice that this 'task' of his, this 'vocation', is nothing but the result of his faith in weighty philosophical books of knight-errantry.[371]

With reference to which, we might comment that Barthes's 'writing degree zero' is but another example of that desire for just such a philosopher's stone, etc. Max Stirner and Barthes to the contrary, Marx and Engels, and the way that de Man read Marx and Engels, show that, as regards the language of morality, religion, metaphysics and so on, the unity of a consciousness and its objects is nothing but a play of language as arbitrary as the shape of the constellations, which share a common plane only as the result of an optical appearance.

Coda: Aesthetics, Rhetoric, Ideology

As we saw a while ago, de Man valued aesthetic theory as 'critical philosophy ... the critique of the critiques'.[372] We should not forget that *The German Ideology*,

---

370 Marx and Engels, *The German Ideology*, MECW 5, pp. 446–7. In his 'Comments on James Mill, *Éléments d'économie politique*', 1844, his first essay dealing with human nature, Marx makes a distinction between the 'direct language' of man's 'essential nature' – man not estranged from but self-confirmed in his 'own activity', 'own life', 'own spirit' and 'own wealth' as a social being – and the language that represents the 'extent' to which man has become 'estranged from [his] essential nature', 'the estranged language of material values', the language of 'our objects in relation to each other' – or the language in which 'things [*Gegenstand*], reality, sensuousness are conceived only in the form of the *object*, or of *contemplation*, but not as *human sensuous activity*, *practice* not subjectively'. See Marx, 'Comments on James Mill, *Éléments d'économie politique*', MECW 3, pp. 227–8, p. 217; see also Marx, *Theses on Feuerbach*, Thesis 1, MECW 5, p. 5, p. 6.
371 Marx and Engels, *The German Ideology*, MECW 5, p. 447.
372 'Hegel on the Sublime', AI, p. 106.

as de Man reads it, not only provides the model text for demystifying ideology – 'in the language of the critique of the totality, of the critique of history'[373] – but also a model of 'critical aesthetic theory' or 'aesthetic thinking' similar to or in keeping with Kant's in the *Third Critique*. Which is to say, as de Man puts it in 'Hegel and the Sublime', that Marx and Engels, like Kant, identified the aesthetic as providing not only 'a necessary, though problematic articulation ... of the schemata of theoretical reason [to do with questions about our knowledge of the world, the necessary conditions of sense perception] with those of practical reason [to do with questions of freedom and morality]' but also 'the inescapable *burden* [emphasis added] of any linkage between political discourse and political action'.[374]

The aesthetic was central to de Man's thinking about politics and ideology and, as he saw it, central to Marx's also. However, it's difficult to tell from the published corpus just how far and how deeply he had read in Marx's writing on the aesthetic. Though, as far as I can tell, he makes no reference to it, I guess he must have known that Marx's most sustained thinking about the aesthetic is to be found not in *The German Ideology* of 1845 but in the *Economic and Philosophical Manuscripts* of 1844. It's here that Marx gets to grips with the way in which bourgeois political economy, by ignoring the direct relation between worker and production, conceals how separated, estranged or alienated he is from his productive activity, from the objects produced by it, from other men and from himself. Also, it's here that Marx takes the aesthetic as an essential aspect and measure of man, of what it is to be a human being, and uses it to clarify how much man has lost and stands to gain in the move from Capitalism to Communism. Two passages are especially vivid and worth reading.

The first passage I have in mind is in the last section of the First Manuscript of the *Economic and Philosophical Manuscripts*. As always, Marx goes back to basics: 'The worker can create nothing without *nature*', he says, '*without the sensuous external world*. It is the material in which his labour realizes itself, in which it is active and from which and by means of which it produces'.[375] Sensuous nature is the object of man's activity. Man, as we've seen, like the animals, must intervene in nature to satisfy his basic need to survive and reproduce his species. At first, this intervention, this life producing life or life activity, seems to man just that, only the means to survive and reproduce.[376] But whereas an

---

373   Debord 2006, Thesis 204.
374   AI, p. 106.
375   Marx, *Economic and Philosophical Manuscripts*, MECW 3, p. 273, see Marx 1975, trans. Benton, p. 325.
376   Marx, *Economic and Philosophical Manuscripts*, MECW 3, p. 276, Marx 1975, trans. Benton,

animal is immediately at one with its species life activity and its species-specific bit of nature, man takes his life activity and the whole of nature (including the life activities and species-specific bits of nature of the other species) as an object of and for his consciousness and will. Only man is free to do this, to everywhere act free of the satisfaction of the basic animal needs to eat, drink, find shelter, procreate, and so on. Intervening in nature in this way, man has made a human world out of and *of* nature. In doing so, he has transformed himself for, to the extent that he's part of it, he humanises nature and rises above it. He produces himself as a 'conscious being', and thus 'his own life is an object for him'.[377] He becomes a human being with a human subjectivity, and 'only because of that is his activity free activity'. Estranged labour reverses the relation that a human being has with his productive life activity by reducing it to 'a mere means for his existence'.[378] Then comes this:

> The practical creation of an *objective world*, the *fashioning* of inorganic nature, is proof that man is a conscious species-being, i.e. a being that treats the species as its own essential being or itself as a species-being. It is true that animals also produce ... But they produce only their immediate needs or those of their young; they produce one-sidedly, while man produces universally; they produce only when immediate physical need compels them to do so, while man produces even when he is free from physical need and truly produces only in freedom from such need; they produce only themselves, while man reproduces the whole of nature; their products belong immediately to their physical bodies, while man confronts his own product. Animals produce only according to the standards and needs of the species to which they belong, while man is capable of producing according to the standards of every species and of applying to each object its inherent standard; hence man also produces in accordance with the laws of beauty.[379]

A useful gloss on what Marx means by 'inherent standard' with reference to a specific object and its relation to the 'laws of beauty' can be read in the Third Manuscript in the section dealing with private property and Communism:

---

      p. 328.
377 Ibid.
378 Marx, *Economic and Philosophical Manuscripts*, MECW 3, p. 276, Marx 1975, trans. Benton, pp. 328–9.
379 Marx, *Economic and Philosophical Manuscripts*, MECW 3, pp. 276–77, Marx 1975, trans. Benton, pp. 328–9.

> The *manner* in which they [*objects*] become his [become for him the *objectification of himself*] depends on the *nature* of the *object* and the nature of the *essential power* that corresponds to *it*; for it is just the *determinateness* of this relation that constitutes the particular, *real* mode of affirmation. An object is different for the *eye* from what it is for the *ear*, and the eye's object *is* different from the *ear's*. The peculiarity of each essential power is precisely its *peculiar essence*, and thus also the peculiar mode of its objectification, of its *objectively real*, living *being*. Man is therefore affirmed in the objective world not only in thought but with *all* the senses.
>
> On the other hand, let us look at the question in its subjective aspect: only music can awaken the musical sense in man and the most beautiful music has *no* sense for the unmusical ear, because my object can only be the confirmation of one of my essential powers, i.e., can only be for me in so far as my essential power exists for me as a subjective attribute (this is because the sense of an object for me extends only as far as *my* sense extends, only has sense for a sense that corresponds to that object).[380]

I very much like the example he gives here of 'the dealer in minerals [who] sees only the commercial value, and not the beauty and peculiar nature of the minerals', who 'lacks a mineralogical sense'.[381] This merchant sees only the mineral's value with reference to the price he paid for it and the price he will charge when selling it on to realise a profit. He doesn't value the mineral object's distinct or essential character or quality for the pleasure it gives as it strikes his eye, etc., but only with regard to its commercial value in the market place. Indeed, he is so estranged from the object, as such, that he takes no such pleasure from it. As far the merchant is concerned, the mineral makes no sense for him.

---

380   Marx, *Economic and Philosophical Manuscripts*, MECW 3, p. 301, Marx 1975, trans. Benton, pp. 352–3.

It's worth pointing out that Marx's thinking here in the *Economic and Philosophical Manuscripts* was taken into Modernist art theory and criticism by Clement Greenberg who put it to use in the fourth and fifth sections of his seminal essay of 1940 'Towards a Newer Laocoon', see Greenberg 1986, pp. 30–2. Jones 2006, pp. 80–3, shows how Greenberg probably took this bit of Marx from Lifshitz 1938, pp. 78–9. At this moment – his beginning as a critic of art and culture – Greenberg thought it was 'necessary to quote Marx word for word': see Greenberg, 'Avant-Garde and Kitsch', *Partisan Review*, fall, 1939, in Greenberg 1986, pp. 22–5 at p. 22.

381   Marx, *Economic and Philosophical Manuscripts*, MECW 3, p. 302, Marx 1975, trans. Benton, p. 353.

Man's senses, as they were wrested from man's immediate at-oneness with nature, were made human senses: senses freed from the imperative to be consumed in the satisfaction of basic, physical needs. Man, unlike animals, was everywhere free to confront objects – natural objects and objects of his own devising – in their specificity and apart from any immediate, natural, basic need to do so. Because human beings are free in this way, 'man therefore also forms things in accordance with *the laws of beauty* [emphasis added]'. He comes to realise that the sensible form of objects affords a kind of knowing for its own sake, just for the pleasure it gives: the pleasure of finding things beautiful. Indeed, forming things – as we'll see in a moment, Marx means not only forming physical things but also forming mental representations of things and even, in this instance, forming abstract concepts – in accordance with *the laws of beauty* is the ultimate expression of human freedom.

Following on from what de Man said about Marx and Engels's *The German Ideology* being made of 'aesthetic thinking' along the lines of Kant's *Third Critique*, it seems to me that this section of the *Economic and Philosophical Manuscripts* would have been unthinkable without Kant. It's *as if* Marx is giving a historically materialist account of the disinterestedness and universality, freedom from need and utility, that Kant claimed for aesthetically based logical judgments of beauty. Which is to say, it's *as if* he's bringing Kant's analysis of why and how we find something beautiful back from the sphere of the ideal to reality.

The second passage I have in mind, which could be read as confirming that *as if*, can also be found in the Third Manuscript of the *Economic and Philosophical Manuscripts*, in the section on private property and Communism. Here Marx points out that the history of man has been a history of the cultivation of the senses. The sense organs constitute the natural and biological basis of the human senses but it's their social character that distinguishes them from the animal. And they have their history in natural science and anthropology, in nature and human society. The human senses have developed as human senses as a result not only of natural evolution but also of the socio-historical development of man. 'The cultivation of the five senses is the work of all previous history'.[382] The *human* value of an object is the value it has for the *human* senses. And the senses have value as *human* senses only if they have *human* objects to value.

---

[382] Marx, *Economic and Philosophical Manuscripts*, cw, 3, pp. 301–2, Marx 1975, trans. Benton, p. 353.

In Capitalism, man is related to the objects produced by his labour and to objects of nature as alien objects. Estranged labour produces 'marvels', 'palaces', 'beauty' for the rich 'but deformity for the worker'.[383] Thus deformed, 'Sense which is [now] a prisoner of crude practical need has only a *restricted* sense'.[384] It would be hard to say how man's deformed senses now differ from those of animals for in Capitalism 'all the physical and intellectual senses have been replaced by the simple estrangement of all the senses – by the sense of *having*'.[385] The economy's domination of social life has reduced *being* to *having*.[386] Or, as Moses Hess, to whose *Philosophie der Tat* we're directed, put it: 'an object is "ours" only when we have it – when it exists for us as capital or when it is eaten, drunk, worn, inhabited, etc.'[387]

After their long history of development, the human senses have to be released from the restrictions imposed on them by private property and capital. At which point Marx says, and this is the second passage I have in mind:

> The supersession of private property is therefore the complete *emancipation* of all the human senses and attributes; but it is this emancipation precisely because these senses and attributes have become *human*, subjectively as well as objectively. The eye has become a *human* eye, just as its *object* has become a social, *human* object, made by man for man. The *senses* have therefore become *theoreticians* in their immediate praxis. They relate to the *thing* for its own sake, but the thing itself is an *objective human* relation to itself and to man, and vice-versa. Need or enjoyment have lost their *egoistic* nature, and nature has lost its mere *utility* in the sense that its use has become *human* use.[388]

I wonder what de Man would have made of the way Marx tropes the senses as '*theoreticians* in their immediate praxis'? He'd have certainly found it interesting, especially in light of what he'd said in the fourth Messenger Lecture,

---

383 Marx, *Economic and Philosophical Manuscripts*, MECW 3, p. 273, Marx 1975, trans. Benton, p. 352.

384 Marx, *Economic and Philosophical Manuscripts*, MECW 3, p. 302, Marx 1975, trans. Benton, p. 353.

385 Marx, *Economic and Philosophical Manuscripts*, MECW 3, p. 300, Marx 1975, trans. Benton, p. 352.

386 Debord 2006, Thesis 17.

387 Marx, *Economic and Philosophical Manuscripts*, MECW 3, p. 300, Marx 1975, trans. Benton, p. 352 and note 6. See Moses Hess, *Philosophie der Tat*, in Herwegh 1843, p. 329.

388 Marx, *Economic and Philosophical Manuscripts*, CW, 3, p. 300, Marx 1975, trans. Benton, p. 352.

'Phenomenality and Materiality in Kant', about the way eighteenth-century psychology and philosophy thought of the faculties of imagination and reason as being able 'to *act*, or even to act freely, as if they were conscious and complete human beings?'[389] And, given that, I'm sure he would have drawn our attention to how Marx *italicised* his use of '*senses*' and '*theoreticians*' to alert us to the very personification he's writing here. Both de Man and Marx knew full that the materiality of the mind could exist only in the figure of prosopopeia.

The five senses personified as the *theoria*.[390] In Ancient Greece, the *theoria* was a delegation sent by a city to consult an oracle or take part in a festival at a sanctuary outside its own territory. Their task was to inform curiosity and verify. On their return they would give an account of what the oracle had said or of what they had witnessed. For Marx, as *theoreticians* of their own activity, the function of the *senses* is to sense-and-say or see-, smell-, hear-, taste-, touch-and-tell. Hence, 'in their immediate praxis', in the way they bring sensation and cognition (*seeing* and *seeing … as*) to practical consciousness by and in language, their manner of being material is, precisely, phenomenal. Praxis is a productive activity that involves the *translation* of ideas *into* material effects. It's an activity that is simultaneously subjective and objective, idealistic and materialistic.

Something of this is there in the very first of the *Theses on Feuerbach* (1845):

> The chief defect of all previous materialism – that of Feuerbach included – is that things [*Gegenstand*], reality, sensuousness are conceived only in the form of the *object*, or of *contemplation* [*Anschauung*], but not as *human sensuous activity*, *practice*, not subjectively. Hence, it happened that the *active* side, in contradistinction to materialism, was set forth by idealism – but only abstractly, since, of course, idealism does not know real, sensuous activity as such. Feuerbach wants sensuous objects, really distinct from conceptual objects, but he does not conceive human activity itself as *objective* activity.[391]

And finally, not far away from those 'theoreticians' in the *Economic and Philosophical Manuscripts*, Marx has these two sentences:

---

389 AI, 87.
390 Wlad Godzich has things to say about theory in these terms in his 'Foreword: The Tiger on the Mat', RT, pp. xiii–xiv.
391 Marx, *Theses on Feuerbach*, Thesis 1, MECW 5, p. 6.

> Man's first object – man – is nature, sense perception; and the particular sensuous human powers, since they can find objective realization only in *natural* objects, can find self-knowledge only in the science of nature in general. The element of thought itself, the element of the vital expression of thought – *language* – is sensuous nature.[392]

As Marx theorises it, and as de Man read it in Kant's *Third Critique*, the aesthetic has its being-in-man as a linguistic principle that provides a necessary articulation between subject and object, the sensing subject and the sensed object. And it has its being-in-the-world in and by way of the sensuous nature or sensuous materiality of language.

Insofar as the aesthetic as it comes into being and develops in civil society is taken as the unity of subject and object, the sensing subject and the sensed object, rather than as a linguistic conceptualisation effecting a self-deluded belief in the unity of subject and object, the sensing subject and the sensed object, it too is one more bit of ideology. Aesthetic ideology or the ideology of the aesthetic, that much-vaunted adequation of sensation and knowledge, blinds man to the fact of his deformed existence, to the degree that he is alienated, estranged or separated from his productive activity, his objects, his world and himself.

A year or so after abandoning the notebooks that became the *Economic and Philosophical Manuscripts*, Marx, along with Engels, pointed out in *The German Ideology*, with reference to ideology, how man in his alienated and estranged condition mistakes the sensuous expression of his thoughts, his historically and culturally produced linguistic reality, for his actual material reality. Or, as de Man puts it in 'The Resistance to Theory' – to repeat for the last time something I have said before – he mistakes reference for phenomenalism. This is the confusion that Marx and Engels realised had to be demystified by way of a critical consideration of language, a glimpse that was all but lost to their interests in political economy and the supersession of private property. A spectre was haunting Europe and there were other more pressing matters to address.[393] Nevertheless (and here I'm repeating for the last or penultimate time another thing I have said before), as de Man pointed out, again in 'The Resistance to Theory', that insight provided and still provides the basis for demystifying the always-present false conceptions and ideological aberrations,

---

392 Marx, *Economic and Philosophical Manuscripts*, CW, 3, p. 304, Marx 1975, trans. Benton, pp. 355–6.
393 See Marx, Karl 1848, *Manifesto of the Communist Party*, in Marx, Engels *Selected Works in One Volume*, pp. 35–62.

myths, self-deceptions, *mensonges romantiques* and idealised fictions ... and for understanding the process that produces them ... a process that is 'accomplished by the so-called thinker consciously ... but with a false consciousness'.

For the End ...

Marx had it, I reckon, when he talked of the difference between a 'merely speculative, merely theoretical' thought, and that other kind of enquiry which is in the end an 'appropriation of the world', 'a reproduction of the concrete by way of thought', 'a rich totality of many determinations and relations'[394] ... And ... one distinctive feature of Marx's approach to revolutionary politics was his continuing confidence in the place of theoretical work. An uneasy confidence, a confidence that was fought for and sometimes lost; but a confidence nonetheless.

At certain moments – in the later 1850s certainly – all those years of patient, irascible labour with the Blue Books, the mercantilist tracts, the forgotten tomes of Proudhon, Hegel and Ricardo must have seemed eccentric and futile. And yet in 1864 Marx emerged as the only man capable of putting the first international association of workers into shape, the only man who could give it a programme, a basis for unity, a coherent view of capital and labour.

This is made to sound a bit too magical – out of the Reading Room and on to the barricade! – but it is closer to the truth than the stock image of Marx the Militant.

T.J. CLARK, 'Preliminary Arguments: Work of Art and Ideology'

∴

I dwell in Possiblity –
A fairer House than Prose –
EMILY DICKINSON, 657

∴

---

394   See Marx 1973, pp. 101–2.

Ideology was once, in the late 1970s to early 1980s, a hot topic amongst liberal and supposedly Left academics. However, as society at large moved increasingly to the right so did the Academy. It is germane that, in the mid-1980s – the economy recovering somewhat after the financial crisis of 1980–1 in a market driven restructuring of social life – when academics in the United States of America and Europe were jettisoning their interest in it, de Man was preparing to make his own dedicated contribution to puzzling Marx and Engels's concept of ideology.

Capitalism persists, *mutatis mutandis*, constantly revolutionising the instruments and relations of production and moving the relations of society from crisis to crisis. And with it persists the defect or misplacement in seeing and *seeing ... as* or linguistic conceptualisation that produces the aberration that is ideology and all the ideological aberrations and false conceptions that are determined by it and are specific to it. The so-called thinker thinks consciously, still with a false consciousness.

With the global economy even now struggling to recover from the crash of 2008 ... and with the state strengthening the socio-economic chains that secure us ever more closely to the instability and failures of the Dictatorship of Capital ... we should take de Man's remarks in 'The Resistance to Theory' as pressing directives for the theoretical mind to return to *The German Ideology* and to theorising a materialism that confronts the problem of more accurately *seeing* the material world *as* it *is* ... materialised in and by language ... *as* a phenomenon of that material world ... *as* a burden and a curse ... its materiality and ambiguous ambiguousness, rhetoricity and persistent threat of being misunderstood, fundamental to and essential for one's human being in-the-world, self and social relations ...

Although that return is *necessary*, it is also necessarily *insufficient*. 'Philosophers have only *interpreted* the world in various ways; the point, however, is to *change* it'.[395]

Capitalism's power seems inescapable; but so, once, did 'the motley feudal ties that bound man to his "natural superiors"', absolute monarchy, aristocracies and theocracies, etc.[396] 'Revolution is our obligation: our hope of evolution';[397] and 'any human power can be resisted by and changed by human beings'.[398]

---

395 Marx, *Theses on Feuerbach*, Thesis 11, MECW 5, p. 8.
396 Le Guin, Ursula K., National Book Award Medal for Distinguished Contribution to American Letters Acceptance Speech, 2014, in Le Guin 2018, pp. 383–84 at 384; Marx, *Manifesto of the Communist Party, Selected Works in One Volume*, p. 37.
397 Le Guin 2002, p. 296.
398 Le Guin 2014.

As we've seen, de Man theorises the 'burden of any linkage between discourse and action' as 'inescapable'.[399] Even if one could overcome the resistance to theory, one could not – one cannot – make a revolution by theorising it into being. Or by writing a manifesto, not even one that speaks 'to our hearts like a poem'. As Shevek, Ursula K. Le Guin's anarchist hero of *The Dispossessed*, said, 'You cannot buy the Revolution. You cannot make the Revolution. You can only be the Revolution. It is in your spirit, or it is nowhere'.[400] And 'it is for all, or it is nothing'.[401] And it will persist, for 'if it is seen as having any end, it will never truly begin'.[402] Though Marx and Engels expose the ideological false conceptions of German philosophy, they're aware, of course, that that theoretical struggle is no substitute for the material struggle against material actuality. 'Liberation' – not just 'liberating "man" from the domination of … phrases' – can only be achieved in the material world by material means.[403] It 'is a historical act not a mental act, and it is brought about by historical conditions … in accordance with the different stages of their development … when their development is sufficiently advanced'.[404] In other words, to bring back something de Man said in 'Genesis and Genealogy (Nietzsche)' and apply it slightly out of context here, the Revolution will be an event or occurrence or moment of such radical discontinuity and disruption of the linearity of the temporal process that it will neither contain nor reflect it, neither be contained by it nor reflected in it.[405] Mindful of the distinction that Heidegger drew between *Geschicht* and *Historie*, which so attracted de Man: we might say that when it happens the Revolution will be an event or occurrence (*Geschicht*) effected by the destiny (*Geschick*) of the proletariat, not a divined reckoning that will happen at such and such a moment according to the presuppositions of historical explanation (*Historie*).

The theoretical mind, having theorised false consciousness and the always-formed false conceptions, aberrations, myths, *mensonges romantiques*, self-deceptions and idealised fictions effected by it as problems of the tension between freedom and perfectibility, perfectibility and language, language and man, and man and political society, will not by its own efforts shake our chains to earth. However … the theoretical mind, once liberated in itself and press-

---

399 AI, p. 106.
400 Le Guin, 2002, p. 248.
401 Le Guin, 2002, p. 296.
402 Le Guin, 2002, p. 296.
403 See Marx and Engels, *The German Ideology*, MECW 5, p. 38.
404 Ibid.
405 AR, p. 81.

ing back against the pressure of reality, *must* emerge as will from Amenthes's shadow-world and turn against the worldly actuality that exists outside it ...[406] and make that worldly actuality anew. But patience is required. Sufficient patience, that is, to dwell in Possibility while we pursue the conclusions of Marx and Engels's poetic thought to their end ...

406   Marx, 'Notes to the Doctoral Dissertation', in Marx 1997, p. 61.

Bibliography

Aaron, Daniel 1968, *Writers and Partisans: A History of Literary Radicalism in America*, New York: Wily.

Althusser, Louis 1970, 'Sur le Contrat Social (Les déclages)' in *Cahiers pour l'Analyse*, 8, *L'impensé de J.J. Rousseau*: 5–42.

Arent, Arthur, (and 137 other signatories) 1938, 'The Moscow Trials: A Statement by American Progressives', *New Masses*, 3 May, 1938: 19.

Barr Jr., Alfred H. 1952, 'Is Modern Art Communistic?', *New York Times Magazine*, 14 December: 22–3, 28–30.

Barthes, Roland 1973 [1957], *Mythologies*, selected and translated by Annette Lavers, Granada Publishing: Paladin.

Barthes, Roland 1967 [1953], *Writing Degree Zero*, translated by Annette Lavers and Colin Smith, New York: Hill & Wang.

Battcock, Gregory (ed.) 1968, *Minimal Art: A Critical Anthology*, New York: E.P. Dutton.

Baxandall, Michael 1985, *Patterns of Intention: On the Historical Explanation of Pictures*, New Haven and London: Yale University Press.

Beckett, Samuel 1958, *Endgame*, London: Faber & Faber.

Beckett, Samuel 1956, *Waiting for Godot*, London: Faber & Faber.

Beckley, Bill with David Shapiro (eds.) 1998, *Uncontrollable Beauty: Toward a New Aesthetics*, New York: School of Visual Arts, Allworth Press.

Benjamin, Walter 1977 [1963], *The Origin of German Tragic Drama*, translated by John Osbourne, London: Verso.

Bensaïd, Daniel 2002 [1995], *Marx for Our Times*, translated by Gregory Elliott, London: Verso.

Bottomore, Tom, et al. 1983, *A Dictionary of Marxist Thought*, Oxford, Blackwell.

Breton, André and Leon Trotsky 1938, 'Manifesto: Towards a Free Revolutionary Art', *Partisan Review*, 6, 1, fall: 49–53.

Cage, John 1961, *Silence*, Middleton: Wesleyan University Press.

Caruth, Cathy and Deborah Esch (eds.) 1995, *Critical Encounters: Reference and Responsibility in Deconstructive Writing*, New Brunswick: Rutgers University Press.

Castleman, Riva 1986, *Jasper Johns: A Print Retrospective*, New York: Museum of Modern Art.

Cézanne, Paul 1978, edited by P.M. Doran, *Conversations avec Cézanne*, Paris: Macula.

Clark, T.J. 1976, 'Preliminary Arguments: Work of Art and Ideology', unpub. discussion paper, College Art Association Annual Conference, Chicago, IL, 1976.

Clark T.J. 2001, 'Phenomenality and Materiality in Cézanne', in Cohen, Tom, et al. (eds.), *Material Events: Paul de Man and the Afterlife of Theory*, Minneapolis and London: University of Minnesota Press, 93–113.

Cohen, Tom, Barbara Cohen, J. Hillis Miller, Andrzej Warminski (eds.) 2001, *Material Events: Paul de Man and the After Life of Theory*, Minneapolis and London: University of Minnesota Press.

Coleridge, S.T. 1816, *The Statesman's Manual or, The Bible the best guide to political skill and foresight: a lay sermon, addressed to the higher classes of society, with an appendix, containing comments and essays connected with the study of the inspired writings*, first Edition, London: Gale and Fenne, J.M. Richardson, and Hatchard.

Crichton, Michael 1977, *Jasper Johns*, New York: Harry N. Abrams in association with Whitney Museum of American Art.

Danchev, Alex (editor and translator) 2013, *The Letters of Paul Cézanne*, London: Thames & Hudson.

Davis, Whitney 1996, with the editorial assistance of Richard W. Quinn, *Replications: Archaeology, Art History, Psychoanalysis*, University Park: Pennsylvania State University Press.

De Antonio, Emile and Mitch Tuchman 1984, *Painters Painting: A Candid History of the Modern Art Scene, 1940–1970*, New York: Abbeville Press, a transcript of interviews with artists in the movie directed by Emile de Antonio *Painters Painting: The New York Art Scene 1940–1970*, 1972.

De Graef, Ortwin 1993, *Serenity in Crisis: A Preface to Paul de Man 1939–1960*, Lincoln and London: University of Nebraska Press.

De Man, Paul 1996, *Aesthetic Ideology*, edited with an introduction by Andrzej Warminski, Minneapolis and London: University of Minnesota Press.

De Man, Paul 1979, *Allegories of Reading: Figural Language in Rousseau, Nietzsche, Rilke and Proust*, New Haven and London: Yale University Press.

De Man, Paul 1983 [1971], *Blindness & Insight: Essays in the Rhetoric of Contemporary Criticism*, 2nd ed., revised by Wlad Godzich, Minneapolis: University of Minnesota Press, London: Methuen & Co.

De Man, Paul 1989, *Critical Writings 1953–1978*, edited with an introduction by Lindsay Waters, Minneapolis: University of Minnesota Press.

De Man, Paul 1986, *The Resistance to Theory*, edited with an introduction by Wlad Godzich, Minneapolis: University of Minnesota Press.

De Man, Paul 1984, *The Rhetoric of Romanticism*, New York and Guildford: Columbia University Press.

De Man, Paul 1993, *Romanticism and Contemporary Criticism*, edited by E.S. Burt, Kevin Newmark, and Andrzej Warminski, Baltimore and London: The Johns Hopkins University Press.

Debord, Guy 2006 [1967], *The Society of the Spectacle*, translated by Donald Nicolson-Smith, Brooklyn: Zone Books.

Degras, Jane (Tabrisky) 1965, *The Communist International 1919–1943: Documents Volume 3*, London and New York: Oxford University Press.

Delbanco, Andrew 2007, 'Scandals of Higher Education', *The New York Review of Books*, 29 March: 42–7.

Derrida, Jacques 1988, 'Like the Sound of the Sea Deep within a Shell: Paul de Man's War', *Critical Inquiry* 14, spring: 590–652.

Dickinson, Emily 1997, *Emily Dickinson. Selected Poems*, selected and edited by Helen McNeil, London: J.M. Dent, Everyman's Poetry.

Dodge, Peter 1979, *A Documentary Study of Hendrik de Man, Socialist Critic of Marxism*, Princeton: Princeton University Press.

Dodge, Peter 1966, *Beyond Marxism: The Faith and Works of Hendrik de Man*, The Hague: Nijhoff.

Domhoff, G. William 1978, *The Powers That Be: Processes of Ruling Class Domination in America*, New York: Random House.

Domhoff, G. William 1967, *Who Rules America?*, Englewood Cliffs: Prentice Hall.

Duchamp, Marcel 1975, *The Essential Writings of Marcel Duchamp*, edited by Michel Sanouillet and Elmer Peterson, London: Thames & Hudson.

Eagleton, Terry 1992, 'Capitalism, Modernism and Post-modernism', in *Modern Criticism and Theory: A Reader*, edited by David Lodge, London and New York: Longman.

Eagleton, Terry 1983, *Literary Theory: An Introduction*, Oxford: Blackwell.

Eagleton, Terry 1984, *The Function of Criticism*, London: New Left Books.

Eagleton, Terry 1990, *The Ideology of the Aesthetic*, Oxford and Cambridge: Blackwell.

Eastman, Max 1934, *Artists in Uniform*, New York: Alfred A. Knopf.

Empson, William 1947 [1930], *Seven Types of Ambiguity*, London: Chatto and Windus, 2nd revised edition.

Empson, William 1935, *Some Versions of Pastoral*, London: Chatto & Windus.

Engels, Frederick 1991 [1876], 'The Part Played by Labour in the Transition from Ape to Man', in *Karl Marx & Frederick Engels, Selected Works in One Volume*, London: Lawrence & Wishart, 339–49.

Engels, Frederick 1976 [1878], *Anti-Dühring (Herr Eugen Dühring's Revolution in Science)*, translation of the third German edition, 1894, Peking: Foreign Languages Press.

Engels, Frederick 1955 [1878–82], translated by Clemens Dutt, *Dialectics of Nature*, London: Lawrence & Wishart.

Euripedes 2011, *Electra, Phoenician Women, Bacchae, Iphigenia at Aulis*, translated by Cecelia Eaton Lusching and Paul Woodruff, Indianapolis and Cambridge: Hackett Publishing Co., Inc.

Freud, Sigmund 1976 [1900], *The Interpretation of Dreams* (1900), translated by James Strachey, Harmondsworth: Penguin Books, The Pelican Freud Library, Volume 4.

Fried, Michael 1968 [1967], 'Art and Objecthood', in *Minimal Art: A Critical Anthology*, edited by Gregory Battcock, 116–47.

Gasquet, Joachim 1991 [1978], *Joachim Gasquet's Cézanne: A Memoir with Conversations*, translated by Christopher Pemberton, London: Thames & Hudson.

Girard, René 1965 [1961], *Deceit, Desire and the Novel*, translated by Yvonne Freccero, Baltimore and London: Johns Hopkins University Press.

Girard, René 1961, *Mensonge romantique et vérité romanesque*, Paris: Grasset.

Goodnough, Robert 1951, 'Pollock Paints a picture', photographs by Hans Namuth, *ARTnews*: 50, 3, 38–41, 60–1.

Greenberg, Clement 1993 [1951], 'Cézanne and the Unity of Modern Art', in *Clement Greenberg. The Collected Essays and Criticism, Volume 3, Affirmations and Refusals, 1950–1956*, edited by John O'Brian, London and Chicago: University of Chicago Press, 82–91.

Greenberg, Clement 1993 [1967], 'Complaints of an Art Critic', *Artforum*, in *Clement Greenberg. The Collected Essays and Criticism*, Volume 4, *Modernism with a Vengeance, 1957–1969*, edited by John O'Brian, London and Chicago: University of Chicago Press, 265–72.

Greenberg, Clement 1993 [1963], *Three New American painters: Louis, Noland, Olitski*, in *Clement Greenberg. The Collected Essays and Criticism*, Volume 4, *Modernism with a Vengeance, 1957–1969*, edited by John O'Bian, London and Chicago: University of Chicago Press, 149–53.

Greenberg, Clement 1986 [1940], 'Towards a Newer Laocoon', in *Clement Greenberg. The Collected Essays and Criticism*, Volume 1, *Perceptions and Judgments, 1939–1944*, edited by John O'Brian, London and Chicago: University of Chicago Press, 23–38.

Gruen, John 1972, *The Party's Over: Reminiscences of the Fifties – New York's Artists, Writers, Musicians, and their Friends*, New York: The Viking Press.

Guilbaut, Serge 1983, *How New York Stole the Idea of Modern Art: Abstract Expressionism, Freedom, and the Cold War*, Chicago: The University of Chicago Press.

Gunn, Thom 2017, 'Sunlight', from *Moly* (1971), in *Thom Gunn, Selected Poems*, edited by Clive Wilmer, London: Faber & Faber, 98–9.

Hansen, J. et al. 1969, *Leon Trotsky: The Man and His Work. Reminiscences and Appraisals*, New York: Merit Publishers.

Hanson, N.R. 1972, *Patterns of Discovery: An Inquiry into the Conceptual Foundations of Science*, London: Cambridge University Press.

Harrison, Charles and Fred Orton (eds.) 1984, *Modernism, Criticism, Realism: Alternative Contexts for Art*, London: Harper & Row.

Hegel, G.W.F. 1977 [1807], *Phenomenology of Spirit*, translated by A.V. Miller, Oxford and New York: Oxford University Press.

Heidegger, Martin 1993 [1978], *Martin Heidegger: Basic Writings*, translated by Frank A. Capuzzi and J. Glen Gray, revised and expanded edition, edited by David Farrell Krell, London: Routledge & Kegan Paul.

Heidegger, Martin 1992 [1927], *Being and Time*, translated by translated by John Macquarrie and Edward Robinson, Oxford: Blackwell.

Heidegger, Martin 1982 [1959], *On the Way to Language*, translated by Peter D. Hertz, San Francisco: Harper Collins.

Heidegger, Martin 1971, *Poetry, Language, Thought*, translated by Albert Hofstadter, New York: Harper & Row.

Hellstein, Valierie 2011, 'Abstract Expressionism's Counterculture: The Club, the Cold War, and the New Sensibility', New York: The Museum of Modern Art, 25 February, available at www.moma.org/docs/calendar/Hellstein2.25.11MoMApaper.pdf

Herwegh, Georg 1843, *Einundzwanzig Bogen Aus Der Schweiz*, Zürich: Wintethur.

Hess, Thomas B. 1972, *Barnett Newman*, London: Tate Gallery Publications.

Hess, Thomas B. 1968, *Willem de Kooning*, New York: The Museum of Modern Art.

Hollinger, David A. 1975, 'Ethnic Diversity, Cosmopolitanism and the Emergence of the American Liberal Intelligentsia', *American Quarterly*, 27, 2: 133–51,

Homberger, Eric 1986, *American Writers and Radical Politics, 1900–1939: Equivocal Commitments*, New York: St. Martin's Press.

Hopps, Walter 1965, 'An Interview with Jasper Johns', *Artforum*, *3*, March: 32–6.

Huelsenbeck, Richard 1951 [1920], 'En Avant Dada', in *The Dada Painters and Poets: An Anthology*, edited by Robert Motherwell, New York: Wittenborn, Schulz, Inc., 22–48.

Inwood, Michael 1999, *A Heidegger Dictionary*, Oxford and Malden: Blackwell.

Jachec, Nancy 2000, *The Philosophy and Politics of Abstract Expressionism 1940–1960*, Cambridge: Cambridge University Press.

Jameson, Frederic 1974, review of V.N. Volosinov, *Marxism and the Philosophy of Language*, *Style*, 8, 3: 535–43.

Johns, Jasper 1964, *Jasper Johns*, New York: Jewish Museum, and London: Whitechapel Art Gallery.

Johns, Jasper 1974 [1965], interview by David Sylvester with Jasper Johns, in *Jasper Johns Drawings*, London: Arts Council of Great Britain, 7–19.

Johns, Johns 1965, interview by Walter Hopps, 'An Interview with Jasper Johns', *Artforum*, March: 32–6.

Johns, Jasper 1958, quoted in 'Art. Trend to "Anti-Art"', *Newsweek*, 31 March: 96.

Jones, Caroline A. 2006, *Eyesight Alone: Clement Greenberg's Modernism and the Bureaucratization of the Senses*, Chicago and London: Chicago University Press.

Kant, Immanuel 1968, *Werkausgabe 10: Kritik der Urteilskraft*, edited by Wilelm Weischedel, Frankfurt: Suhrkamp Verlag.

Kant, Immanuel 1968, *Logik* in *Werkausgabe 6: Schriften zur Metaphysik und Logik 2*, edited by Wilelm Weischedel, Frankfurt: Suhrkamp Verlag.

Kant, Immanuel 1951 [1790], *Critique of Judgement*, translated and with introduction and notes by J.H. Bernard, New York: Hafner Press.

Kant, Immanuel 1992 [1800], *Lectures on Logic*, translated and edited by J. Michael Young, Cambridge: Cambridge University Press.
Kostelanetz, Richard 1971, *John Cage*, London: Allen Lane, The Penguin Press.
Landau, Ellen G. 1989, *Jackson Pollock*, New York: Harry N. Abrams.
Larrain, Jorge 1979, *The Concept of Ideology*, London: Hutchinson & Co.
Léger, Fernand 1935, 'The New Realism', lecture given at The Museum of Modern Art, New York, during the retrospective *Fernand Léger: Paintings and Drawings*, 30 September–24 October, 1935, translated by Harold Rosenberg, *Art Front*, December: 10.
Le Guin, Ursula K. 2002 [1974], *The Dispossessed*, London: Gollancz, SF Masterworks.
Le Guin, Ursula K. 2018, *Dreams Must Explain Themselves. The Selected Non-Fiction of Ursula K. Le Guin*, London: Gollancz.
Lehman, David 1992, 'Paul de Man: The Plot Thickens', *New York Times*, 24 May: 9.
Lenin, V.I. 1970, *Lenin on the United States: Selected Writings by V.I. Lenin*, New York: International Publishers.
Lentricchia, Frank 1983, *Criticism and Social Change*, Chicago: University of Chicago.
Lifshitz, Mikhail 1938 [1933], *The Philosophy of Art of Karl Marx*, translated by Ralph B. Winn, New York: Critics Group.
Loesberg Jonathan 1977, 'Materialism and Aesthetics: Paul de Man's *Aesthetic Ideology*', *Diacritics*, 27, 4: 87–108.
Lukács, Georg 1967 [1920], *History and Class Consciousness: Studies in Marxist Dialectics*, translated by Rodney Livingstone, London: Merlin Press.
McEvilley, Thomas 1984, 'Doctor Lawyer Indian Chief: "Primitivism" in 20th. Century Art at the Museum of Modern Art in 1984', *Artforum*, November: 54–61.
McQuillan, Martin 2001, *Paul de Man*, London and New York: Routledge.
Macksey, Richard and Eugenio Donato (eds.) 1970, *The Languages of Criticism and the Sciences of Man: The Structuralist Controversy*, Baltimore: Johns Hopkins University Press.
Mantel, Hilary 2012, *Bring Up the Bodies*, London: Fourth Estate.
Marie, Annika 2006, *The Most Radical Act: Harold Rosenberg, Barnett Newman and Ad Reinhardt*, unpublished PhD dissertation, Austin: The University of Texas.
Markiewicz, Henryk 1972, 'The Limits of Literature', *New Literary History* 4: 5–14.
Marx, Karl 1976 [1867], *Capital 1: A Critique of Political Economy*, translated by Ben Fowkes, Harmondsworth: Penguin/NLR.
Marx, Karl 1992 [1885], *Capital 2*, translated by David Fernbach, Harmondsworth, Penguin/NLR.
Marx, Karl 1976 [1844], 'Comments on James Mill, *Éléments d'économie politique*', in *Karl Marx, Frederick Engels, Collected Works* Vol. 3, 1843–1844, translated by Clemens Dutt, London: Lawrence & Wishart, 211–28.
Marx, Karl 1975, *Early Writings*, translated by Gregor Benton, introduction by Lucio Colletti, Harmondsworth: Penguin Books/*New Left Review*.

Marx, Karl 1975 [1844], *Economic and Philosophical Manuscripts* of 1844, translated by Martin Milligan and Dirk J. Struik, in *Karl Marx, Frederick Engels, Collected Works*, Volume 3, 1843–4, London: Lawrence & Wishart, 229–346.

Marx, Karl 1977 [1871], *The Civil War in France*, Peking: Foreign Language Press.

Marx, Karl 1973 [1857–8], *Grundrisse, Foundations of the Critique of Political Economy (Rough Draft)*, translated by Martin Nicolaus, Harmondsworth: Penguin/*New Left Review*.

Marx, Karl 1991 [1848], *Manifesto of the Communist Party*, in Karl Marx, Frederick Engels *Selected Works in One Volume*, London: Lawrence & Wishart, 35–62.

Marx, Karl 1997 [1839–41], 'Notes to the Doctoral Dissertation', in *Writings of the Young Marx in Philosophy and Society* [1967], edited and translated by Lloyd D. Easton and Kurt H. Guddat, Indianapolis: Hackett Publishing Co. Ltd., 51–66.

Marx, Karl 1976 [1845], *Theses on Feuerbach*, in *Karl Marx, Frederick Engels, Collected Works*, Volume 5, 1845–7, translated by Clemens Dutt, W. Lough, C.P. Magill, London: Lawrence & Wishart, 6–8.

Marx, Karl and Frederick Engels 1976 [1845–7], *The German Ideology*, in *Karl Marx, Frederick Engels, Collected Works*, Volume 5, 1845–7, translated by Clemens Dutt, W. Lough, C.P. Magill, London: Lawrence & Wishart, 19–450.

Marx, Karl and Frederick Engels 1975, *Selected Correspondence, 1846–1895*, translated by Dona Torr, Westport: Greenwood Press.

Marx, Karl and Frederick Engels 1991 [1968], *Karl Marx & Frederick Engels, Selected Works in One Volume*, London: Lawrence & Wishart.

Merleau-Ponty, Maurice 1975 [1948], 'Cézanne's Doubt' (1948), in Maurice Merleau-Ponty, *Sens et non-sens* (1948), translated by Hubert L. Dreyfus and Patricia Allen Dreyfus, *Sense and Non-Sense* (1961), excerpted in *Cézanne in Perspective*, edited by Judith Wechsler, Englewood Cliffs: Prentice-Hall, Inc., 120–4.

Milner, Marion 1957, *On Not Being Able To Paint*, 2nd ed., London: William Heinemann.

Monroe, Gerald M. 1973, 'Art Front', in *Archives of American Art Journal*, 13, 3: 13–19.

Motherwell, Robert 1965, 'An Interview with Robert Motherwell', *Artforum*, 4, September: 33–7.

Motherwell, Robert (ed.) 1951, *The Dada Painters and Poets: An Anthology*, New York: Wittenborn, Schulz, Inc.

Motherwell, Robert and Harold Rosenberg, Pierre Chareau and John Cage (eds.) 1947, *Problems in Contemporary Art*, 4, *Possiblities*, 1, winter 1947–8, New York: Wittenborn, Schulz, Inc.

Naifeh, Steven, and Gregory White Smith 1989, *Jackson Pollock: An American Saga*, New York: Clarkson N. Potter.

Norris, Christopher 1988, *Paul de Man: Deconstruction and the Critique of Aesthetic Ideology*, New York and London: Routledge.

O'Brien, Elaine Owens 1997, *The Art Criticism of Harold Rosenberg: Theaters of Love and Combat*, unpublished PhD dissertation, New York: City University.

Orton, Fred 1992, 'Action, Revolution and Painting', *Oxford Art Journal*, 14, 1: 3–17.

Orton, Fred 1991, 'Footnote One: The Idea of the Cold War', in *American Abstract Expressionism*, edited by David Thistlewood, Liverpool: Liverpool University Press, 179–92.

Orton, Fred 1989, 'On Being Bent Blue (Second State): An Introduction to Jacques Derrida/A Footnote on Jasper Johns', *Oxford Art Journal*, 12, 1: 35–46.

Orton, Fred 1987, 'Present, the Scene of … Selves, the Occasion of … Ruses', *Block* 13, winter: 5–19.

Orton, Fred 2004, 'SUSPENSA VIX VIA FIT: Jasper Johns' catenary, the everyday self, the work of art/aesthetic self, and the art object', *Oxford Art Journal*, 27, 1: 79–93.

Orton, Fred 1994, *Figuring Jasper Johns*, London: Reaktion Books and Harvard University Press.

Orton, Fred 1996, *Jasper Johns: The Sculptures*, Leeds: Centre for the Study of Sculpture, Henry Moore Institute.

Pells, Richard H. 1973, *Radical Visions and American Dreams: Culture and Social Thought in the Depression Years*, Middletown: Wesleyan University Press.

Phillips, William and Philip Rahv 1936, 'Private Experience and Public Philosophy', *Poetry: A Magazine of Verse*, 48, 2, May: 104.

Podro, Michael 1990, 'The Landscape Thinks Itself in Me', *The International Review of Psycho-Analysis*, 17, 4: 401–10.

Thirty Years of Poetry: A Magazine of Verse. Index to Volumes 1–60, October 1912-September 1942 Index to Volumes 1–100, 1912–1962, 1963, New York: AMS Reprint Company.

Polt, Richard 1999, *Heidegger: An Introduction*, London: UCL Press.

Redfield, Marc 1990, 'De Man, Schiller, and the Politics of Reception', *Diacritics*, 20, 3, autumn: 50–70.

Rewald, John 1961, *The History of Impressionism*, New York: The Museum of Modern Art.

Robbins, Christa Noel 2012, 'Harold Rosenberg on the Character of Action', *Oxford Art Journal*, 35, 2: 195–214.

Rose, Barbara 1979, 'Hans Namuth's Photographs and the Jackson Pollock Myth: Part One: Media Impact and the Failure of Criticism', *Arts Magazine*, 53, 7, March: 112–13.

Rosenberg, Harold 1983, *Act and the Actor, Making the Self*, New York, World Publishing Co. 1970; Chicago: The University of Chicago.

Rosenberg, Harold 1976 [1973], *Discovering the Present. Three Decades in Art, Culture and Politics*, Chicago: The University of Chicago, Phoenix Edition.

Rosenberg, Harold 1982 [1959], *The Tradition of the New*, Chicago: The University of Chicago, Phoenix Edition.

Rosenberg, Harold 1973, *Willem de Kooning*, New York: Harry N. Abrams.

Rosenberg, Harold 1937, 'Aesthetic Assault', a review of Jules Romains' *The Boys in the Back Room*, *New Masses*, 30 March: 25.

Rosenberg, Harold 1935, 'Artists Increase their Understanding of Public Buildings', *Art Front*, November: 3, 6.

Rosenberg, Harold 1936, 'Cubism and Abstract Art', *Art Front*, June: 15.

Rosenberg, Harold 1939, 'Marx and "The People"', *Partisan Review*, 6, 4, summer: 21–5, 124.

Rosenberg, Harold 1939, 'Myth and History', *Partisan Review*, 6, 2, winter: 19–39.

Rosenberg, Harold 1935, 'The Front', *Partisan Review*, 2, 6, January–February: 74.

Rosenberg, Harold 1934, 'The Men on the Wall', *Poetry: A Magazine of Verse*, April, 44, 1: 3–4.

Rosenberg, Harold 1961, 'The Search for Jackson Pollock', *ARTnews*, 59, 10, February: 59–60, review of Bryan Robertson's *Jackson Pollock*, New York: Harry N. Abrams.

Rosenberg, Harold 1931, 'Myth and Poem', *The Symposium*, 2, 2, April: 179–91.

Rosenberg, Harold 1933, 'Note on Class Conflict and Literature', *The New Act*, 1, January: 3–10.

Rosenberg, Harold 1936, 'Peasants and Pure Art', *Art Front*, January: 5–6.

Rosenberg, Harold 1937, 'Portrait of a Predicament', *New Masses*, 9 February: 24.

Rosenberg Harold 1939, (with other members of the League for Cultural Freedom and Socialism), 'Statement of the LCFS', *Partisan Review*, 6, 4, summer: 125–27.

Rosenberg, Harold 1937, 'The Melancholy Railings', *New Masses*, 20 July: 20.

Rosenberg, Harold 1939, (contribution), 'The Situation in American Writing', *Partisan Review*, 6, 4, summer: 47–9.

Rosenberg, Harold 1937, 'What We May demand', *New Masses*, 23 March: 17–18.

Rosenberg, Harold 1936, 'The Wit of William Gropper', *Art Front*, March: 7–8.

Rosenberg, Harold 1932, Review of Kenneth Burke's *Counter Statement* and Montgomery Belgion's *The Human Parrot and Other Essays*, *The Symposium*, 3, 1, January: 116–18.

Rosenberg, Harold 1931, Review of William Empson's *Seven Types of Ambiguity*, *The Symposium*, 2, 3, July: 412–18.

Rosenberg, Harold 1933, Review of Jules Romaine's *Men of Good Will*, *The Symposium*, 4, 4, October: 511–14.

Rosenberg, Harold 1933, 'Sanity, Individuality and Poetry', *The New Act*, 2, June: 59–75.

Rosenberg, Harold, and Robert Motherwell 1947–48, 'Possibilities', *Possibilities*, 1, winter: 1.

Rosenberg, Harold, and William Rubin 1967, exchange of letters, *Artforum*, April: 6–7 and especially that of May, 4, concerning Rubin's 'Jackson Pollock and the Modern Tradition', *Artforum*, February: 14–22.

Rousseau, Jean-Jacques 1964, *Oeuvres Complètes*, III, ed. Bernard Gagnebin and Marcel Raymond, Paris: Gallimard, Bibliothèque de la Pléiade.

Rousseau, Jean-Jacques 1993 [1750–62], trans. and intro. G.D.H. Cole, revised J.H. Brumfitt and John C. Hall, Rousseau, *The Social Contract and Discourses*, London: Everyman and Rutland: Charles E. Tuttle.

Richard Shiff 1984, *Cézanne and the End of Impressionism*, London and Chicago: University of Chicago Press.

Shiff, Richard 1978, 'Performing an Appearance: On the Surface of Abstract Expressionism', in Michael Auping, *Abstract Expressionism: The Critical Developments*, New York: Harry N. Abrams in association with Buffalo: Albright-Knox Art Gallery, 94–123.

Solomon, Alan R. 1964, 'Jasper Johns', *Jasper Johns*, New York: Jewish Museum, 6, and London: Whitechapel Art Gallery, 4–25.

Solomon, Deborah 1988, 'The Unflagging Artistry of Jasper Johns', *The New York Times Magazine*, 19 June: 1–42.

Solomon, Deborah 1987, *Jackson Pollock: A Biography*, New York: Simon and Schuster.

Stevens, Wallace 1951 [1942], 'The Noble Rider and the Sound of Words', in Wallace Stevens, *The Necessary Angel: Essays on Reality and the Imagination*, New York: Vintage Books, 1–36.

Steinberg, Leo 1972 [1962], 'Jasper Johns: The First Seven Years of His Art', in *Metro*, 4/5, in Leo Steinberg, *Other Criteria: Confrontations in Twentieth-Century Art*, New York: Oxford University Press, 17–54.

Stoekl, Allan 1985, 'De Man and the Dialectics of Being', *Diacritics*, 15, 3, autumn: 36–45.

Suzuki, D.T. 1948 [1934], *An Introduction to Zen Buddhism*, translated by Constance Rolfe, with a preface by Carl Jung, London: Buddhist Society/Rider & Co.

Tomkins, Calvin 1980, *Off the Wall: Robert Rauschenberg and the Art World of Our Time*, New York: Doubleday.

Trotsky, Leon 1938, 'Art and Politics', *Partisan Review*, 5, 3, August–September: 3–10.

Trotsky, Leon 1947 [1939], *The Living Thoughts of Karl Marx*, published separately as *Marxism in the United States*, New York: Workers Party Publications.

Trotsky, Leon 1970, *Writings of Leon Trotsky (1937–38)*, New York: Pathfinder Press.

Vaihinger, Hans 1924 [1911], *The Philosophy of As if: A System of the Theoretical, Practical and Religious Fictions of Mankind*, translated by C.K. Ogden, New York: Harcourt Brace.

Volosinov, V.N. 1986 [1929], *Marxism and the Philosophy of Language*, 1929, translated by Ladislaw Matejka and I.R. Tituni, Cambridge and London: Harvard University Press.

Waters, Lindsay 1995, 'Professah de Man – he dead', *American Literary History*, 7, 2, summer: 284–303.

Waters, Lindsay and Wlad Godzich (eds.) 1989, *Reading de Man Reading*, Minneapolis: University of Minnesota Press.

Watts, Alan 1932, *An Outline of Zen Buddhism*, London: The Golden Vista Press.

Watts, Alan 1936, *The Spirit of Zen: A Way of Life, Work, and Art in the Far East*, London: John Murray.

Wechsler, Judith (ed.) 1975, *Cézanne in Perspective*, Englewood Cliffs: Prentice-Hall, Inc.

Wilczynski, J. 1981, *Encyclopaedic Dictionary of Marxism, Socialism and Communism*, Berlin and New York: De Gruyter.

Wimsatt Jr., W.K. and M.C. Beardsley 1946, 'The Intentional Fallacy', *The Sewanee Review*, 54, 3, July–September: 468–88.

Wittgenstein, Ludwig 1966 [from notes transcribed in 1938 by Yorik Smythies, Rush Rees and James Taylor], *Lectures on Aesthetics* (1938), in *Lectures and Conversations on Aesthetics, Psychology, and Religious Belief*, Oxford: Basil Blackwell.

Wittgenstein, Ludwig 1958 [1953], *Philosophical Investigations*, translated by G.E.M. Anscombe, Oxford: Basil Blackwell.

Wittgenstein, Ludwig 1974 [1921], *Tractatus Logico-Philosophicus*, translated by D.F. Pears & B.F. McGuiness, London: Routledge & Kegan Paul.

Wollheim, Richard 1968, *Art and its Objects*, Harmondsworth: Penguin Books Ltd.

Wollheim, Richard 1987, *Painting as an Art*, London: Thames & Hudson.

Wollheim, Richard 1970, 'The Work of Art as Object', *Studio International*, 180, 928, December, also in Richard Wollheim, *On Art and the Mind*, Cambridge, MA: Harvard University Press, 1973, 112–9, and Harrison and Orton (eds.) 1984, *Modernism, Criticism, Realism*, 10–17.

Wood, Allen W. 2004, *Karl Marx*, 2nd ed., Abingdon: Routledge.

Wordsworth, William 1939 [1850], *The Prelude; or, Growth of a Poet's Mind; An Autobiographical Poem*, in Thomas Hutchinson (ed.), *The Poetical Works of Wordsworth*, London: Oxford University Press, 633–752.

Young, Joseph E. 1969, 'Jasper Johns: An Appraisal', *Art International*, 13, 7, September: 50–56.

www.astrosurf.com/luxorion/report-aberrations.htm (24 October, 2008)

www.olympusmicro.com/primer/anatomy/aberrationhome.html (24 October, 2008)

www.scienceworld.wolfram.com/physics/OpticalAberrations.html (24 October, 2008)

http://www.telescope-optics.net/eye_aberrations.htm (24 October, 2008)

warholstars.org/abstract-expressionism/abstractexpressionism.html

Index

Adorno, T.W.   xxii
Althusser, Louis   119
Apollinaire, Guillaume   58
Art & Language   ix, xi, xv, xix
Atkinson, Terry   ix, x, xi

Babbitt, Irving   111
Bach, Johann Sebastian   7
Baldwin, Michael   ix
   see also Art & Language
Barthes, Roland   85, 98–9, 103, 106, 109–10, 112–20, 135, 147, 150, 153, 154, 160, 164
Bataille, Georges   148
Baudelaire, Charles   29
Baxandall, Michael   3, 7, 8, 20
Beardsley, M.C.   *see* Wimsatt Jr., W.K. and M.C. Beardsley
Beaufort, Jean   92
Beckett, Samuel   1
Benjamin, Walter   xv, 24, 82
Bentham, Jeremy   161, 162
Bernard, Émile   40
Blunt, Anthony   ix
Bostetter, Edward Everett   111
Brancusi, Constantin   20
Browder, Earl   50
Burke, Kenneth   85
Burnham, James   47

Cage, John   69
Caro, Anthony   20, 32
Cervantes, Miguel de   106
Cézanne, Paul   viii, x, xix, xx, 22–41
Chareau, Pierre   69
Clark, T.J.   x, xi, xx, xxii, 172
Coleridge, S.T.   22–3, 26, 33
Creuzer, Friederich   26

De Kooning, Willem   xviii, 11
De Man, Henrik   87
De Man, Paul   viii, xiii, xv, xviii, xx–xxii, 6–7, 33–4, 35, 40, 41, 81–175
Dali, Salvador   52
Dante   7
Darwin, Charles   137
David, Jacques-Louis   7

Day, Gail   xx
Debord, Guy   89
Derrida, Jacques   xiii, xv, xxi
Dickinson, Emily   172
Dondero, George A.   xiii, 72
Dostoevsky, Fyodor   62

Eagleton, Terry   xx
Edwards, Jonathan   24
Eliot, T.S.   19, 111
Empson, William   91–2, 94–9
Engels, Frederick   81, 91, 117, 128–31, 156
   see also Marx, Karl and Frederick Engels

Feuerbach, Ludwig   64, 154, 170
Flaubert, Gustave   106
Frank, Waldo   50–1
Frankenthaler, Helen   xv, 20
Fried, Michael   24, 31–2, 40

Gasquet, Joachim   22, 28–31, 35, 36, 37
Gauguin, Paul   x, 29, 30
Giotto   7
Girard, René   106–12, 118, 127, 135
Goethe, Johann Wolfgang von   63
Greenberg, Clement   xii, xiii, xiv, xvi, xvii, 7, 25, 31, 40, 43
Gropper, William   52
Gunn, Thom   27

Harrison, Charles   ix, xv
   see also Art & Language
Hays, H.R.   47
Haeckel, Ernst   130
Hegel, G.W.F.   57, 78, 82, 90, 92, 95, 110, 118, 127, 145, 152, 159, 165, 172
Heidegger, Martin   86, 89–95, 97, 99–101, 103, 106, 144, 151, 152, 174
Hepworth, Barbara   6
Herbert, George   94–5
Hess, Moses   169
Hitler, Adolf   74
Huelsenbeck, Richard   69–70
Hulme, T.E.   111
Husserl, Edmund   100, 151

INDEX

Jakobson, Roman   115
Jameson, Frederic   xx
Johns, Jasper   viii, xv–xii, xix, 1–21

Kant, Immanuel   29, 82, 86, 118, 127, 141–6, 151, 158, 163, 165, 168, 170, 171
Kierkegaard, Søren   78, 85
Kleist, Heinrich von   82

Larrain, Jorge   116
Lavers, Annette   113
Le Guin, Ursula K.   174
Lenin, V.I.   67–8
Lévi-Strauss, Claude   140–1, 145, 150
Levin, Harry   87
Louis, Morris   8, 25
Lukás, Georg   103–5, 111, 114

McEvilley, Thomas   2
Mann, Thomas   54
Marvell, Andrew   95
Marx, Karl   viii, xii, xiii, xiv, xv, xviii, xx, xxi, xxii, 42, 55, 57, 61–70, 78, 81, 85–8, 91, 92, 93, 97, 99–105, 106, 110, 111, 117, 128–29, 130, 131, 147, 161, 162, 165–71, 172
Marx, Karl and Frederick Engels   xxi, 57, 85, 86, 88, 91, 92, 102, 105, 106, 110, 117, 118, 131, 135, 152–64, 165, 168, 171, 173–74, 175
Matisse, Henri   8
Mehring, Franz   81, 156
Merleau-Ponty, Maurice   36, 41, 151
Milner, Marion   38–9, 40
Mills, C. Wright   72
Monet, Claude   xix, 40
Montaigne, Michel Eyquem de   148–52
Moore, Harriet   47
Moore, Henry   6
Motherwell, Robert   69
Mozart, Wolfgang Amadeus   7

Namuth, Hans   70
Newman, Barnett   xviii, 20, 42, 71, 80
Nietzsche, Friedrich   110, 129, 137, 138, 139, 174
Noland, Kenneth   25, 32

Olitski, Jules   25, 32
Orton, Fred   viii–xxiii

Phillips, William   47
Picasso, Pablo   20
Pissarro, Camille   29
Pollock, Griselda   x, xiii, xiv
Pollock, Jackson   xiv, xviii, 11, 70–1
Proust, Marcel   106, 107, 138, 139, 157

Rahv, Philip   47
Ramsden, Mel   ix
  see also Art & Language
Raposa, Joe   22
Rauschenberg, Robert   xviii
Rilke, Rainer Maria   136, 138
Rivers, Larry   xv
Roberts, John   xx
Robbe-Grillet, Alain   110
Rosenberg, Arthur   54
Rosenberg, Harold   xii–xiv, xvii, xviii, 42–80
Rosso, Stefano   83–5, 102, 119
Rothko, Mark   xiv, 8
Rousseau, Jean-Jacques   41, 85, 86, 119–31, 135, 143, 152, 155, 158–60
Rubin, William   2–3

Sartre, Jean-Paul   92, 99, 100
Schapiro, Meyer   xvii
Schiller, Friedrich   82, 86, 104, 119, 145
Shakespeare, William   62, 94
Sollers, Philippe   110
Solman, Joseph   51
Somerville, Mary   137, 144
Spivak, Max   51
Sprinker, Michael   xx
Stalin, Joseph V.   49, 53, 54, 58
Stella, Frank   xv, 20
Stendhal   106, 107
Stirner, Max   163–4
Stevens, Wallace   58–9, 69, 71, 74
Sylvester, David   5, 14, 15

Tolstoy, Leo   7
Trotsky, Leon   viii, xiii, xiv, 53–5, 67, 68

Van Gogh, Vincent   x
Varnedoe, Kirk   2

Wainwright, Philip   47
Waters, Lindsay   90

Werckmeister, O.K. xi, xvii
Williams, Hank 161
Wimsatt Jr., W.K. and M.C. Beardsley 1–3
Wittgenstein, Ludwig xiii, xv, xxi, 4, 10, 16
Wollheim, Richard xxi, 3–4, 6, 7, 8, 11, 16
Wordsworth, William 21, 34

Young, Joseph E. 1

Zychlinski, Franz Zychlin von 164
Zola, Émile 29

Printed in the United States
by Baker & Taylor Publisher Services